I WAS A HERO ONCE

I WAS A HERO ONCE

Peter P Mahoney

atmosphere press

*To the men and women of VVAW
who taught me how to fight for what I believe in.*

*To my family,
Natasha, Daniel, and Anastasia,
who gave me the thing in life worth fighting for.*

I was a hero once
Or so it seemed
My life was gripped in the vise of commitment
And Truth was my name

It was all so long ago
The tilted windmills of my youth still smugly sit atop the hill
My wide-eyed innocence lies smashed upon the rocks below
You cannot change the world
If you cannot change yourself

So now I chase the American Dream
I never wanted
Marinating in suburban mediocrity
Struggling to keep up with the Joneses
A task to which the Mahoneys
Are never quite equal
My life defined
By the endless repetition of mindless tasks
Mow the yard
Wash the car
Fix the sink
Tend the garden

I still have my ideals
I tell myself
Lamely
When on occasion I ponder who I am
But principles without actions are like the kiss of a whore
Or the handshake of a politician
I cannot think of these things now
The weight may crush me
Besides,
My nap awaits
But I will awake, my friend
I will awake

- Peter P Mahoney, 2015 -

Contents

Author's Note

Storytelling has been an integral part of the human experience since we first gazed around at our world and tried to make sense of it. It has been our way of conveying history and knowledge from one generation to the next, connecting the generations to each other and to all those that have preceded them. In Australia, for example, this tradition has continued in Aboriginal culture for over sixty thousand years.

Of course, official history has always been the version of events concocted by the victors. The official history of the United States is one of progress and accomplishment, of "taming the wilderness" and "manifest destiny." Our history books talk little, if anything, about the fact that the United States was created through the enslavement of one race and the genocide committed against another. Those little details contradict the America-is-always-the-good-guy description of history that is an essential element in Americans' belief about ourselves.

One of the things I've learned is that there are usually as many versions of any historical event as there are people who participated in it. I've managed to be a Gump-like witness to a number of the major historical incidents of the latter half of the twentieth century, yet when I've read in books or newspapers accounts of these things, I always walk away thinking, "That's not the way I remember how things went down." When something happens, we each filter it through our own experiences and our own biases. How that event affected me is different from how it affected the person next to me.

This is where the storytellers come in. Storytellers can relate an alternative version of the facts that can enrich and complement the dominant narrative or, when necessary, challenge and contradict it. This role has become even more essential in our modern world, where the tools and technology of authoritarianism are being used by those in power to snuff out any version of history that does not align with their own.

I am a storyteller. From barstools to back porches, from kitchen tables to campfires, from podiums to park benches, I have spun my yarns to audiences both big and small, both rapt and bored. I didn't start out that way. I was just a dreamer, quietly imagining myself as something special, as someone who would "make a difference" in the world. But the fact is, I was just an ordinary person leading an ordinary life. Then, partly by design, partly by happenstance, I was thrust into a series of adventures and circumstances beyond anything I had ever dreamed.

It all started when I ran away from home at eighteen and hitchhiked around the country. Then I joined the Army, became an infantry lieutenant, and went to Vietnam. After Vietnam, I tried to become a hippie, got involved with Vietnam Veterans Against the War (VVAW), and became a National Coordinator for the organization. I was subsequently indicted for conspiracy to incite a riot at the Republican Convention in 1972—the so-called Gainesville Eight case—and one of my best friends turned out to be an FBI informer who testified against me at the trial. In the early eighties, I was involved with the New York Vietnam Veterans Memorial Commission, which built a memorial for Vietnam veterans in New York City and published the book *Dear America: Letters Home from Vietnam.* In the late eighties, I was part of a delegation of Vietnam veterans who went to the Soviet Union to meet with Soviet veterans of their Afghanistan War. I fell in love with a woman from Russia, married her, and spent nine years living there, during which time I fathered two children, then brought my family back to the U.S. and the suburban middle-class life I had left so many years before. The adventures ultimately, inevitably perhaps, ended, and like Samwise Gamgee, I returned to an ordinary life once they were over. The only thing I had left from that special time was the stories.

There is a particular type of narrative structure called the Hero's Journey. The term was first used by Joseph Campbell in 1949 in his book *The Hero with a Thousand* Faces. In my opinion, the one step of the Hero's Journey that is missing from many stories is the return to ordinary life once the adventure is over. Of course, "ordinary life" is not as exciting, as compelling, as the adventure, so you don't want to end a good yarn with all the boring details of the post-adventure everyday life. So, "... and they all lived happily ever after" became a standard ending. For me, the post-adventure life is a key element to my story, providing the perspective and the voice with which I relate it. It seemed to me that the only way I could include this in an interesting way was to alternate chapters of my present life with those of my past, the juxtaposition providing a contrast between the two as well as showing the continued influence each has had on the other. For those of you, dear readers, who might prefer a strictly chronological timeline, this structure may be a bit perplexing, even Brechtian in its alienation effect, but I need to tell my story my way. This is my version of events.

When I was young, the word *hero* had a very specific meaning for me. It designated a man, usually a soldier, of strength and courage who was willing to sacrifice his own well-being for the protection of others. Of course, many so-called "heroes," when asked about it, will tell you that the primary motivating factor for their actions was fear, not courage, but whatever the reason, they acted, and others benefited from it. Over the years, it seems the criteria for designating one a hero have been diluted. I am not a hero because I served in Vietnam. I, like tens of thousands of others, merely survived the ordeal. But if I were to be called a hero, then it should be for the things I did *after* Vietnam. Those, I think, may be worthy of the designation.

I wrote this book for two reasons. First and foremost, I wrote it for my children. Their experience of me is as a slightly boring "soccer dad," ordinary and unremarkable. I wanted them to know who I was and what I did before I became their dad. More importantly, I hope the book can be inspiring to the entire younger generation they represent, who will have to deal with the mess of a world that we have left them. The second reason is that when I was young, I had hoped that my actions would "make a difference," but I'm not so sure if they amounted to "a hill of beans," as Humphry Bogart famously intoned. If my actions did not change the world, then I dream that maybe my stories can.

Chapter 1

Death of the Man

The call came sooner than expected. The last prognosis had been six months, yet it had barely been three. I knew instinctively what the call was about as soon as I heard my mother's voice. Joseph Richard Mahoney—the *man*—my father, had died.

My first reaction was self-recrimination, guilt being one of the primary motivators for Irish Catholics, even lapsed ones like me. I hadn't been to see him one last time, to tell him all the things I had never spoken of, to exchange finally all the father-son confidences we had never shared. The truth is, we wouldn't have said much more to each other than we ever did. Even if I had tried, by then he was in the last stages of Alzheimer's, too late for shared intimacies and heartfelt talks.

Beyond that, I realized I wanted to remember him as he had been, a physically strong yet gentle man, not what he had declined into in his last months. I had seen him the year before, in 2006, when he and my mother came up to Long Island for the funeral of his sister. Alzheimer's hadn't yet taken over; he was still *there* a lot of the time. He would sit in the room with others and seem to drift off into his own world, but if you addressed him directly, he was alive, engaged, and even self-deprecating about his inability to remember simple things. He had frequent bathroom accidents and needed help at the dinner table, but the spark of Joe Mahoney still glowed.

When things finally went downhill, my mother said, it seemed like he had just given up.

What is my father's legacy? Of all the fine things I learned from him—hard work, family loyalty, humility—his greatest lesson was to be ordinary. He had his chance—as did I—to break free of the patterns that life had set for him, to reach beyond what was expected, to strive for greatness, but he chose to be ordinary. I struggled with the same thing. For years, I dreamed of being someone extraordinary, but my fate has been the same as his—a brief shooting star of astonishing experience, followed by the mundane existence of an ordinary man. I have fought mightily against the suburban life for which my father strived. His mantra was always *What will the neighbors think?* He was afraid to be different or to be seen as different, afraid to show how unique he was.

I realized all this a few years before my father died. I was at my house in Vermont—a summer weekend vacation home, one of my prized possessions, the mortgage paid for by skiers renting it in the wintertime. My brother Henry was visiting, another of the Mahoney clan who'd once had visions of greatness. Henry loved music. He had attended Berklee College of Music with dreams of becoming a composer, eking out his tuition as a back-up road musician. The money ran out before he could graduate, however, and he managed finally to earn a degree in music education a few years later at a state college. He worked for a number of years as a high school music teacher, excelled at the job, but when his marriage fell apart, he chose to live in New Hampshire so he could be near his daughter and continue to be a father to her. Music education, however, wasn't much of a priority in New Hampshire, so Henry, the aspiring composer and inspiring music teacher, ended up as an oft-unemployed construction worker. I would invite him to my home from time to time, with some home improvement project in store, and we would spend the weekend talking trash and building something.

At the end of one of our construction days, Henry and I were drinking beers, roaming around the splotchy patch of grass, weeds, and moss in my front yard, talking about improving the look of it. Henry was telling me about what he did with a similar patch in front of his rented trailer. Suddenly, we looked at each other with wry smiles of recognition. Here we were, two middle-aged former rebels who had fled suburbia, desperate to escape the stifling, keep-up-with-the-Joneses mindset, contemplating lawns on a sultry summer evening. Drinkin' beer and talkin' about lawns, thinking about how far we had traveled to get to the same place.

In one of those excruciating ironies that life sometimes throws at us, on the morning of my father's wake, I was closing on my first house in the suburbs. The closing was in Westborough, Massachusetts, and my father's wake was in the afternoon on Long Island. My wife, Natasha, and I signed all the papers in the lawyer's office and then drove to the too-expensive piece of property we had just purchased for a quick walk-through and look-see. As we drove up to the house on the quiet suburban street, I noticed that the lawn hadn't been mowed for some time. My first thought was, *Gotta mow that lawn; what will the neighbors think?* My father's mantra had become mine.

Then it was on to Long Island for the gathering of the Mahoney clan. My four brothers and two sisters were there, along with my mother and a considerable assortment of uncles, aunts, cousins, nieces, and nephews. Irish Catholic families of my parents' generation tended to proliferate. There were eight children in my Uncle Jack's family and five in my Aunt Virginia's, both on my father's side. My Aunt Justine, on my mother's side, had six children.

Also in attendance was my father's best friend, Seymour Epstein, Uncle Sy we called him, and his wife, Gloria, who had flown in from Las Vegas. Joe Mahoney and Sy Epstein were quite a pair. Born and raised in Brooklyn, they met in the South Pacific in 1944, having enlisted in the UDTs—Underwater

Demolition Teams—the precursor to the Navy SEALS. The mission of a UDT was as simple as it was maniacally dangerous. Dressed only in swim trunks, a diving mask, and fins, with a Ka-Bar knife strapped to their waists and satchels of explosives bound to their backs, they would swim up to beaches of Japanese-held islands, recon the area, and blow up any obstacles in the path of the Marines before they waded ashore.

After the invasion of the Tarawa Atoll in the Gilbert Islands in November 1943—where over a thousand Marines were killed and over two thousand wounded—the need for pre-assault recon and demolition of natural and man-made obstructions became clear. The UDTs were created for this purpose. After Tarawa was the island of Kwajalein. The original plan called for night reconnaissance, but Rear Admiral Richmond K. Turner, the commander of the amphibious forces in the South Pacific, was determined to avoid a repeat of Tarawa; he wanted to know about the coral as well as any blockages the Japanese may have emplaced around the island. UDT 1 was ordered to perform two daylight recons. In keeping with the Seabee tradition of doing whatever it took to accomplish the job while not necessarily following the rules, UDT 1 did both. The mission was to follow standard procedure with each two-man team in a rubber boat—wearing full fatigues, boots, life jackets, and metal helmets—paddling to the beach to make pertinent observations. Team 1 found the coral reef was preventing the craft from getting close enough to shore to ascertain the beach conditions. Ensign Lewis F. Luehrs and Seabee Chief Bill Acheson, anticipating this potential problem, had worn swim trunks beneath their fatigues. Stripping down, they swam forty-five minutes undetected across the reef.

Upon their return, they brought sketches of gun emplacements and other vital intelligence directly to Rear Admiral Turner's flagship and gave their report, still in their trunks. Admiral Turner concluded that the only way to obtain this kind of granular intelligence was to send out individual swimmers, and he relayed these thoughts to Admiral Chester W. Nimitz, Commander in Chief of all Allied air, land, and sea forces during World War II. Because of these men's ingenuity, their recon improvisation proved to be a flashpoint in UDT history, changing the mission model and training regimen of Naval Special Warfare forever, with a new emphasis on developing strong swimmers, daylight reconnaissance, and training without lifelines. The uniform of diving masks and swim trunks became the lasting image of the UDTs as "Naked Warriors," among which Ensign Lewis F. Luehrs and Seabee Chief Bill Acheson were the first.

Members of UDT 4. Joe Mahoney, standing, second from left.
Sy Epstein, crouching, lower right.

My father and Uncle Sy were in UDT 4 during the invasion of Guam, and they famously left a sign on the beach as a joke to greet the landing Marines: "Welcome Marines AGAT USO two blocks Courtesy UDT-4." My father was a very quiet man, and like many veterans, he didn't speak often about his World War II experiences, but Uncle Sy was the opposite. An inveterate storyteller, he loved to regale us with tales of the adventures of Sy and Joe in the South Pacific while my father would sit there and roll his eyes, shifting uncomfortably in his chair as Uncle Sy would talk about how they had smoked marijuana or chased Hawaiian booty. I suspect many of Sy's yarns had been embellished over the years. One of his favorite tales was about how he and Joe had schemed to get extra beer money. Sy was a small, wiry guy whose physical presence was not overwhelming. He was, however, like my father, strong as an ox, a key requirement for the type of work they did in UDT. They would challenge other sailors to a heavy-lifting contest between Sy and the strongest from among their adversaries. The other sailors would take one look at Sy and figure they were in for some easy money. Sy, of course, always won—or at least he always won in his retelling of it. Now, Sy swore that this was my father's idea, but it is hard to believe that the fast-talking little Brooklyn Jew who later went on to a highly successful career as a criminal attorney in New York City wasn't the brains behind that operation.

Sy would also tell the story of when my father first met my mother. Back in the States after the war, while waiting to be discharged, they attended a dance in their white sailor suits. Sy said my father took one look at my mother and was immediately smitten. Sy saw the two of them leave the dance floor, and when they came back a short while later, Sy swore that my father's white sailor pants were covered with dirt because he had dropped to his knees and proposed. When I asked my mother about this, she just smiled and shook her head.

"Uncle Sy has a vivid imagination," she said.

My father and I did not see eye to eye on politics and lifestyle choices, but as his oldest son, I thought it was my place to deliver the eulogy at his funeral. My mother, however, had asked Henry instead. I didn't know if this was a not-too-subtle dig at my black-sheep status in the family—something my mother enjoyed reminding me of—or whether she just assumed I wouldn't find the time to sit down and write it. I was a little hurt by this until Henry's words rang out:

> *The streets of heaven are crowded tonight—Earth is a little less*
> *   interesting—*
> *Joe Mahoney has gone.*
> *He was an Irish lad ... a Brooklyn boy.*
> *He was a Frogman ... a courageous man ... a demolition man*
> *A jazzman ... a music-loving man ... a dancing man.*
> *He was a hard-working man ... a shipfitter man*
> *A fun-loving man ... a beer-drinking man*
> *A religious man ... a righteous man*
> *A weight-lifting man ... a powerful man.*
> *He was a family man ... a humble man*
> *A stoic man ... a quirky man.*
> *He was a sharp-dressed man ... an outdoorsman*
> *A traveling man ... a fisherman.*
> *He was a blue-collar man.*
> *He was a man among men ... he was a one-woman man.*
> *Above all, he was always a gentleman.*
> *Husband ... Father ... Grandfather ... Great-Grandfather ...*
> *   Brother ... Uncle ... Friend ...*
> *We were all blessed to have Dad in our lives.*
> *Thanks for everything, Dad.*
> *You will be missed.*
> *We love you so much ... We love you madly.*

Whatever my mother's reason, she had made the right choice.

A few months after my father's funeral, my wife, kids, and I were still settling into our new suburban existence. I was sitting at home on a Friday night, watching the Knicks lose another basketball game, when Natasha came to me with the phone. "It's someone who wants to talk to you about some genealogy survey," she said, handing me the phone.

I was wary as I put the phone to my ear; I don't like to take calls from strangers. The voice on the other end of the line was somewhat hesitant and unsure, not the pseudo-cheery, aggressive salesperson type, and had a strong hint of a Southern accent. He explained that he was doing a genealogy survey and was looking for a Peter Mahoney who had lived at some point in Louisiana. I affirmed that I had lived in Louisiana in the distant past, and he continued to be very vague. I kept waiting for the pitch line, waiting for him to tell me what he was selling so I could hang up the phone. Finally, I asked him straight out what this was about, and he paused, then said a name and asked me if I had ever known that person. It was as if he had punched me in the gut. I started to panic. My first thought was that somehow this man was going to try to sue me, blackmail me, or otherwise try to get money from me. I said nothing and hung up the phone. I sat there for a number of minutes staring at the phone, dreading that it would ring again. The man didn't call me back.

I was utterly stunned, my emotions in total turmoil. As I started to think it all through, however, the pieces began to fall into place. I checked the phone log and saw the caller's name and phone number there. I checked the area code and saw it was for Northern Louisiana. A quick Google search on the name gave me some basic information about him. He lived in Monroe, Louisiana, and worked as a security manager for a regional grocery store. The relative ordinariness of him gave me some level of comfort that perhaps it wasn't a scam or a shakedown. I didn't sleep much that night, going over and over in my mind the risks and rewards of calling him back. On one level, I was terrified that the call could be a life-changing one, that the existence I had constructed for my family and myself would be irrevocably altered by this unexpected blast from my past. On the other hand, an irresistible curiosity tugged at me. Could it really be true? What would it mean? Who was this man? There was a risk, to be sure, but one I couldn't avoid. I had to call him back.

The next day, I waited until the afternoon when Natasha and the kids were out of the house, and I called him back.

"Hi, Chris, I'm the guy you called last night," I said.

"Yes." Noncommittal, expectant.

I plunged in, no small talk. I was afraid I might lose my nerve.

"So let me ask you this, is this woman you mentioned your mother?"

"She's my biological mother, yes."

"Well, then I guess I'm probably your father."

"Yes, I know."

Chapter 2

Escape from Suburbia

Suburbia, the apotheosis of the American Dream! It's where I grew up. Row upon row of single-family houses surrounded by lawns and flowers and ornamental trees, with pools and patios and two-car garages, everything a middle-class family could want.

I hated it.

I hated the enforced conformity, the flatulent culture, and the accumulation of possessions as the principal indication of success. Mostly, I hated the fact that the Mahoneys never could quite keep up with the Joneses, and our pile of possessions always seemed smaller than everyone else's. I had fled the place as a young man, and I never expected to live there again. So, how did I end up back in the suburbs with a wife and two children? It was a long, strange trip.

I am a baby boomer, a member of the enormous demographic bubble created when the Greatest Generation turned its attention from defeating fascism to making babies. For Joe Mahoney, it meant turning away from any intimations of greatness that his military service might have sparked in him to embrace the comfort and security of family life instead. Other members of his UDT team used the G.I. Bill to go to college and become doctors, lawyers, and CEOs; Joe Mahoney went back to the shipyards as a shipfitter. Perhaps, after a childhood lived during the Depression and a young manhood spent in war in the South Pacific, the vision of normalcy was too great an attraction for him. It was one of those questions I never managed to ask him.

I was the second of his and Julia's children—my sister Kathy having preceded me into the world by a year and a half. There would ultimately be seven of us—five boys and two girls—as Irish appetites clearly won the day over Catholic rhythmic birth control. The one veterans' benefit my father took advantage of was the G.I. mortgage. Our family joined the great urban exodus of the early fifties, as the ascendancy of the motor vehicle and the economic prosperity of the post-war years spurred people to abandon their inner-city tenements to chase the dream of owning their own home. We all had our little pink houses. Of course, for most people, the bank was the real owner of the real estate, but the brilliant illusion fit in well with the emerging American culture: perception was reality. What you looked like was who you really were.

When I was about two, we moved out of the temporary veterans' housing in Brooklyn's Gerritsen Beach to a little town on Long Island called Williston Park, close to the city, an older suburb consisting of single-family soapbox houses on small plots of land. You could have a house of your own with a lawn, a backyard, and a garage, but no privacy. The houses were crammed so close together that it was almost like living in a horizontal apartment building. You always knew what was happening in your neighbors' lives, and they always knew what was going on in yours.

In 1959, when I was in the fifth grade, my family moved again, having by then expanded to five children and outgrown the little soapbox in Williston Park. The Mahoneys headed for greener pastures in Suffolk County, a town called Commack, which literally offered green pastures. When we first moved there, it was mostly woods and potato farms. The endless sub-divisions and shopping centers that now encompass the area were just breaking ground.

Housing development companies bought up huge tracts of land, and each had their own model houses for families to view. You would choose the model you wanted, and the house would be built. The Mahoneys bought a house with a half-acre of land in Parkview Estates for the sum of $14,990. We were among the first families to move into Parkview Estates.

My mother faced an existential crisis when we moved to Commack: there was no Catholic school in town. St. Ann's, in Brentwood, the next town to the south, was the closest, but they were reluctant to take pupils who didn't live in Brentwood. She begged and pleaded with the nuns and finally persuaded them to take my sister Kathy and me, but there was simply no room in the third grade for my brother Henry. He was forced to attend the public school in Commack. The big difference, for Henry, between the two school systems—other than religious content and the outfits the teachers wore—was that the public school curriculum included a music program and the Catholic school did not. Henry was introduced to music, and he was on his way.

My father had sacrificed a lot to bring us to the suburbs, namely, time spent with his family. His work in the shipyards was always far from where we lived. He was up and away at five or six in the morning, long before his children ever stirred from bed. He didn't return to the nest until six-thirty or seven at night, tired and uncommunicative, except on occasional paydays, when the lure of a few beers with the boys was greater than that of Friday nights with the family. When home, he would usually retreat to his record collection with a can or two or three of beer, not to be bothered by the produce of his loins. For hours on end, he would meticulously catalog his massive and ever-growing collection of jazz LPs and 78s by song, artist, and album as he listened to the music, recording the play date of each album on its cover. It wasn't exactly "little boy blue and the man in the moon," but it was close.

Despite the emotional distance between us—or maybe because of it—I idolized him when I was growing up. He was an avid weight lifter, and continued to pump iron two or three times a week well into his seventies, yet I never saw him use his impressive physical strength in an aggressive way. His reticence to speak about his military experience only added to his aura in my eyes. He was a powerful swimmer, a vestige of his time in UDT. A big part of my father's routine when we went to the beach would be to "take his swim." He would go out from the shore about a hundred yards and swim back and forth, parallel to the shore, counting his strokes. He would do this twice during the afternoon, the first for a warm-up swim, the second for the number of strokes he had set as a goal for that day. Once, when I was twelve years old, we were at Callahan's Beach—the local town beach on Long Island Sound—and my father was out taking his second swim. I was with my brothers, running around in the sand, and I stepped on something sharp, perhaps a broken piece of glass or a shell, and I sliced my heel really badly. I was sitting on our blanket, bleeding profusely and trying not to cry, when some people came over and asked me what had happened. I showed them my foot, and they called over the lifeguards. I told them I was there with my father and pointed out to sea.

"That's him swimming out there."

The two lifeguards jumped in the water, but they just couldn't catch him. We had to wait until he was finished taking his swim before I could get my foot stitched up.

I guess I didn't feel deprived of my father's attention because my mother showered me with enough love for them both. At various times, my mother worked as a school bus driver, a meat cutter in a supermarket, and an Avon lady in an effort to augment the family's income. We weren't poor by any means, but money always seemed to be tight. I suspect my parents would have been quite comfortable financially if a new mouth to feed hadn't popped out of my mother every few years.

Life of a suburban boy. Little League,
Boy Scouts, varsity basketball team.

The town of Commack, meanwhile, was a young boy's dream, flanked by hundreds of acres of woods and fields filled with all manner of wildlife and potential adventure. An industrious kid could build treehouses or secret forts in the forests or search for arrowheads in a clearing we called Indian Valley. You could find owl pellets, the regurgitation of fur and bones after an owl consumed a rodent. You could catch a box turtle for a pet, shoot birds with a BB gun, irritate a flying squirrel into taking flight, or startle a deer at every turn in the road. Hoyt Farm Boy Scout Camp was nearby, with miles of hiking trails and a ranger who loved giving nature lectures and who would display in his nature museum the owl pellets and arrowheads we had found.

My life revolved around religion and sports; I was sufficiently athletic that I did well in most sports I tried, though I seldom took the time to learn the intricacies of the games I played. I was meticulous about following all the rules and ceremonies of Catholicism, even becoming an altar boy. I joined the Cub Scouts, then the Boy Scouts, and worked my way through the ranks of both.

Growing up, I always thought I was destined to be something special, fueled by idealism rooted in an unshakeable belief in my country and my religion. I knew my country was the greatest one on earth and that everyone in every other country wanted what we in America had. I knew that Catholicism was the one true religion, and I felt sorry for all those Protestants who didn't realize this and would probably go to hell as a result. I felt utterly privileged that I was a Catholic in America—we had even just voted a Catholic in as president. I had the best of everything, and I was determined to follow my ideals to greatness.

In the eighth grade, much to the delight of my mother and the nuns at St Ann's, I announced that I wanted to be a priest. The road to the priesthood was a long one: six years in a minor seminary—the equivalent of four years of high school and two years of college—then six more years studying theology at a major seminary. The minor seminary for the Diocese of Rockville Center—the diocese that covered Long Island— was St. Pius X Seminary, located in the town of Uniondale in Nassau County, a two-hour bus ride from where I lived. In those days in New York State, you were required to take a test similar to the Scholastic Aptitude Test (SAT) in order to get into a Catholic high school. I applied to the seminary as my first choice in the fall of 1961 and put Chaminade—a Catholic boys' school in Mineola, Long Island—as my second, only because you were required to put more than one choice on the application. I ended up scoring the highest of any person who applied to Chaminade that year, so they offered me a full four-year scholarship. This caused a huge dilemma for me because I wanted to go to the seminary, but a scholarship was no small thing for my family. So, my mother wrote a letter—purportedly from me—to Bishop Walter Kellenburg, the head of the Diocese of Rockville Center, explaining the situation. The bishop agreed to transfer the scholarship from Chaminade to St. Pius X.

After a year at the seminary, I pretty much knew I didn't want to be a priest. It finally dawned on me that I had chosen the seminary because it was what my mother wanted me to do, not what I really wanted for myself. I was just beginning to discover girls, and boys who attended the seminary were not allowed to have girlfriends under pain of expulsion. The allure of the opposite sex was not the only reason for my loss of vocation. I was inspired by the words of Christ in the New Testament: the Beatitudes, the Good Samaritan, the Prodigal Son, the camel through the eye of a needle. I was enamored with the Christian ideal, yet the more I learned about the history of the institution that had been created in Christ's name—the obscene wealth, the power struggles, the brutality of the Inquisition and the Crusades—the more I realized that Catholicism as a religion had little to do with the teachings of Christ. This began a lifelong trend of me being attracted to an ideal and then becoming disillusioned when I was confronted with the reality behind the ideal.

I continued to attend the seminary for another two years. I displayed all the outward appearances of the perfect son, except I wasn't. I had a whole secret life—from my parents, at least—that began as normal boyish mischief but was gradually evolving into criminality by the time I was a teenager. In addition to the woods and fields, my neighborhood was also a giant construction site. I would sneak out after everyone had gone to bed, climb through my bedroom window and shimmy down the drainpipe. I would meet up with my two friends Mark and Bill, and we'd explore and, when the spirit moved us, vandalize one of the many half-built houses. One house on our block was fully constructed, but the people who had bought it had reneged on the contract, so it was left vacant for a long period of time. We set up our base of operations in the attic. Some nights, we would just hang out for a few hours, listening to Cousin Brucie on the radio—that's Bruce Morrow, a legendary rock 'n roll DJ in NYC—and maybe leaf through *Playboy* magazines and smoke cigars. On other nights, we would break into houses after making sure nobody was home. We weren't really interested in taking anything of value, although we had acquired the radio, the cigars, and the *Playboy* magazines that way. Usually, we'd just raid the refrigerator; we were just into the adventure of the thing. Then, in a simple twist of fate, I was unable to meet my friends one night, and that was the night they were caught. Mark and Bill ended up with criminal records, and I did not, even though I had been involved in virtually all of their escapades. I can't imagine what a scandal it would have been had a seminarian been busted for breaking and entering.

In late 1964, Secretary of Defense Robert McNamara announced the closure of the Brooklyn Navy Yard, the place where my father worked. At the end of my junior year in 1965, my father got a job with General Dynamics in Quincy, Massachusetts, and the family moved to Rhode Island. This provided a convenient excuse for leaving the seminary, as I had been unable to muster the courage to tell my mother the priesthood no longer interested me. What I still couldn't tell her was that the day I left the seminary, I had also left the Catholic Church.

In 1966, I graduated from Bishop Hendricken, another all-boys Catholic high school, in Warwick, Rhode Island, and in the fall of that year, I entered Providence College—again, at that time, an all-boys Catholic school. In my first semester, I made the Dean's List. In those days, if you made the Dean's List during the first semester, you were allowed unlimited cuts to classes in the second semester. I proceeded to use this privilege with abandon, and about halfway through the term, I was so far behind in all my classes that there was little chance I would ever catch up.

I was feeling restless and imprisoned by the limitations of doing what was expected of me. I had dreams of breaking away, of setting out on some sort of adventure, a quest to find myself, but it seemed it was only a dream, and, perhaps like my father, I just didn't have the courage to take that step. Then, fate intervened.

I was out in the family car with Henry and some of our friends, and I had a small fender bender accident in a parking lot. This provided me with the excuse I needed. So, I told my brother that I was not going home; I was running away. Henry, when he realized I was serious, quickly called my mother and put me on the phone with her. Of course, she convinced me to come back home. I spent many hours that night talking back and forth with her. I told her I didn't know what I wanted to do about college, although I didn't mention the fact that I had been skipping classes for weeks. By the time the conversation ended and my mother went to bed, she was convinced she had again bent me to her will, and I wasn't going anywhere. I thought so, too.

The next morning, however, I was supposed to get up earlier than the rest of the family to go to my part-time job in a restaurant, and almost without thinking, I packed a bag, put about twenty-some dollars in my pocket, and stood at the door with my hand on the doorknob. Was I really going to do this? It felt like I stood there for hours, but it was probably just minutes. Finally, I opened the door and left the norm behind.

Almost immediately, I began having second thoughts. My initial plan was to hitchhike around the country, but first, I wanted to visit my girlfriend, Cassandra, at my old stomping grounds on Long Island. I hitched rides all the way to Commack, which took about half a day. Cassandra met me at the front door of her house but didn't invite me in. She didn't seem particularly pleased to see me. I blurted out what I was planning to do, hoping, perhaps, she would talk me out of it. Her response was like a slap in the face: "Why should I care about what you do?"

Years later, I found out that the only reason she had shown any interest in me at all was that she had a crush on my brother Henry, and since he wasn't paying much attention to her, she hung out with me in order to be close to him. So much for that relationship.

I was walking down the road after the kiss-off from Cassandra and starting to seriously question if this whole adventure was a good idea. Maybe I should just go home with my tail between my legs and resume the life I was running away from. Then a car passed me by and began beeping furiously, then pulled over to the side of the road. The driver wildly waving at me was Mark, my old sidekick.

Mark and I had been inseparable all through grammar school. After the nuns at St. Ann's had accepted me and my sister, a deluge of students from Commack began attending the school, Mark among them. We were partners in mischief. Whenever we got caught, my mother was always convinced it was Mark's fault, that he had somehow led her poor innocent boy astray. Actually, it was usually the other way around. Mark was always ready to participate in any crazy ploy I came up with. He even followed me to the seminary for a year, but dropped out when he couldn't hack the academics. We drifted apart after that, even more so when my mother forbade me to see him after he and Bill had been arrested.

I told him my plan to hitchhike around the country, and immediately he was all in. He was working some low-level job, hanging out in bars at night (in those days, the drinking age in New York was eighteen), and generally doing nothing but waiting around to see if he got drafted. He wanted some excitement in his life as much as I did. Quickly, my whole perspective changed. Having a partner was exactly what I needed to pull this off.

Needless to say, Mark's mother was not enthused when he brought me home and announced to her our plans. She had recently separated from her long-time husband, who had left her for a younger woman, and she was preparing to pack up and head for her hometown of Denver. She was expecting Mark to help her with the move. Mark promised to meet up with her in a few months' time in Denver and help her settle in. She wasn't mollified by this, but there wasn't much she could do. Meanwhile, I never communicated with my parents about where I was going or what I was planning to do. My life to that point had been all about conformity and obedience; I was relishing my newfound freedom and was afraid I would lose my resolve if I heard my mother's voice beckoning me home.

I hung around Mark's house for two or three days until he received his last paycheck, and then we headed out. Florida was our first destination. Our plan was to hitchhike until our money ran low, stop and work for a while to replenish our funds, and then get back on the road. We soon realized that this hitchhiking thing was not going to be so easy. We got a ride or two and reached New York City, but you can't hitchhike in a city, so we had to walk across Manhattan, then north to the George Washington Bridge, and walk across the bridge to New Jersey. At the end of the first day, we found a barn in central rural New Jersey with a haystack inside, where we burrowed for the night.

At some point, the owner of the barn came in and turned on the lights. I don't know if it was a routine check or if he suspected something. We huddled in the haystack, holding our breath, hoping we hadn't left any signs of our entry and that the farmer didn't have a shotgun and was of a mind to spray some buckshot into the hay. He must not have detected us, because he turned off the lights and left.

Don't let anyone tell you that being covered with hay protects you from the cold. We woke up miserable: cold, tired, achy, and sort of wondering what the hell we were doing. It was the middle of March, when the relatively pleasant temperatures during the daytime would plunge towards freezing at night. Mercifully, we found a roadside diner and went inside to warm up. Mark ordered a cup of coffee, and I followed suit, more from the desire to get my hands around something warm than anything else. It was the first cup of coffee I'd ever had in my life, but it was the beginning of a lifelong love affair between me and the bewitching black brew.

After about an hour in the diner, we were back out on a secondary road, not an interstate, heading south. Before we could hitch our first ride, a state police car pulled over, and the officer informed us that hitchhiking was illegal in New Jersey, even on secondary roads. He ordered us into the back of the car, but instead of hauling us into a police station, he gave us a ride all the way to the Delaware Memorial Bridge. We managed to get across the bridge before the end of the day, but then met another state trooper—this time in Maryland—who shooed us off the interstate and told us to stay on secondary roads. We had little luck getting anywhere on secondary roads—folks driving on those roads were usually going short distances—so we decided to call it a day. Mark insisted we check into a motel rather than spend another night in a barn. I didn't have a lot of money with me; at least Mark had his final paycheck, so he was a bit more affluent, but I didn't resist his suggestion.

The next morning, feeling refreshed from a good night's sleep, we set out once again. After a couple of short-distance hitches, we seemingly lucked out and got picked up by two guys in their mid-twenties who said they were driving all the way to Florida. As we rode along, however, it became clear that maybe we hadn't been so lucky after all. Mark and I were sitting in the back seat of a two-door sedan, which meant we were essentially trapped in the car with no way out unless the two in the front seat decided to let us out. The second thing was that our hosts quickly informed us that they were heading to Florida because they were fleeing from some unspecified crime they had committed in New York, which was why they were driving on secondary roads rather than Interstate 95.

We managed to keep an apprehensive but cordial relationship with them, laughing at their jokes, even the ones with an edge of menace to them delivered by the guy in the passenger seat. We drove straight through the night and into the next day. This was my first trip out of the Northeast, and I was amazed when we found ourselves at some godforsaken gas station in rural Georgia in the middle of the night and I couldn't understand a word the young gas station attendant was saying. His accent sounded like he was speaking a foreign language.

We finally made it to their destination—West Palm Beach, where the mother of one of the guys lived—in the late afternoon of the next day. We were trying to locate the street his mother lived on when we saw the flashing lights of a cop car behind us. I guess seeing four men in a car with New York plates driving somewhat aimlessly around town was a bit too much provocation for this West Palm Beach police officer. I was trying to work out in my mind how Mark and I were going to separate ourselves from the two fugitives in the front seat when they got arrested. To my surprise, it was Mark and I who got arrested—or at least detained—and the cop let the two fugitives drive off. Mark was still on probation from the breaking and entering charge in Commack, and this information caused the cop to focus on us rather than the criminals in the front seat. Mark had cleared the trip with his probation officer—that was part of the business he took care of before we left—but we had to sit around the West Palm Beach police station for a couple of hours while the local cops made sure he was telling the truth. The incident at least had the advantage of getting us away from our host/captors. Eventually, we were able to leave the cop station; from there, we checked into a fleabag hotel. We only had about ten dollars between us, so this would be one of our stop-and-work places.

We survived for a week eating peanut butter as we scanned

the help-wanted ads in the local newspaper. We went to an unemployment office, and they sent us out on a job interview to be busboys at the Bath and Tennis Club in Palm Beach. I had no idea what we were walking into. The Club had been built in 1927 by the financier Edward F. Hutton and his wife, Marjorie Merriweather Post, who had founded General Foods and was then considered the richest woman in America. It was built right next to Post's sumptuous mansion, Mar-a-Lago, which was later bought by Donald Trump in 1985 and turned into his own infamous private club in the early nineties after he had been ridiculed and roundly snubbed by the Palm Beach old guard. It was exclusively WASP, no Blacks or Jews allowed. The Bath and Tennis Club was one of the swankiest oases for upper-crust society in America and, indeed, one could say in the world.

I was amazed that Mark and I—two drifters who had basically wandered in off the sidewalk—were hired to work there. We bussed lunch in the café during the afternoon and, occasionally, some private functions at night. Even more amazing, at least for us, the club provided room and board for its employees, so even though our wages were paltry, we had almost no expenses, so we could save just about every dime we made. This was important because Mark and I had decided, after our eventful trip to Florida, to end our hitchhiking careers and buy a car for the continuation of our adventures. The season at the club ended in late May, and the place shut down as the Palm Beach crowd headed out to wherever they spent the summers. This coincided nicely with our plans to move on.

We started spending our off-hours wandering along a strip of used car lots along Route 1 in West Palm Beach, checking out vehicles and prices. We were hoping to find a vehicle between $300 and $500, which would leave us with a few hundred dollars for the road. The pickings in that price range were pretty slim.

One day, passing by a service station, we were stopped cold by a vision in the parking lot—a 1953 Cadillac hearse, canary yellow with a black vinyl roof and silver landau bars on the sides. We fell in love. It was in pristine condition inside and out. The front seats were red leather, and the back of the hearse was lined in purple velvet. Mark asked the service station manager if the hearse might be for sale.

The manager pointed to a young man standing nearby and said, "Ask him; he's the owner."

We approached the guy, making the requisite oohs and ahhs about the hearse. As expected, he said unequivocally that it wasn't for sale. We nodded sagely in agreement, noting that if we owned it, we wouldn't consider selling it either. We engaged in a bit of small talk, then Mark and I started to leave. As a complete afterthought, Mark turned and gave him a phone number where we could be reached, saying that if he happened to change his mind in the next couple of weeks to give us a call.

About a week later, the owner called and said something had come up, and he needed to sell the hearse. He was asking $1,500. Way more than we could afford, we told him. Okay, how much can you offer? The guy must have really needed money. $500, we said. How about $750? $700? Done. We were now the proud owners of a yellow Cadillac hearse, except that now we had only $100 for the road.

When the season ended, we drove up the Florida coast and across the Panhandle into Alabama. Everywhere we went, the hearse was the center of attention. The added bonus was that we could sleep in the back, although in addition to the plush purple velvet on the floor, there were also rollers on which to slide coffins, and the rollers were not particularly comfortable to sleep on.

We made it as far as New Orleans before the money ran out. A friendly gas station owner allowed us to park the hearse in the back for a few days, and we survived by shoplifting from grocery stores and siphoning gas from parked cars while we looked for work. Finally, we both got jobs at a Burger King in Metairie, a suburb of New Orleans. I think the manager thought the hearse was cool; he wanted us to park it out front to attract customers while we were working.

At Burger King, we met Etta Jo, a fortyish Southern belle with hair dyed red and piled high on her head, seemingly frozen in place by masses of hair spray. She was sweet as molasses, with a bit of spice when she'd had a few drinks, and when we told her that we were sleeping in the back of the hearse, she wouldn't hear of it. She and her husband, Elmo, offered us a place to stay for $50 a month, a little fishing shack across the river, over the Huey P. Long Bridge, in the town of Westwego. The shack was situated on a sliver of land between the levee and the river, so if Old Man River decided to rise overnight, we'd be floating out of our beds in the morning.

Mark and I worked until midnight, but were still full of youthful adrenaline when we finished. One night, along with two other night-shifters, we grabbed some white culinary jackets from the kitchen and drove the hearse downtown. In those days, Bourbon Street was not a pedestrian mall; cars were driving down the street twenty-four hours a day. I got out of the hearse where Bourbon met Canal and started walking down Bourbon. Mark circled back around in the hearse and drove down Bourbon behind me. As the hearse drew even with me, I started coughing and gagging, then grabbed my chest and fell to the ground, feigning death. The two night-shifters jumped out of the hearse in their white jackets, picked me up off the sidewalk, and threw me into the back. We drove off, laughing, much to the startled amazement of the partying onlookers. The driver of the car behind us must have been curious because he followed the hearse through the streets of the French Quarter until I finally sat up and waved to him through the back window.

There was a girl who worked the night shift—Gerry—who

had just graduated from high school. She was clearly on the prowl for a husband and made it clear that she was interested in me. After three years at the seminary, a final year of high school at an all-boys school, and then the all-boys Providence College, I didn't have much of a clue how to respond to a woman's overt flirtations. Gerry finally lost patience with my lack of response and took matters into her own hands, and in short order, we became lovers. Gerry lived at home with her parents, so our time together was at the fishing shack, which made things more than a little uncomfortable for Mark. He was itching to get back on the road, and I was more and more settling in. Gerry was reeling me in; she was my first sexual relationship, and needless to say, I was enjoying it. Finally, in response to expectations, I bought Gerry a cheap engagement ring and asked her to marry me.

That was the last straw for Mark. He announced he had bought a train ticket for Denver and was leaving. He didn't care about the hearse and said I could have it. I drove him to the train station, and we didn't say much to each other. I shook his hand, said goodbye, and that was the last I ever saw of him.

Once Mark was gone, I started to realize what I was getting myself into. I had again succumbed to the burden of expectations, and I was hurtling down a path that I didn't want to take. I had embarked on my life's great adventure and then had allowed myself to be sidetracked. Marriage was the last thing I wanted or needed at that stage of my life. I was painting myself into a corner, and I did the only thing I knew to escape.

I ran.

A few weeks after Mark left, unbeknownst to Gerry, I parked the hearse next to the little fishing shack—like Mark, never to see it again—hitch-hiked down to the recruiter's office in New Orleans, and on April 15, 1968, I enlisted in the Army. Unbeknownst to me, I had left something of myself behind that I would find out about in a phone call more than forty years later.

Chapter 3

The Family Man

Running away. It seems I've been running away from things for much of my life. Running away has been my go-to solution when things get too hard, too complicated, or too boring. Even now, as I sit here writing this, safely ensconced in the bosom of my middle-class family, the urge can hit me. Get into my car and drive off alone. Keep on going, head for the horizon, and don't turn back.

Don't get me wrong; I love my family. My wife and children are the most wonderful thing that have ever happened to me in my life. The good thing about having a family is that you're almost never alone; that's also the bad thing about having a family. A family keeps you tethered to responsibility, mired in routine, a slave to love given and returned.

In my mind, the choice was always clear: chase your dreams or settle down. You could logically say that it doesn't have to be such a stark choice. My sitting here typing these words is my way of trying to chase my dreams without giving up my family. This "book" I've been writing for about forty years seems no closer to reality than when I started. Sure, I have pages and pages of unconnected thoughts and something of a story worth telling, but I don't know if it will ever be more than digital scribblings that will disappear when my hard drive is reformatted after I'm dead.

The fact is, I'm done running. If the choice, indeed, is chasing dreams or settling down, then I have made my choice. I wonder if my father ever had dreams he wanted to chase. I wonder if he ever thought he could be more than a shipfitter, more than a working stiff hanging on by his fingernails in the suburbs. I never saw it, but maybe he did. Funny thing, he never chased his dreams, and I did, yet we both ended up in the same place. I wonder which of us made the wrong choice.

In 2018, Natasha and I celebrated our twenty-fifth wedding anniversary at a romantic little restaurant in Warren, Vermont. I should say we celebrated one of our two wedding anniversaries. There were two ceremonies, a civil one and a church one, about six months apart. Natasha, never one to overlook an opportunity for celebration, makes sure we observe both. The twenty-fifth anniversary of the civil ceremony, which happened first, was celebrated with a full-blown party; thirty or so guests crammed into our house—eating, drinking, dancing, and whatever else was happening in the dark corners. The second one was a more intimate affair, just the two of us. We drank champagne and reminisced about our twenty-five years together. After the dinner, we went out to the little bridge in the middle of town for a kiss, which had become a ritual of our relationship. Our first kiss had been on a bridge, and now we kiss on every bridge we cross. It's amazing to me that I still love her as much as or more than when I first met her.

Natasha and I have two children, a boy and a girl. As can be expected, I love them both, passionately, unequivocally, unconditionally. Their presence in my life changed everything: my thoughts, my plans, my decisions, my actions. My first consideration in everything became not what was good for me but what was good for them.

The decision to move to the suburbs—the last place in the

world I would choose to live for myself—was made for them. We assumed that suburbia was where the good schools were, and I was gladly willing to submit myself to the stifling suburban lifestyle I had fled as a teenager for the chance to get my kids the opportunity for the best education. It was, of course, an illusion, as so much of life in the suburbs has always been. The facilities were impressive enough, with manicured athletic fields and state-of-the-art classrooms, but how could I expect an environment that requires conformity as the central organizing factor of life to teach anything other than that in its schools? I had a huge argument with my son's math teacher in high school, who had lowered his grade on a final test because he had used a pen rather than a pencil to complete it, against her instructions. I raged at the teacher, saying that a final test was to measure his comprehension of math and that whether he used a pen or a pencil had nothing to do with his understanding of the material. The teacher curtly replied that he hadn't followed the rules and was penalized for it. I asked her if following the rules was more important than understanding math, but she just turned and walked away. Perhaps she thought it was a rhetorical question.

What bothered me most about moving back to the suburbs was how easily I slipped back into the lifestyle. I tried to console myself with the idea that I was just playing the game, playing a role that I knew so well for the sake of my children, but the fact is I had become the role I thought I was playing: middle-class suburban dad.

After years of scuffling for money and living in cramped apartments, Natasha and I were both working at well-paying jobs, and we lived in a spacious McMansion surrounded by the requisite accouterments of suburban life: a shiny new propane grill on the deck, a riding mower for the lawn, and a gas-powered snow blower for the driveway. We were, apparently, the new darlings of the credit card companies, and almost daily, there was a new credit card offer for one or the other of us in the mailbox. The amount of space in our house was, perhaps, three or four times as much as any of our previous abodes. There was ample room to start accumulating living room sets and dining room sets and bedroom sets and entertainment centers and bookcases and treadmills, all acquired with the simple flash of a piece of plastic at one of the big boxes that surrounded us. I used a credit card to buy Natasha a Mercedes for her birthday—her dream car—a pre-owned one, to be sure, but enough of a status symbol for the Joneses to try to keep up with us. As the credit card debt ballooned, we started to play credit card roulette, transferring funds from high-interest cards to one of the zero-percent cards we were getting offered each week. When the introductory zero-percent offer ran out, we would just transfer the money to the latest zero-percent offer we had received.

The Family Man. From left, Daniel, Natasha, Peter, Anastasia.

My son was born in 1995, and my daughter a year and a half later. Like me when I was young, Dan was naturally athletic. I pushed him into basketball—perhaps trying to play out, through him, my own failed attempts at the sport. I held weekly training sessions with him, signed him up for all manner of basketball teams and basketball camps, and even coached one of the teams he was on. In grade school, he was the tall kid with better-than-average jumping skills, so he always played the center position. He stopped growing at about fourteen, and the 6'2" height he attained was actually short for higher-level basketball. That and his lack of competitive fire caused him to soon lose interest in the sport, and after being the only freshman to make the junior varsity team in high school, he announced in his sophomore year that he didn't want to play on the school team anymore. His passion was computers, and that's where he wanted to spend his time and energy.

It is, of course, very common for a teenager to, at some point, shrug off his parents' expectations and begin to assert his own ambitions. I wanted to give him the space to find himself, but I couldn't help feeling deeply disappointed when his expectations didn't match mine. It's a sometimes painful struggle—like a butterfly struggling to free itself from the cocoon, that struggle giving it the strength to fly. As a father, I wanted him to learn from my mistakes, but I soon realized that as he chose his own path, he would only—hopefully—learn from his own. I've come to realize that the things about him that most disappoint me are the things where he is most like me, that he is that way because that is what I taught him, and that my disappointment is at myself.

Through high school, Dan's mantra was to do the absolute minimum necessary to get by. The classes he enjoyed—like computer science and math—he did well in, but he barely attained passing grades in many of his other classes. He wanted to get into a high-level polytechnic institute—like Worcester Polytech Institute, which was a half hour's drive from our house—to pursue a computer science degree, but his GPA was not something that would impress college admissions departments, although his scores on the SATs somewhat made up for it. In the end, he settled for the state university in Worcester and graduated in five years. Throughout the summer after his graduation, I was pushing him to blanket the computer programming job market with résumés. He had attended a mediocre school and gotten mediocre grades. He would be competing with the top recruits graduating from the top schools. I tried to convince him that a volume approach to his job search was his only chance. He bided his time through the summer, then sent out a single résumé in August, and was hired. So much for a dad's sage advice.

My daughter, Anastasia, was the opposite of my son. She wasn't as naturally gifted as he was, but she more than made up for it by working harder than anyone else. She flitted from one interest to another when she was young, from figure skating to horseback riding to gymnastics, before she finally fell in love with ballet. Starting ballet training at thirteen is not particularly conducive to making a career of it, but she plugged away at it throughout high school and managed to get accepted to a joint Fordham University/Alvin Ailey BFA dance program. Although Ailey was not a ballet school, Anastasia plunged into the modern dance curriculum it offered. Anastasia was a good dancer but not a great dancer, and, of course, at Ailey, she was surrounded by great dancers. She worked hard to keep up, but she had to function at the absolute outer edge of her physical ability, leaving her totally exhausted and often injured during her four years there. After graduation, she headed off to Israel to try to establish her dance career but was met with disappointment and the onset of COVID. After a year, the spark of passion for dance was extinguished, and she came home to an ordinary life without dance.

As I write this, my two children are both in their mid-twenties, and much will change in their lives as they grow older. Lord knows, I was a very different person when I was thirty than I was when I was twenty. But I see in them similar paths to those chosen by me and my father. Like my father, my son, Dan, never strove to be anything special; he settled for ordinary and seemed perfectly content with his choice. Like me, my daughter, Anastasia, tried to follow her dream and break out of the patterns set out for her, but she too, like me, fell short of her dream.

And what of my other inadvertent offspring? Those two telephone conversations we had years ago are the only times we have ever talked. We exchanged a couple of emails and some pictures along the way, and we even made some plans to meet when he and his family were coming north for a vacation, but it never panned out. He made it clear that I was his biological father but that his "real" father was the man who raised him. His biological mother had given him up for adoption when he was born, but after he was an adult, she apparently felt the urge to find him and showed up on his doorstep one day and announced she was his mother. She gave him my name, and a little Internet searching led him to me.

After the initial excitement of connecting, I don't think either of us was sure what to do next. Each of us had forged a life completely separate and independent of the other, and neither of us particularly fit well in the other's life. Northern Louisiana is not particularly high on my list of places to visit, so the chances of our ever meeting seem slim. Perhaps we will meet someday, perhaps not.

Chapter 4

You're in the Army Now

Running away from the complications I had imposed on myself was a big part of my decision to join the Army, but it was more complex than that. When I dropped out of college, I lost my student deferment, and my draft board had been sending draft notices to my parents' house, which my mother—in a fit of pique over my clandestine departure—had been sending back to the draft board marked "Addressee Unknown."

But there was more to it than that. Part of it was a residue of working-class patriotism, one of the strong ideals I had grown up with. Mahoneys had been serving in the military since the Civil War. My great-uncles had served in the Civil War, my grandfathers served in World War 1, and my father and uncles served in World War II. Hey, Vietnam was my war. It was a no-brainer.

Mostly, though, I needed to prove myself, to establish my manhood in the quintessential American way: by participation in a war. My father kept his military service mementos in an old sea trunk in the attic. Once, my brother Henry and I had convinced him to open it, and among the pictures and uniform remnants, we saw the medals my father had been awarded, including a Bronze Star with a "V" device denoting heroism, the fourth highest military decoration. We asked him what he had done to receive it, and he joked that it was for jumping overboard to save a case of beer. He never did tell us the reason, which only added to its aura. The medals were tangible proof that my father had faced the test of courage and not been found wanting. I wanted medals, too, so no one could ever doubt my bravery.

Set squarely against this patriotic zeal and the need to prove myself was another set of ideals that continued to gnaw at my conscience. My generation—many of us fueled by the inspiring words of John Kennedy, "Ask not what your country can do for you …"—had championed movements for free speech, civil rights, and women's rights. I had never actively participated in any of these causes but had cheered from the sidelines as others did. In February of 1968, the greatest cause of the Boomers—the anti-war movement—exploded into the national consciousness. The NVA and Viet Cong had launched the Tet Offensive, a massive coordinated series of attacks on most of the major cities, towns, and military installations in South Vietnam. Although the offensive was ultimately a huge military defeat for the enemy, it was an even greater political defeat for the United States. It shattered the illusion that all was going well and that an American victory was just around the corner. It soured large portions of the American public on their political and military leaders, showing them up as naïve Pollyannas at best or downright liars at worst.

What had started out as small student protests against the draft burgeoned into massive multi-generational demonstrations to end the war, as the horrors being perpetrated in Vietnam were nightly televised into American living rooms and the lies of the government became too obvious to ignore. It was the major turning point in the war. Although I was aware of all of this—even felt sympathetic towards it—it didn't sway me from my chosen course.

The first stop in my military odyssey was Fort Polk, somewhere in Central Louisiana, a million miles from nowhere, except a nondescript little town called Leesville, whose main purpose was to service the soldiers at Polk. The five-hour bus ride from New Orleans was filled with Southern boys, both Black and White, many of them never having spent any length of time in close proximity to anyone from another race. I don't remember there being a whole lot of tension, at least not at first. In retrospect, this seems a bit surprising since barely two weeks earlier, on April 4, 1968, Martin Luther King Jr. had been assassinated in Memphis, Tennessee, setting off massive violent demonstrations across the country. Also surprisingly, there was almost no talk about Vietnam during the bus ride to Polk. I was not the compulsive news hound then that I became later in life, and what was happening in Vietnam was little more than background noise to the personal foibles confronting me. Everyone on the bus—a mixture of country boys from Mississippi, Cajuns from Louisiana, and urban Blacks from the projects in New Orleans—was feeling much like me—scared, excited, and confused. It was like a high school field trip, all macho posturing and false bravado. Vietnam seemed too far away to worry about.

That bus ride was my first introduction to the word *fuck* as the most significant word in the English language. I had heard it before, but growing up in a homogenized suburban Catholic environment, *damn* and *hell* were the curse words of choice, with an occasional *shit* when things were really bad. Uttering *fuck* was something of a guilty pleasure, a word that teenage boys would say under their breath, then giggle nervously and look around to see if any adult had overheard them. On that bus ride to Polk, every other word was *fuck*. *Fuck* was used as a noun, a verb, and an adjective. If something needed a bit more emphasis, then *motherfuck* upped the ante. I was a bit taken aback but quickly adjusted my vocabulary, and it soon became a habit I have not broken to this day. Whenever my emotions are elevated—when I'm happy, or angry, or scared, or sad— then the *fucks* and *motherfucks* come flowing out of my mouth in an endless stream of vulgarity.

During the Vietnam War, Polk was infamous among infantry soldiers for a training area called Tigerland, a small portion of the land consisting of dense, jungle-like vegetation that, along with the heat, humidity, and precipitation in that part of Louisiana, closely replicated the conditions in Vietnam. More soldiers were shipped to Vietnam from Fort Polk than from any other American training base, a fact that the drill sergeants who met our bus when we arrived immediately drummed into our heads. If you trained at Tigerland, you were going to Vietnam. The specter of the war suddenly became very real to all of us.

We took our first baby steps of indoctrination at Fort Polk's reception center, where they buzz-cut your hair, gave you a uniform and bedding, and generally abused and belittled you. Like everyone there, I barely knew what was going on most of the time. I just went where I was told and did what was demanded. We were subjected to endless sessions of filling out paperwork, assembly-line inoculations, and a whole battery of different tests. After one such test—probably the Armed Services Vocational Aptitude Battery (ASVAB) test—they called out the names of maybe five of us out of two hundred, directed us into another room, and said we'd just qualified for Officer Candidate School (OCS). Did I want to be an officer? I was barely nineteen years old, and the Army was offering me the opportunity to lead men into battle. I didn't have any idea what that meant, and I really didn't know if I wanted to be an officer. When I joined, I hadn't signed up for any particular MOS (Military Occupation Specialty). I had only requested jump school. As part of proving myself, I had decided I needed to do the things I was most afraid of, and I was deathly afraid of heights. So, I had figured that jumping out of airplanes would be the perfect cure.

We were given a few days to think about it. During that time, we received a little card listing the pay grades, i.e., the salaries according to each level of rank. I looked at the salary of an E-1—$109 a month—the lowest level of an enlisted soldier, and then I looked at the salary of an O-1—$343 a month—the lowest level of an officer. That's when I decided I was going to Officer Candidate School. OCS was also supposed to be tough. If I could get through OCS, I'd be strong enough to get through anything.

The last night at the reception station, before they split us up into companies and marched us off to the actual eight weeks of basic training, I got involved in a pick-up basketball game and sprained my ankle. Next morning, I went on medical call, expecting that I would be sitting in the reception station peeling potatoes for a few weeks until the ankle healed. The medic handed me an Ace bandage and told me to get back in formation. So, I went through the first several weeks of basic training on a sprained ankle.

The drill sergeants woke us up at four or five o'clock in the morning for a several-mile run, then calisthenics, and then we'd run everywhere all day to each training session, not to mention the endless push-ups whenever you or someone in your platoon fucked up. I had thought I was in good shape when I joined. I wasn't even close, and doing it all on a sprained ankle didn't help, but I found out I was physically capable of much more than I ever imagined.

My MOS was Eleven-Bravo—infantry—so after basic training at Fort Polk, I was sent to Fort Dix, New Jersey, for another eight weeks of Advanced Infantry Training (AIT). I had never really fired a weapon other than BB guns and a .22 rifle at Boy Scout camp. In basic, we were all taught how to shoot the M-16, the standard Army weapon. In AIT, I was trained to use a number of other weapons: the M-60 machine gun, the M-79 grenade launcher, the M-72 LAW (Light Anti-Tank Weapon), the M18A1 Claymore mine, the .50 caliber machine gun, and the .45 caliber pistol. At the time, I never really connected the firing of weapons to the task we were ultimately being trained for, namely to kill other human beings before they killed you.

For me, it was just another sport, a test of skill. I found out I was pretty good with a rifle, and I got an expert rating in both the M-16 and the M-60 machine gun, which allowed me to pin two Army expert qualification badges to my then medal-barren uniform.

At the end of AIT, I had a ten-day leave before the start of OCS. I spent the time at my parents' house. All had been forgiven me after I joined the Army. Although my parents were disappointed that I had dropped out of college—I was the first in the family to attempt higher education—joining the military was an acceptable alternative, and I was back on a path of doing what was expected. I felt uncomfortable in the role of soldier-son and hero-brother that I needed to play while I was there, but it was easier to hide behind that façade than to try to articulate the self-doubts and worries that were plaguing me at the time.

I was about to embark on twenty-three weeks of rigorous Officer Candidate School training. The dropout rate of this training was significant; forty to fifty percent of those who started were unable to finish. If you were able to survive it—and I do mean *survive*—then you would graduate as an infantry second lieutenant. I was worried that I would not be able to handle the training and would drop out. I was terrified that I would complete the training and be unable to handle the responsibility that being an infantry officer would require.

So, in early September 1968, shortly before my twentieth birthday, I headed to Fort Benning, Georgia, to begin OCS. The Army had an interesting way of training men to be leaders. During the first eighteen weeks of OCS, you were treated like the lowest piece of shit on the planet. You were shown absolutely no respect, you had no status, you were just a nothing. Lording it over you were the Tac Officers, short for Tactical Officers, who were the lieutenants in charge of the candidates. Virtually all of the Tac Officers were recent OCS graduates, so they saw it as a chance to do to the new candidates what had been done to them, which became a self-perpetuating cycle. Most Tac Officers didn't know their ass from their elbow. A lot of foolish lieutenants got the idea that this was how you ran a platoon, by treating the men under your command the way you were treated during OCS, which, in some cases, led to young lieutenants dying from gunshot wounds in their backs or grenades under their bunks from their own men in Vietnam.

A big part of the Tac Officers' job was to enforce the often sophomoric discipline code of OCS. This included the precise placement of every single item in a candidate's room, with prescribed distances between boots and shower shoes under your bunk and specific folding patterns for the clothes in your dresser drawers. I was once denied a weekend pass because a pair of underwear was not properly folded. At meals, candidates were required to sit at attention, eyes straight ahead, and forbidden to speak to one another. You had to eat a "square meal," which consisted of grasping the fork from its precise location on the table, lifting the food directly vertically from the plate, then directly horizontally into your mouth, then retracing that path to place the fork back into its original position on the table. There it stayed until you chewed and swallowed the food in your mouth before repeating the same cycle once again. To complicate this further, meals were strictly regimented to last exactly thirty minutes. Since the mess hall could accommodate perhaps half of the OCS company, the rest had to stand at attention in line outside the mess hall until a place was freed up for the next in line to enter. At the end of thirty minutes, the mess hall was cleared, oftentimes leaving those at the back of the line shit out of luck as far as that meal was concerned.

The reason for all this, they said, was to teach men to think under pressure. An infantry lieutenant in a combat situation needed to make decisions under tremendous pressure, so during OCS, they kept you in a state of constant, never-ending stress to see how you'd react. But this method didn't teach how to think; it taught how to obey—blindly and unquestioningly.

We had to try to reconcile this obedience with another crucial lesson: everything in Officer Candidate School was against the rules, so you had to learn how to break them in order to get things done. The mess hall protocols, which usually left large portions of the company hungry by the end of the day, were an integral part of this stressful environment. We dealt with it by having "pogie runs," pogie being the nickname for illegal food. Someone would collect money, then sneak out of the barracks at night, go into town, buy food, and then come back and share it with everyone.

Most of the guys in OCS were fresh recruits like me. Sprinkled in among us, however, were maybe ten or fifteen guys who had been in the military for four or five years—a couple had already been to Vietnam and back—and they had decided that they wanted to become officers. There was one guy who was a former Special Forces sergeant. He had been to Vietnam twice, and he had previously been stationed at Benning, so he knew a lot of people and knew his way around the post. He was the guy who usually made the pogie run because he knew how to get things done.

One night, he got caught making the run. Of all the guys in my OCS class, everybody was convinced that he would really make an excellent officer; he was a natural leader. They kicked him out of OCS for making the pogie run; unauthorized absence from the company area was considered a major breach of the rules. That was one of the other central lessons of OCS: you have to break the rules to get things done, but don't get caught. Lt. Calley, who would later be found guilty of overseeing the My Lai massacre, went through Officer Candidate School at Benning and graduated in 1967. In my opinion, the type of training he received during Officer Candidate School very much prepared Calley to do what he did, but he broke one of the cardinal rules; he got caught.

Freshly minted officer and gentleman.

After eighteen weeks, those who were left became senior candidates, at which point we began to have certain privileges like occasional weekend passes, and we received treatment a bit more like the officers we were about to become; junior candidates now had to salute us when we passed. Most of those who survived to the eighteenth week made it the rest of the way. I survived, and on March 15, 1969, I became an infantry second lieutenant.

Had Officer Candidate School prepared me to lead men in battle? Probably not. I had learned a bit more about the military and about certain types of weapons. We had to learn how to call in artillery, how to use a compass, and how to read a map. OCS did a pretty good job of teaching these technical things, and guys who couldn't deal with them washed out. Where I thought that the school utterly failed was in two areas. The first was small unit tactics, how you maneuver your forces in a battle situation. Those of us who graduated from Infantry Officer Candidate School didn't have a clue about how to lead a platoon in battle. It would be strictly OJT—on-the-job training—when we got to Vietnam. The second failure was with regard to leadership. A platoon leader was on intimate terms with all the men in his command, twenty to thirty men of differing ages, races, backgrounds, and needs, and the cast of characters was constantly changing as guys rotated in and out or were wounded or killed. How do you motivate them, how do you create a team from this motley group, how do you keep up their morale, how do you deal with their personal problems, how do you maintain their respect? There was no training in OCS about any of that.

So, ready or not, the Army had made me an officer, if not quite a gentleman. I had originally signed up for three years. By pure luck of scheduling, my various trainings took place back-to-back, so I actually graduated from OCS eleven months after I had joined the Army, which cut a month off my total military commitment. At the time, an officer had a two-year obligation from the day he graduated from OCS. Some draftees tried to finagle the system. If they were in for an original two-year commitment, they would try to remain in OCS by failing and starting over until they had less than a year left in the Army, then they would drop out. Since the tour of duty in Vietnam was for a year minimum, they couldn't be sent to Vietnam with less than a year's service remaining. Eventually, the Army changed it to a three-year commitment from the day you started OCS, regardless of whether you graduated or not.

Although I had signed up for jump school when I enlisted, once I agreed to go to OCS, jump school was not guaranteed, but I requested it for assignment after OCS, and I was accepted. The first week, Ground Week, was easy, primarily focused on learning how to execute a PLF, a parachute landing fall. This consisted of endlessly jumping off a three-foot high platform until, hopefully, the mechanics of the PLF—hitting the five points of contact: balls of feet, calves, thighs, buttocks, pull-up muscles—became second nature. There was, of course, a significant amount of PT, but after OCS, I was in the best shape of my life, so all the running and push-ups were of no consequence to me.

The second week of jump school was Tower Week. This is where I first had to confront my fear of heights. There were two towers to jump from. The thirty-four-foot tower was designed to simulate jumping from the door of the plane. Four students would jump in quick succession to practice group coordination. In a real parachute jump, there was a limited amount of time over a drop zone with no room for any delay between individuals exiting the plane. The focus on speed and technique kept me from thinking too much about height—that and the pain in my crotch from the harness we had to wear. The harness replicated the harness of a parachute, but unlike an actual jump, where you were constantly falling so there was little weight exerted on the harness, the harness on the thirty-four-foot tower was hooked to a pulley that ran along a cable. When you jumped from the tower, your full body weight jammed the harness up into your balls, where it stayed as you traversed the seventy-five or so yards to the end of the cable.

Next up was the two-hundred-fifty-foot tower. With a fully opened parachute above you, students were lifted from the ground to the top of the tower by cables, then the cables released, and the students floated back to the ground. This was very similar to the famed Coney Island Parachute Jump, the key difference being the cables remained fastened to the parachute in the amusement park. There was no distraction here from the perception of height, except perhaps, closing your eyes on the ascent. I forced myself to keep my eyes open, utterly scared and utterly thrilled by the experience. The surge of adrenaline that resulted was the beginning of my addiction to that hormone.

The third week was Jump Week. The C-123 aircraft we jumped from had no windows, so that lessened the sense of being 1,250 feet from the ground. Still, sitting in the plane as we headed for the drop zone for that first jump, my hands were trembling and my stomach was threatening to eject the contents of my breakfast all over the floor. I held it together, primarily because I didn't want to be seen as a "pussy" in front of the others, but I suspect most of them were going through the same shit as I was. Finally, the command came from the Jump Master, "Stand up! Hook up!" We all stood and hooked up our static lines—fifteen-foot-long lines attached at one end to the bag on your back that the parachute was in and at the other end to a cable running down the middle of the plane. The moment had arrived. Again, the Airborne School's focus on speed, technique, and group dynamics didn't give you time to think about fear. As the two lines of trainees shuffled towards the two rear doors, you were pushing against the back of the man in front of you, and the guy behind you was pushing against you. You were no longer an individual making individual decisions, just a mindless automaton being carried along by the momentum of the "stick." When you got to the door, you jumped because there was nothing else you could do. At least, that's how I got through it.

The adrenaline rush I got dropping from a tower was nothing compared to jumping out of an airplane. The first four or so seconds were a combination of ecstasy and terror as you waited for the gentle tug on your harness that told you your chute had deployed. Then you found yourself hanging in the air surrounded by dozens of others like yourself, screaming, singing, and laughing maniacally at the pure lunacy of what you had just done. On the first jump, there were usually one or two trainees who didn't wait long enough for the main chute to open and deployed their reserve chute prematurely, suffering the ignominy of hanging beneath two canopies as they descended to the ground.

Ah, the ground, Earth, the fabled place of safety for those who fly or those who sail! Except it was rushing up at you at a speed of about twenty-five feet per second. The initial exhilaration once the chute opened was short-lived, usually less than a minute. You quickly realized you weren't flying; you were falling, and reaching the safety of the ground was the most dangerous part of the whole enterprise. You hoped to remember the mechanics of the PLF from Ground Week—legs together, knees flexed, hit the five points of contact. On my first jump, one unlucky trainee hit the ground with his legs apart and knees locked. He broke both his legs. I managed a reasonable PLF on my first jump. Although I only hit three of the five points of contact—balls of the feet, buttocks, pull-up muscles—I arrived intact.

You had to make five jumps during Jump Week to get your jump wings. There were four so-called Hollywood jumps, that is, jumps without any equipment, and one so-called combat jump with a full load of equipment similar to what you would carry into a battle. On my third jump—a Hollywood jump—I sprained my ankle on the landing, the same ankle I had sprained just before basic training. I was afraid if I reported the sprained ankle to anyone, they would wash me out of jump school, so I made my final two jumps—one of which was the combat jump—on a sprained ankle. I got my jump wings, but now, over fifty years later, my ankle will never let me forget that decision.

My unit assignment after OCS and jump school in April of 1969 was the 197th Infantry Brigade at Fort Benning. The 197th was a lackluster group assigned to impersonate the roles of enemy combatants in the training of the U.S. Army Infantry School. Nicknamed "the Big Red Dud" for the design of the unit's shoulder patch and the fact that their role as aggressors required them to fire blanks during training exercises, it was not considered a plum assignment for a newly minted lieutenant. Worse still, it was predominantly a "leg" unit, not an airborne unit, so my jump wings would be little more than a uniform decoration, and I would not get the extra "jump pay" available to those assigned to an airborne unit. There was, however, one airborne company attached to the 197th: Company A, 75th Infantry (Ranger). In February 1969, all U.S. Army Long Range Reconnaissance Patrol (LRRP) units were reorganized as the 75th Infantry Regiment (Ranger). Thirteen Ranger companies were in Vietnam, each attached to a division or separate brigade, acting as the eyes and ears of those units. LRRPs collected intelligence, discovered enemy troop locations, surveilled trails and enemy hot spots, directed artillery and air strikes, made bombing damage assessments, and performed ambushes and sniper attacks. Additionally, Rangers recovered prisoners of war, captured enemy soldiers for interrogation, mined enemy trails and roads, and tapped wire communications of the North Vietnam Army and the National Liberation Front for South Vietnam (Vietcong) on the Ho Chi Minh Trail. Two companies, Company A and Company B, were kept stateside in strategic reserve. When I walked through the door of the 197th Brigade headquarters, garrisoned at Kelley Hill Barracks at Fort Benning, it just so happened that Company A needed another junior officer. And so, just like that, I became a LRRP platoon leader.

I spent four months at Company A, basically in a holding pattern until my orders for Vietnam came through. The mission of Company A was as mundane as the rest of the 197th, playing aggressor for the Infantry School. Company A, however, had the distinction of playing aggressors for the Ranger School at Camp Merrill near Dahlonega, Georgia. Ranger School was probably the toughest training the Army had to offer; the attrition rate was even greater than OCS. In those days, over sixty-five percent of those who started didn't finish. You didn't have to graduate from Ranger School to be assigned to a LRRP company, but it was prestigious if you had. I wanted to try it, so I put in a request for Ranger School while I was in Company A. But my company commander had washed out of Ranger School, so he didn't see the benefit of it and denied my request. Nevertheless, I got to experience a little bit of Ranger School from the other side, and frankly, I'm not sure if I would have been able to complete it.

My time in Company A was probably the best training I ever had. I was in charge of a platoon, most of whom had already served in Vietnam. Purple Hearts and Silver Stars abounded among them. I was the nominal leader of these men, but they were all aware that I was a so-called "shake-and-bake" lieutenant, Army slang for an OCS graduate. I knew almost nothing but wanted to learn, and they were willing to teach me. I think I was able to earn the respect of these men, not for my knowledge, leadership, or skills, but because I never tried to pretend to be anything more than I was. Even my crusty old platoon sergeant, who actually ran the platoon but rigidly adhered to military protocol, insisted that I was the one in charge and spoke to me deferentially: "Sir, don't you think we ought to do things this way?"

In October of 1969, I got my orders. First, I would go to Fort Bragg, North Carolina, to attend Advisor School, then on to Fort Bliss, Texas, for three months of Vietnamese language school, and then on to Vietnam, where I would be assigned as an advisor to a unit of the South Vietnamese Army.

The Vietnam War went through a number of different phases during its prolonged duration. After Nixon was elected in 1968, the war moved into what was called the Vietnamization phase. U.S. troops began slowly to be withdrawn, and the theory was that South Vietnamese troops would be trained and upgraded to assume the role of front-line fighters. The cynical description of this process among ordinary soldiers was "changing the color of the corpses." By late 1969 and early 1970, a significant number of those being sent to Vietnam were being sent as "advisors," and I was slotted into that group.

Advisor School was nothing much, merely the Army trying to teach, in its clumsy manner, Vietnamese cultural sensitivity to men who had spent many months getting indoctrinated with the refrain, "The only good gook was a dead gook," a sentiment that, despite my embrace of many of the macho elements of military life, disgusted me. Racism, of course, is as American as apple pie, and the dehumanization of the enemy was an essential element of military training in order to make it easier to kill them. Many soldiers in Vietnam resolved the ambiguity of who exactly was the enemy by simply assuming that ALL Vietnamese were the enemy, and the military, with its free-fire zones and search-and-destroy missions, heartily encouraged such thinking.

For me, the highlight, if you want to call it that, of Advisor School started the night before graduation. I was barhopping with a few of the other young lieutenants, and we ended the evening at the Airborne Bar on base. I was the only qualified airborne officer in the whole group and had been putting up with "leg" jokes for much of the night ("The only two things that fall out of the sky are paratroopers and bird shit"). As we were getting up to leave, emboldened by our presence in the Airborne Bar, I announced that I could chug a pitcher of beer in one go. Since we were on our way out, I assumed it would be an idle boast, but my companions took me up on it. One of them passed a hat and collected enough money to buy one last pitcher. So—I chugged it.

The next morning, we gathered in some sort of auditorium, and as part of the ceremony, they announced the outstanding student for the training cycle—me. So, I was supposed to come up on the stage and stand at attention while a letter of commendation that was to become a permanent part of my military record was read to the assembly by the commander of the school. About halfway through the reading, however, the effects of my alcohol consumption caught up with me, and I fainted dead away. In true military fashion, the proceeding continued while I lay on the floor for a few seconds until the letter reading was finished, and then I managed to stumble off into the wings. There were, perhaps, a few snickers that followed after me, most likely from my comrades of the previous evening.

Language School at Fort Bliss was a three-month course in Vietnamese that only provided us with a limited vocabulary of military terms, as opposed to the sixty-four-week course at the Defense Language Institute in Monterey, California, designed to produce fluent speakers. The joke among the students was that we were learning enough Vietnamese to get into trouble but not enough to get out of it.

Finally, in March 1970, I boarded the plane for Vietnam. By this time, I had no illusion that we were there to win anything. The U.S. was pursuing Nixon's "Peace with Honor" strategy, essentially a transition to getting our asses out of there while acting as if the ten or so years we had spent mired in the rice paddies had somehow been productive. I knew the war was wrong and that my participation in it was an exercise in futility. I knew the moral course of action would be to protest against the war rather than fight in it, but I had made a conscious decision to do my duty until I was no longer a soldier.

Chapter 5

International Development

The suburban lifestyle I chose for my family required a certain level of income to sustain. In 1993, I began my career in "international development." This is where the U.S. government spends massive amounts of "foreign aid" in other countries, ostensibly to "do good." When I first started working in this field, I thought I had found the ideal job for me—working to help others achieve a better life while being paid a rather handsome salary to do so. In some ways, it was similar to the work I had been trying to do in Vietnam. I was, again, an advisor, the all-knowing American descending from on high to work among the natives, dispensing wisdom and goodies to those willing to toe the U.S. government's line. In short order, I came to realize that my efforts in international development were as empty and worthless as my efforts in Vietnam had been.

I've had various jobs for various organizations over the years, but mostly, I worked as a senior contracts officer for a non-profit organization that received ninety-nine percent of its funding from the U.S. government. In order to receive the money, you had to follow a pile of rules and regulations about as high as a basketball rim. My job was to know these regulations and to make sure that everyone in my organization followed them.

That was not all there was to the job, of course. Most of the projects required us to distribute smaller amounts of money to other organizations, acting as the government's cashier and overseer for projects that were too small for the government to be bothered to deal with itself. This required setting up a process to choose who would receive the money, negotiating and drafting agreements, and endless training sessions on the rules and regs associated with signing the agreements. The training gave me the opportunity to travel to numerous countries around the world, like Haiti, Honduras, Angola, Congo, Uganda, Nigeria, Tanzania, Zimbabwe, Swaziland, South Africa, the Philippines, and Kenya. These were strange and fascinating and exotic and enormously interesting places that I never would have considered visiting otherwise. The travel was among the most enjoyable elements of the job.

On a training mission to Kenya.

There was another element of the job that I enjoyed. The rules associated with receiving U.S. government funds were byzantine and highly restrictive. Just about anything that could be done that might actually be of benefit to the people we were supposed to be helping was somehow against the rules or required specific written approval from a U.S. government contracts officer. Many of these government contract officers were divorced from the realities of the projects being supported, wallowing in murky regulatory backwaters, quick to deny any request that didn't comply with their interpretation of the rules, regardless of the efficacy of the request for the project. Some of the greatest enjoyment I got out of the job was finding ways within the regulations to thwart this obtuseness.

The reality of international development is that foreign aid money was primarily spent to further the foreign policy interests of the United States, not to "do good," although, on some rare occasions, the two goals did actually coincide. It's not that there weren't many good and decent people both in and out of government who worked in foreign aid and whose motivation was a genuine desire to help people less fortunate; it's just that the occasional good that actually came about from those efforts occurred in spite of the system we worked in rather than because of it.

Sprinkled in among the idealists and do-gooders was a healthy smattering of mindless bureaucrats, foreign aid whores, and the inevitable petty tyrants and micro-managers who were encountered in almost every field of endeavor. The bureaucrats were in love with the rules. They were not interested in what you could do or what you needed to do; they were only interested in what you couldn't do. The bureaucrats sat in their little cocoon offices surrounded by volumes of regulations, finding new and better ways to put roadblocks in the way of those trying to do good. What was right or what was necessary was not of interest to them, only what was allowed. Most contracts officers in and out of government are bureaucrats. I kept trying to convince myself that even though contracts officer was my title, it was not my calling. I wanted to see myself as a champion of the do-gooders, the one who could find the loopholes through the roadblocks thrown up by the regs-obsessed bureaucrats, the one who could clear the path for the righteous to succeed. The fact that I could beat the bureaucrats at their own game, however, only meant I was a better bureaucrat than they were.

Many of the foreign aid whores had started out as idealists but sank into cynicism under the weight of the indifference they confronted. They consoled themselves by saying that it's a business. That allowed them to then concentrate on following the money and disassociating themselves from any consequences of their work. The whores were not interested in results; they were interested only in pleasing the donor. It was a perfect symmetry, actually. If you were able to please the donor without actually producing any tangible results, then the donor would keep giving you money to do the same thing. I went to numerous countries that had been receiving U.S. foreign aid for decades. The assistance programs being run there were almost exactly the same ones that were run thirty years ago. The jargon was new, the acronyms were new, but the basic programs were the same, with the same results—or rather, the same lack of results.

It wasn't insane when you thought about it. It was designed that way. Most of the money in foreign aid was actually given to American organizations, not to the countries we were supposedly helping. The central purpose of U.S. foreign aid was to further the foreign policy interests of the United States, and the foreign policy interests of the United States were to keep these countries dependent on and subservient to the United States.

There's a question I could never answer, though. I didn't say it was a business; I just said it was a job. At some point, I lost the idealism about what I did; I became utterly unconcerned about any "results" associated with my work. I just wanted that paycheck deposited into my bank account every two weeks, and I only wanted the money to finance my family's lifestyle. I was fond of saying to my colleagues, "My work is not my life; my life begins when I walk out the door to this office building." Was that a whoreish way to think?

I was at a dinner with some colleagues in South Africa. We were interviewing a potential candidate for a senior technical position in Lesotho, a small mountainous country completely surrounded by the country of South Africa. The candidate was a medical doctor originally from India who had been working for another organization in Lesotho for several years. I did not know much of his background when we were first introduced before dinner, so I judged him to be a medical professional, a "country doctor" type doing good work among the natives. As he began to speak at dinner, however, I realized he was "one of us," a development professional, utterly at home with the acronym-laden, obfuscating, dehumanizing development-speak lingo that we used to discuss our work. He rattled on about OVCs and COPs and CSOs and FBOs and targets and indicators and the like. As the wine we were drinking began to take hold, I started realizing how disconnected we were from the values and ideals that had motivated most of us to get involved in this work in the first place. I mean, we were running a program where we were trying to help small communities deal with and support children who had been orphaned by the HIV/AIDS epidemic—a fine, humanitarian undertaking—yet anyone listening to our conversation wouldn't have a clue that the alphabet-soup jargon we were using had anything to do with a "fine humanitarian undertaking."

At one point, the doctor—perhaps trying to impress us with his commitment—stated loftily that his life was his work. I was fully in the grasp of the grape by then and blurted out that my work was not my life, that my work *financed* my life. The others at the table looked at me quizzically; such an attitude was decidedly uncommon in our line of work and frankly frowned upon. The world of non-profit development was mostly populated by unmitigated workaholics, ready to totally commit their time, effort, and resources—their lives—to the next project that came down the road. Few stopped to examine whether the projects we ran actually did any good, other than to keep large numbers of development professionals off the unemployment line. We established our indicators, reached our targets, reported our numbers to our funders in approved templates, and trumpeted the worth of our projects in success stories and fancy final reports. Few ever questioned the fact that the "system" in which we worked—the international development system—was in and of itself one of the greatest obstacles to success we would encounter.

I wanted to scream at my colleagues, "Guys, I've been there. I know what it's like; I know how noble it feels, how liberating, to forsake the personal for a higher cause. I also know how 'higher causes' can become petty in reality, how noble passion can get ground down into smirking cynicism in the details of day-to-day execution. I've had my idealism smashed on the rocks of reality too many times to risk the voyage again so easily. I want to believe, again, guys, just like you, but I know too much." Instead, I mumbled a bit to my colleagues' stares about my family being the most important thing in my life.

At another point in the conversation, someone referred to me as "the rules and regs guy." It is perhaps one of the greatest ironies of my life that after spending a large portion of my adult life as a self-identified rebel, more interested in breaking the rules than following them, my work was now to ensure that others followed the rules and complied with the regulations. I tried to tell myself that the worth of my work was in trying to find ways to keep the rules and regs from interfering with success, but it was a losing battle, and the "success" was dubious, to begin with. The rules and regs guy: was it any wonder my life was NOT my work?

But there's another side to this dilemma. A friend of mine told me about a young man who listened to a Les Paul record and was so taken with the sound of Paul's guitar that he determined that he was going to practice until he could duplicate the sound that Les Paul made. He practiced for years, perfecting the sound, then one day managed to meet Les Paul in person. He showed Paul what he had accomplished, and Paul was flabbergasted. Paul explained that in order to get the sound on the record, his guitar had been overdubbed numerous times. The young man was able to succeed in duplicating that sound because he didn't know that it was not possible to do so.

That is the beauty of idealism: young idealists do not know it is not possible to succeed; therefore, very often, they succeed. The cynics know it is not possible to succeed; therefore, invariably, they don't. So how does a cynic—most cynics are, like me, disillusioned idealists—recapture the naïveté that seems so necessary to maintain idealism? How do you slough off a lifetime of experience watching the bad guys win, the good guys slowly turning bad, and maintain the courage and enthusiasm to keep fighting for your ideals? I don't seem to have the answers to these questions. I continue to lurch between bouts of idealism and bouts of cynicism. The big problem is that cynicism is easier because it does not require you to take action. It is the quintessential excuse for laziness. And I am, if anything, a very lazy man.

Chapter 6

Next Stop Is Vietnam

The first thing I noticed about Vietnam was the heat, stepping out of the plane and being blasted in the face by a surge of blisteringly hot air. The next thing was the smell, a kind of sickly-sweet smell that permeated everything, a mixture of rotting vegetation and smoldering human shit that stung the nostrils but quickly became integrated into your senses as an unnoticed norm of the environment.

My first weeks in-country were taken up by endless army processing, then a brief in-country advisor training, which merely repeated most of the points already made during advisor training at Fort Bragg. The most vivid memory I have of this period was sitting in some Officers' Club, listening to the Armed Forces Network as Willis Reed made his way onto the basketball floor for the seventh game of the NBA championship. I felt goosebumps from the Madison Square Garden ovation he got as I was sitting in that hovel of a bar halfway around the world. As I listened to the Knicks pummel the Lakers to win the championship, I was, for that brief time, transported away from the war, the military, and the events that awaited me in the coming year and was just an ordinary guy rooting his favorite team onto victory.

Near the end of my in-country training, I received my assignment orders. I was to be sent up to I Corps to serve on a

Mobile Advisory Team. South Vietnam was divided into four areas of operation, and I Corps was the northernmost of them, comprised of the provinces of Quang Tri, Thua Thien, Quang Nam, Quang Tin, and Quang Ngai. The ancient imperial city of Hue was located in Thua Thien province, and the city of Da Nang was in Quang Nam province. I was flown to Da Nang, the headquarters for I Corps, then on to the city of Hue to take up my military duties. The plane from Da Nang was a single-engine mail plane that left me off at a small airport in the citadel of Hue. No one was there to meet me. The place seemed deserted, and the plane quickly took off again, leaving me alone next to the short runway. I walked towards a cluster of sheds near the edge of the airstrip and a helicopter parked there. The pilot was enjoying an afternoon nap. I woke him up, and he called down to the Military Assistance Command Vietnam (MACV) headquarters; in about half an hour, a jeep driven by a brisk, young S-1 officer picked me up.

S-1 was the Army support unit dealing with personnel and was strictly an administrative assignment, but the young S-1 officer liked collecting medals. On the trip to the MACV compound across the river, he bragged about the air medal he earned by tagging along on routine mail delivery flights to the various MACV district headquarters. At the time, you earned an air medal for every twenty-four "flight hours" you logged. "Flight hours" were standardized for each type of flight mission: a quarter of an hour for administrative flights, half an hour for regular duties, and hazardous duty counted for an hour. The officer told the story of hearing gunfire on the ground on one of his mail delivery flights, so he was able to count it as a hazardous duty flight. He assured me that during my tour, I would earn my Combat Infantryman's Badge (CIB).

My first assignment was as team leader for Mobile Advisory Team I-44—MAT 44 in I Corps lingo—assigned to Phu-Tu district, an area dotted with rice paddies southeast of Hue City along the coastline of the South China Sea. MATs were designed to be six-man advisory units comprised of two officers, three non-commissioned officers (NCOs), and a Vietnamese interpreter, although most of the MATs had only three or four people at any one time.

A Vietnamese province was basically equivalent to a U.S. state, and the province was divided into districts, roughly equivalent to counties. The district was run by the District Chief, who was advised by the District Senior Advisor. A MAT was assigned to a certain district at the disposal of the District Senior Advisor who could deploy the MAT team in whatever way necessary for that particular area.

My MAT in Phu Tu was given the assignment to train the South Vietnamese Regional Forces and Popular Forces—nicknamed "Ruff Puffs"—in the district in the use of M-16 rifles, which were just being issued to them. The Ruff Puffs were somewhat similar to the U.S. National Guard and State Militias. Before then, only the Army Republic of Vietnam (ARVN) troops had used M-16s; these local forces, on the other hand, had operated with a motley assortment of M-1s, carbines, Thompson submachine guns, shotguns, and whatever other weapons they could scrounge.

This was part of the "Vietnamization" effort; as U.S. troops were being withdrawn, ARVN troops were supposed to step up and take over the mainline fighting. The RF and PF units would become the local security, previously the responsibility of the ARVN troops. Three such companies were scattered throughout the district, comprising a battalion. We trained individual platoons from each company in weeklong teaching sessions on the M-16, beginning in the classroom and finishing at the shooting range. I taught a class on the basics of the M-16, but I wasn't nearly proficient enough in Vietnamese, so I had to teach it using Han, the team's interpreter. Since I had to teach this class many times over, I started varying my delivery, changing around what I said to keep things interesting for myself. I did understand enough Vietnamese to notice that no matter what I said, Han always said the same thing. So, in reality, it wasn't me who was teaching the class; it was Han. I was just a prop in his class.

On the final day at the shooting range, we would issue a challenge to the trainees. They could pick from among themselves who was the best shot, and he would engage in a shooting contest with me. If he beat me, they would win a case of beer. For whatever reason, I was an excellent shot, at least at targets on a shooting range. I had never owned a weapon as a civilian, but I never lost any of these competitions, except one. I didn't know the kid's name, but he was a young Vietnamese soldier, built like a string bean with a big smile and happy-go-lucky manner. It seemed like he was just playing at being a soldier, not taking any of it seriously, but he was a seriously good shot with an M-16, and he beat me soundly in the shooting competition. We handed over the case of beer to him and his mates, and he was the star of his platoon.

A few weeks later, my MAT—myself, a sergeant, a medic, and Han, our interpreter—were driving down the road on our way to a new training site. We were following the jeep of the Ruff Puff battalion commander, my "counterpart" in advisor-speak, who would be introducing us to the company commander of the unit we were about to train, as well as two jeeps with my counterpart's security detail. The land around us was totally flat. Rice paddies stretched for several hundred meters in every direction, with groves of bamboo scattered here and there. It must have been early in the rice-planting season because little slivers of green were pushing up out of the muddy water.

Suddenly, we heard an explosion from a thicket of bamboo about two hundred meters off to the left. My counterpart's radio started chattering incessantly, and he was yelling back into it. I asked Han what was going on, and he said there had been some contact in the bamboo grove. There was no gunfire, only that initial explosion. The four jeeps stopped, and the security detail quickly deployed around them. I got out of my jeep and approached my counterpart's jeep to learn what was happening, but he ignored me and kept yelling into his radio. After several minutes of this, I got frustrated, and I started heading across the rice paddies towards the grove, much to the alarm of my counterpart and the other members of my team. It was a stupid move on my part, but I was naïve and gung-ho. This was my first "action" in Vietnam, and I didn't want to miss it. I tried to make a beeline across the paddies but quickly realized that slogging through knee-high mud would be much slower than zigzagging along the patchwork of dykes around the paddies. My team members, my counterpart, and his security detail all reluctantly followed me.

There was a knot of about ten or fifteen Vietnamese soldiers standing around in the grove, looking scared and grim. In the midst of them, lying on the ground, was what looked like half a human being. He was lying on his back, staring up at the sky. His body seemed to end at about his waist. Below that was just a mess of bloody meat, broken bones, and entrails. He had stepped on a Bouncing Betty mine. A Bouncing Betty was spring-loaded, so when you stepped on it, the mine sprung about two or three feet into the air before it exploded. It was meant not just to kill, but also to terrorize. Amazingly, the soldier was not dead yet, but it was clear from his injuries he was not going to survive. My medic got on the radio and called for a medevac, but there really was nothing that could medically be done for him. We all just stood around and watched him die as we waited for the medevac chopper to arrive.

In the midst of all this, I noticed the smell of Gauloises, the popular French cigarette that came in a light blue package, which had a distinctive smell completely different from other cigarettes. I don't know whether the dying soldier had smoked them or if one of the soldiers standing around had lit one up. I do know that thereafter, the smell of Gauloises cigarettes became the smell of death for me. These cigarettes are not common in the U.S., but over the years, on several occasions when someone was smoking a Gauloises near me, I was immediately transported back to this scene of death in the bamboo grove in Vietnam.

I remember the eyes of the soldier on the ground, looking around at everyone with what seemed like a mixture of surprise and resignation. I didn't recognize him at first, the features of his face having been distorted by the ordeal he was going through. Han, my interpreter, told me it was the kid who had beaten me in the shooting competition. It was so hard for me to reconcile this bloody piece of half-man shuddering out his last breaths with the laughing, animated young man drinking beer with his comrades and basking in their congratulations only a few weeks earlier.

This was my first glimpse of the horrors of war, and I was completely shaken by the sight and felt sick to my stomach, but I forced myself not to show it. I had to demonstrate to everyone that I was strong and hard and that I was man enough to deal with it. I thought I saw some of the Vietnamese soldiers looking at me with accusation in their eyes, but maybe I just imagined it. More likely, it was a mixture of sadness at the loss of their friend and the thrill and relief that it was him and not them. I didn't feel any guilt at the time. I was too busy pretending to be a soldier, pretending to be hard. It was only later, after several such incidents, that I started to feel that these men were dying because of me.

A short while later, I was transferred to a different MAT team in Phong Dien district, the northernmost district in Thua Thien province, bordering on Quang Tri. This MAT was assigned to a battalion of Ruff Puffs whose main mission was to guard the An Lo Bridge, the largest bridge along Route 1 between Hue and Quang Tri City. The An Lo Bridge was built by American Army engineers across the Song Bo River, about a hundred meters east of the ruins of the old An Lo Bridge, destroyed during the Tet Offensive in 1968 and a grim reminder of the consequences if our mission failed.

This MAT team already had a team leader, so now I was second in command. It took some time for the captain and me to work out our relationship. To him, I was just a civilian in military clothing; he was career military. He was also perpetually pissed off because he thought he should be a company commander, leading American infantry rather than a five-person advisor team. He saw this assignment as undermining his military career, and he took out his frustration on me by giving me shit about my lack of military comportment. He was also completely contemptuous of the Ruff Puffs whom we were assigned to advise, unwilling even to try to "establish rapport"—as Advisor School promoted—with the "gooks," as he called them. Over time, he begrudgingly came to appreciate my efforts to behave respectfully toward the militia's battalion commander—a task he wanted no part of.

In addition to providing security for the An Lo Bridge, the Ruff Puff battalion had an area of operations that included a string of hamlets stretching to the west along the Song Bo River towards the mountains and the "Street without Joy"—a heavily booby-trapped area of sand dunes and marshes to the east made famous by French journalist and historian Bernard Fall in his book by that name. The three hamlets were purportedly the birthplace of some of the senior VC cadre in Thua Thien province, and the battalion's presence there was greeted with sullen resignation.

As part of the Vietnamization program, the South Vietnamese created something called the People's Self-Defense Force (PSDF), a part-time village-level civilian militia ostensibly organized to protect their homes and villages from the Viet Cong (VC) and the North Vietnamese Army (NVA). The theory was that as the ARVNs gradually took over the mainline fighting from the American forces and as the Ruff Puffs moved up to fill the security role previously held by the ARVNs, the PSDF would provide a deterrent from VC infiltration. Despite the known VC leanings of the three hamlets in our area of operation (AO), the district created a PSDF unit from the hamlets, a group of twenty-three teenage kids, fifteen to seventeen years old, the only ones left in the hamlets who could reasonably be organized into some sort of fighting force. My mobile advisory team was given the assignment to train them. We put them through a three-week training course, which included training on the motley assortment of weapons that had been handed down to them from the Ruff Puffs when they got their M-16s. At the end of the training, there was a flashy, province-wide graduation ceremony, with big speeches from the province chief and other dignitaries, and all of the PSDF were given colorful neckerchiefs to wear.

Then one night, about six weeks after the graduation ceremony, a local VC cadre came into the hamlets and apparently made his own speech, and all twenty-three PSDF graduates walked off with him to join the Viet Cong, taking their weapons and our training with them. The daily incident report stated that all of them had been kidnapped. The whole event had a profound impact on me. I already had serious doubts about the American efforts in Vietnam, but here I had personally trained twenty-three kids who ultimately made a conscious choice to fight on the opposite side despite knowing the might and power of the military force arrayed against them. If they believed that strongly, then who was I to tell them to believe differently?

The warfare I experienced was dirty and exclusively one-sided. There were no extended firefights or major unit battles. The enemy booby-trapped us, and we, on rare occasions, caught a few of them in an ambush. There was an individual VC who would lob a mortar round or two at our compound every once in a while just to let us know he was there, but he never got a round closer than a hundred meters to our perimeter. A big part of my responsibility as an advisor was to get our counterpart to undertake aggressive military operations. Captain Hieu, the battalion commander at the An Lo Bridge, was not inclined to do this. During an extended absence of my team leader due to a family emergency back home, I tried my hand at stimulating some military activity. I would visit the battalion commander every night in his bunker, sit and drink tea or the occasional alcoholic beverage, and try to convince him to take up some sort of action.

I would say to him, "Look at the Americans. We are here fighting hard for your country. Why aren't you willing to fight hard for your own country?"

He would answer, "You Americans. You come here for a year, and then you go home. You all want me to win the war in your year. At the end of the year, you go home. I am home. Americans are like a tree. The tree is strong, but when the wind blows hard enough, the tree will break. Vietnamese are like the grass. No matter how hard the wind blows, no matter which direction, the grass will only bend but never break."

After several such sessions, I finally hit upon a solution. His jeep was his prized possession; he kept it spotless and shiny, and he always had a detail of soldiers spiffing it up every evening, cleaning off the mud and dust from the day's travels. He often complained about how difficult it was to get spare parts for the jeep through the Vietnamese supply system. I told him I could just walk into the motor pool at Camp Eagle—the major base camp of the 101st Division south of Hue—and get just about anything I asked for. I would be glad to get him the parts he needed for his jeep if he would return the favor. He understood what I was asking for and nodded his head in reluctant agreement.

I called in my order for chopper support on the designated day. We had planned a hammer-and-anvil operation with all three Ruff Puff companies participating. One company would be flown ahead by the choppers and dropped off to set up a blocking position. The other two companies would then sweep through the area toward the blocking force, the idea being that any of the enemy fleeing in front of the sweeping force would run into the blocking force. It was a basic military maneuver straight out of the Officer Candidate School textbook. In reality, it turned into a classic Vietnamese "search-and-avoid mission." There was almost no chance that any enemies would be caught in this maneuver because the heightened activity involved in preparing the operation virtually eliminated any element of surprise, and there were no major enemy units operating in our area anyway. But we could put on a good show for the local population, "show the flag," and I had something I could put in my weekly report other than training activities. But the mission did have lethal consequences. Some poor soldier stepped on a booby trap, we called in a medevac, and then we all went home. After several such operations—each with the same result—I started to feel more and more guilty that these soldiers were not dying for their country but rather for my performance report.

The ambushes we staged were not much better. Night ambushes were supposed to last all night, but the Ruff Puffs weren't interested in staying out all night, so about midnight or 1:00 a.m., somebody would shoot off his rifle, the ambush would be compromised, and everyone would go home. One night, I was out on an ambush with them on the outer edge of the last of the three hamlets along the river. I was the only American there, a breach of the protocol that required at least two Americans to be present in any military operation. But I wanted to go because it got me away from the incessant oppression of my team leader. As usual, sometime around midnight, one of the men shot off his rifle, and we all got up to head back to camp, when I saw one of the soldiers run up to the leader of the ambush, talking excitedly. The ambush leader started directing his men towards one of the hooches in the hamlet. Suddenly, three men were running from the hooch, with the militia firing wildly in their direction. Two of them were hit and killed; the third one got away.

One of the dead was a well-known local VC cadre; the

other was an NVA soldier. Apparently, two NVA soldiers had come out of the mountains where the mainline units were fighting and hooked up with the local cadreman for a resupply mission. They had skirted around our ambush but apparently hadn't counted on it ending so soon. The next morning, the Ruff Puffs paraded the two dead bodies through the streets of the three hamlets, much to the sullen displeasure of the local inhabitants.

I was heartily congratulated by all the district advisors from the senior advisor on down; it was the first enemy "kill" in the district in months, and the fact that one of the KIAs was a local VC who had operated for years with impunity made it even sweeter. There were the requisite oohs and ahhs at the fact that I had been out on the ambush "alone," and I just shrugged and tried to act nonchalant. Even my team leader slapped me on the back, though I detected a tinge of jealousy in his voice that I, not him, was getting the credit for this. He told me the incident would earn me a Combat Infantryman's Badge, awarded to an infantryman who has been in combat. The adrenaline did not stop pumping for hours.

The CIB was not the end of it. The Americans, as part of the effort to stimulate the Ruff Puffs and reward them for their military action, gave medals to the battalion commander, the company commander, the ambush leader, and the soldier who spotted the three enemies in the hamlet. The Vietnamese, feeling the need to reciprocate, awarded me the Vietnamese Cross of Gallantry. At the time, I didn't dwell on the gallantry associated with killing two enemy soldiers in what was essentially an ambush situation. It didn't matter much to me; I had accumulated sufficient manhood "bling"—no Purple Heart, no Silver Star, but I had Jump Wings, a CIB, a Cross of Gallantry, and the devalued Bronze Star that they gave to just about everyone as a parting gift for leaving Vietnam—to satisfy my craving. I had the symbols of proving myself; it's just that I hadn't really done a whole lot to earn them.

In late February of 1971, I left Vietnam. Eleven months and twenty-two days that would define who I was and what I did for the rest of my life. I had survived. Now I had to decide what to do with it.

69

Chapter 7

Retirement

So, the ax finally fell in 2017. It wasn't particularly a surprise. I had been working as a Senior Contracts Officer for a non-profit international development organization for fourteen years, but the company had lost a number of its contracts, and I was the old guy with the big salary. I had already taken a tentative step towards retirement by reducing to sixty-percent time. I was hoping to leave on my own terms after maybe another year, but I got unceremoniously shown the door along with about seventy other colleagues, and just like that, at sixty-nine years old, I was retired.

It's not as if I had never been fired before. On the contrary, when I look back at my alleged career, termination seems to have been the most common method of my leaving a job. I should have been used to it. Most times, after the initial shock wore off, I just picked myself up and went on to find something better. This was different, though. This wasn't about going out and finding a new job. This was about a major life transition, from working man to retiree.

Oh, I continued to look for work; it was, after all, a requirement for collecting unemployment, and that check every week for six months helped to ease the transition, but I was torn. On the one hand, there was retirement, the Oz of the working man, dreamed about for years, where your time is your own, your choices made for your own pleasure rather than at someone else's direction to earn a buck. I got there; now I just needed to sit back and enjoy what life sent my way.

On the other hand, I had pretty much had a job since I started delivering newspapers at eleven years old. The idea of not having a job—not earning money, not spending the bulk of my time doing someone else's bidding—was scary. For the first few weeks after getting fired, I felt like I was drifting, like my life was about to spin out of control. The basic structure of my life had been provided by my job. It was both my womb and my tomb. The utter routineness of my life had provided a feeling of safety and security that had always been comforting. I could wake up on a Monday morning, flip on the autopilot, and basically sleepwalk through the rest of the week. Maybe ninety-five percent of how I spent my time was determined by someone else. I didn't really have to think about anything; I just showed up, went through the motions, and cruised. In my womb. The other side of this was that any little thing that upset my routine—my slippers not being where they were sup-posed to be, somebody using the last bit of toilet paper without replacing the roll—set me off into a totally maniacal, unreason-able rage that sent my family scurrying for cover.

As you can imagine, such an existence was barely above a dead man walking; hence, it was also my tomb. There was little, if anything, in such a life that had anything to do with what in my heart and soul I believed was the reason for my existence. Now I had to provide my own structure. Each day I awoke, it would be up to me to decide what to do. There was no more shifting into autopilot on a Monday morning and coasting along on the routine rhythms of the workweek through to Friday afternoon. Every day was now the weekend.

Coupled with that was the inevitable financial uncer-tainty of retirement. All my life, I've worried about money. I don't know how NOT to worry about money. It is as much a part of me as coffee in the morning and agonizing over New

York sports teams. I did not pay much attention to things like retirement savings when I was young. I supposed there would be a revolution long before I would be in a position to spend any retirement funds. As I sank back into a middle-class existence, with a wife and children and responsibilities, I dutifully started contributing money to a retirement fund, but I got a late start on it, and while my stash was not too shabby, it was not enough to live in the free-spending, slap-down-the-plastic-whenever-the-whim-hit-me mode that I had become accustomed to. I reckoned I could throw caution to the wind, continue to live that way until the money ran out, and worry about the consequences when they arrived.

But I won't.

More than anything else, perhaps, was the overwhelming feeling I had of loss of purpose, of no longer having any meaning to my existence. I mean, was that it, just trundle off into the sunset, pretending that doing nothing was really having a good time? Why bother? I mean, the ending to every story is, "And then you die." It's only a matter of when and how. If that's it, then why not just take a little walk up into the woods with the gun I purchased when Trump became president and put it to some practical use by blowing my malfunctioning brains out? It sometimes seemed that was a cleaner and more acceptable alternative to desperately clutching at the last vestiges of a meaningless existence.

Again, but I won't.

No, I will continue to struggle to write this book, trying to convince myself that finishing it will impart some purpose to my life, that telling the stories of my experience will somehow make that experience meaningful.

Natasha and I—after numerous stops and starts, deadlines set and reset—were very close (it seemed) to that place where neither of us was working, with our two children both graduating from college, and the horizon was where we chose it to be. We had plans—big plans. We were going to circumnavigate the globe, traveling around the world from west to east, and we were going to do it without leaving the surface of the planet. No airplanes in our itinerary. Boats, trains, and automobiles, with a healthy dose of walking, would be our modes of transportation. If all went well (a big IF), the trip would take about two years and probably most of our savings. It didn't matter. I needed another great adventure, another massive injection of adrenaline, and I would let the future take care of itself. Of course, finishing this book did not seem to fit well into that scenario, but I figured I'd work it out.

COVID, however, sure put a dent in our round-the-world plans, particularly because travel on cruise ships was going to be such a major part of it. We already had our cruise to New Zealand bought and paid for; we were standing at the starting line, waiting to crouch into the blocks and surge at the sound of the starter's pistol. Now, who knows when, or even if, we will chase that dream again? I saw what had happened to my parents. Their dream was to travel all over the North American continent, a trailer hooked to the back of their truck, living life on the road to the next town, the next campsite, the next adventure. They were able to do it for about a year. They even traveled all the way up to Alaska above the Arctic Circle, but my mother's mom died, and they had to settle down to care for my grandfather. The plan had been to get back on the road once my grandfather passed, but he lived to be ninety-nine, and by then my father was in the first stages of Alzheimer's, and their dreams of travel went bust. Who knows what will happen to our plans? When you are young, it's no big deal to wait for next week, or next month, or even next year. When you reach your seventies, the windows of opportunity get smaller and smaller, and the weeks and months and years become fewer and fewer.

The retired country squire with his harvest of garlic.

This is my dilemma. Even before COVID made "social distancing" the accepted norm, it had become my way of life. Once the kids graduated from high school, we fled the suburbs in Massachusetts as quickly as we could get our house on the market and sold. We bought ourselves a serene piece of rural Vermont, and I am totally content, puttering around my property, tackling the endless tasks that a five-acre piece of mountainside presents to me, never leaving for days at a time except for trips to the wood yard or hardware store to purchase materials for the latest project, plowing the driveway in the winter, boiling sap for maple syrup in the early spring, tending the vegetable garden in the summer, floating lazily on any one of many local lakes, waiting for the bass, or the pike, or the trout, or the ever-elusive landlocked-salmon to strike my bait and provide me with a brief fix of adrenaline. It seems I could live out the remainder of my life in this fashion—sedentary, anonymous, unremarkable, the spitting image of retirement. Yet, still, the fire burns inside of me to chase the dreams, to tilt at the windmills, to crash out of my comfort zone and experience again the thrill of confronting the unknown.

So, what will my retirement be: sitting on the porch sipping vodka and cranberry juice, watching the sun set over the horizon, or galloping breathlessly towards that horizon, racing to keep the sun from ever setting?

I'll let you know when I find out.

Chapter 8

Coming Home

I came home from Vietnam a changed man, disgusted and disillusioned. Like my childhood idealism associated with religion, whatever fervor I may have had about serving my country was gone. My patriotism had been spent like chump change in a penny arcade, wasted on a futile effort in a dirty war where survival was the only measure of success. Although I had seen some minimal combat, my experience was not as intense as that of others. I was alive, but I felt no pride or sense of accomplishment from my ordeal. I was simply glad it was over.

I stepped off the plane from Vietnam, and after a flurry of processing, I was discharged from the Army. In less than four days, I went from being a combat soldier in Vietnam to a civilian on the streets of San Francisco. Needless to say, the transition was abrupt and disorienting, but I suppose I had it better than many. I saw more than my share of guys who served with distinction in Vietnam, who had earned sergeant's stripes while in-country but who still had five or six months left to do in the Army when they got back to the U.S. By the time they were discharged, they had been busted back down to private because they just couldn't deal with the petty bullshit associated with barracks life in the States after having been in Vietnam.

Since I had no particular place to go, I flew to my parents' house in Mansfield, Massachusetts. I'd been so focused on surviving one year in Vietnam that I'd given little thought about what I would do afterward. I had a general plan that I would probably go back to college. I'd saved some money while I was there, so I didn't have to look for a job right away. The only major purchase I made was my "Vietnam stereo," which I bought through the PX catalog right before I left and had it shipped directly to my parents' house.

My brother Henry was playing in a rock 'n roll band, and I tagged along to a couple of his gigs. He was somewhat surprised that I smoked pot since I had always been something of a straight arrow when we were younger, and I suppose he figured my becoming an Army officer was a continuation of my straight-arrow ways, but he gladly shared his stash with me and hooked me up with his guy to buy some of my own. Mostly, I just hung around the house aimlessly. After a very short time at my parents' house, I was again feeling stifled. It had been four years since I'd been under my parents' roof, and it was hard for my mother to make the adjustment that I was free and independent and expected to be treated that way. For her, I was still her oldest son, whom she wanted to take care of and make decisions for. It quickly became evident to me that I needed to get away and get out on my own.

I started to formulate plans to take a road trip back down to New Orleans. My little Datsun 2000, which had been sitting in my parents' driveway while I was in Vietnam, was just begging me to get out and cruise. I wanted to look up some folks down there that I had known before I joined up, but mostly, I just wanted to hit the open road.

As I was preparing for my trip, some news on television caught my eye. There was a large group of Vietnam veterans who were staging a series of anti-war demonstrations in Washington, D.C. The group called itself Vietnam Veterans Against the War (VVAW). VVAW was formed in 1967 when six Vietnam veterans met at an anti-war rally in New York City. The group stayed small and confined to the Northeast for the first couple of years, having only a desk and a phone in the office of another anti-war group. Then, in early September 1970, VVAW organized Operation RAW (Rapid American Withdrawal), a "limited incursion" into New Jersey. The veterans marched from Trenton, New Jersey, to Valley Forge, Pennsylvania, over three days, staging guerrilla theater in the villages and towns they passed through, simulating the manner in which American troops passed through villages and towns in Vietnam. A month before my discharge, VVAW held the Winter Soldier Investigation in Detroit, Michigan, from January 31 to February 2, 1971. At that time, the My Lai massacre in Vietnam was making headlines. The trial of Lieutenant William Calley, the officer in charge of the platoon that carried out the massacre of between three hundred and five hundred unarmed Vietnamese civilians in 1968, had begun in November of 1970. As is always the case when American soldiers get caught in war atrocities that are the direct result of American military policy, the military immediately blamed it on the aberration of the individual soldiers involved and court-martialed the young lieutenant. The Winter Soldier Investigation was an attempt by VVAW to organize testimony by over a hundred Vietnam veterans concerning the atrocities and war crimes they had participated in or witnessed in Vietnam. Contrary to the right-wing criticism of John Kerry during his presidential campaign in 2004, the Winter Soldier Investigation was not organized to brand American soldiers as "baby killers." Rather, it demonstrated that atrocities such as My Lai were common and widespread and were the result of American military policy, not the aberrant actions of individual soldiers.

Then, from April 18 to April 23, VVAW organized its most ambitious action to date: Operation Dewey Canyon III, named after two secret Marine incursions into Laos and Cambodia ordered by President Nixon. Over one thousand Vietnam veterans from all over the country descended on Washington, D.C., and camped out on the National Mall for three days. John Kerry emerged as one of the principal spokesmen for VVAW during this time and made his famous speech before the Senate Foreign Relations Committee on April 22, 1971:

We call this investigation the "Winter Soldier Investigation." The term "Winter Soldier" is a play on words of Thomas Paine in 1776 when he spoke of the Sunshine Patriot and summertime soldiers who deserted Valley Forge because the going was rough.

We have come here to Washington because we feel we have to be winter soldiers now ... The country doesn't know it yet, but it has created a monster, a monster in the form of millions of men who have been taught to deal and to trade in violence, and who are given the chance to die for the biggest nothing in history; men who have returned with a sense of anger and a sense of betrayal which no one has yet grasped ...

We are asking Americans to think about that because how do you ask a man to be the last man to die in Vietnam? How do you ask a man to be the last man to die for a mistake?

The demonstrations saturated the national news. The Nixon administration went to federal court to get an order to remove the veterans from the National Mall. It went all the way to the Supreme Court, which ruled in Nixon's favor. The members of VVAW—after debating among themselves for half the night—took a vote on staying or leaving the Mall; the majority voted to stay put. The park rangers refused to go in and remove them. The *Washington Daily News'* front-page headline the next day was "Vets Overrule Supreme Court."

The fact that John Kerry had become the face of VVAW and he was from Massachusetts meant that the events were covered on both the local and national television news at my parents' house. My father was disgusted by it as he sat there

Front page of The Washington Daily News,
April 22, 1971.

with his can of beer, watching the evening news. He parroted Nixon's dismissal of the group as probably not being veterans anyway. I was riveted by the images I saw flashing on the screen, and I told my father that I believed they were veterans and that I wished I were there with them. We had never really discussed politics before, and considering I had just returned from Vietnam, he just assumed that I shared his patriotic working-class support for the war. It was the beginning of a period of strained relations between us; from then on, we were always arguing about politics.

I had planned to leave for New Orleans the week of the VVAW demonstrations. Now there was a potentially new wrinkle to my plans. Did I want to go to D.C. and join in with the other anti-war veterans? I left home on the morning of the second day of the demonstrations and was in D.C. just before nightfall. I drove around Washington, passing by the Mall, trying to get a glimpse of the protesting veterans and trying to screw up the courage to join them.

On the last day of the demonstrations, the Vietnam veterans gathered in front of the Capitol, then each man walked up to the chain-link fence—hastily erected to protect Congress from the men they had sent to fight—and threw back the medals he had won in Vietnam to protest the ongoing war. It was undoubtedly the most powerful anti-war demonstration yet. I did not take part. In the end, I was too scared, too shy, or just wasn't ready to participate. I found the road south out of Washington and headed on to New Orleans.

Operation Dewey Canyon III. Photo by Fred W. McDarrah.

When I said I had no real plans after Vietnam, that's not quite true. I had one principal goal when I got out of the military. I wanted to become a hippie. I had watched from afar all the iconic moments of the baby-boomer generation: Haight-Ashbury, Woodstock, long hair, free love, peace, dope, good vibes. Throughout the crew cut, authoritarian, life-negating military experience, I would fantasize about coming back to join my generation in its distinctive life-affirming choices. The idea kept me going. By 1971, a lot of the good vibes had dissipated—drowning under the weight of drug abuse, rip-offs, egotistical excesses, and the ever-present lure of American materialism—but I believed there were still enough remnants of hippie culture for me to catch up on what I had missed.

The first order of business was to get myself a hippie vehicle.

My little Datsun 2000 sports car did not fill the bill. The vehicle of choice for hippies was a Volkswagen van, and one of my old friends in New Orleans had a brother who was willing to sell one. I bought it, drove my Datsun back to Massachusetts, left it with my brother Henry, and hitchhiked back down to New Orleans to get my van. I took out the back seats, redecorated the interior with as hippie a look as I could muster, lay a foam pad on the floor, and that became my home for the next four months.

The next thing on my list was to attend a rock festival, and there happened to be one called "The Celebration of Life" scheduled to take place on a seven-hundred-acre plantation in the small, unincorporated town of McCrea, Louisiana, on the east bank of the Atchafalaya River in the northwestern portion of Pointe Coupee Parish. Billed as "Eight Days in the Country," the promo material promised a mega-line-up of stars: The Rolling Stones, Sly and the Family Stone, the Allman Brothers, Pink Floyd, B.B. King, and the American Rock Opera Company performing music from *Jesus Christ Superstar*. The event was a total disaster. The promoters faced significant legal problems and stern opposition from the local populace, who were not at all pleased about sixty thousand or so hippies descending on rural Louisiana. The venue was announced only four days before the event, and the promoters were scrambling to get it set up. In addition, there had been little consideration of Louisiana's weather conditions in the middle of summer; the festival started out with heavy rainstorms followed by blisteringly hot days swarming with mosquitos from the nearby river. The swampy waters of the Atchafalaya were the only relief from the heat, but it ran swiftly and dangerously past the festival site; two people drowned in it during the festival. The local police sent numerous undercover agents into the crowd to identify the drug sellers; over a hundred drug arrests were made as people were leaving. Most of the major acts never showed up, and the whole thing shut down after three days.

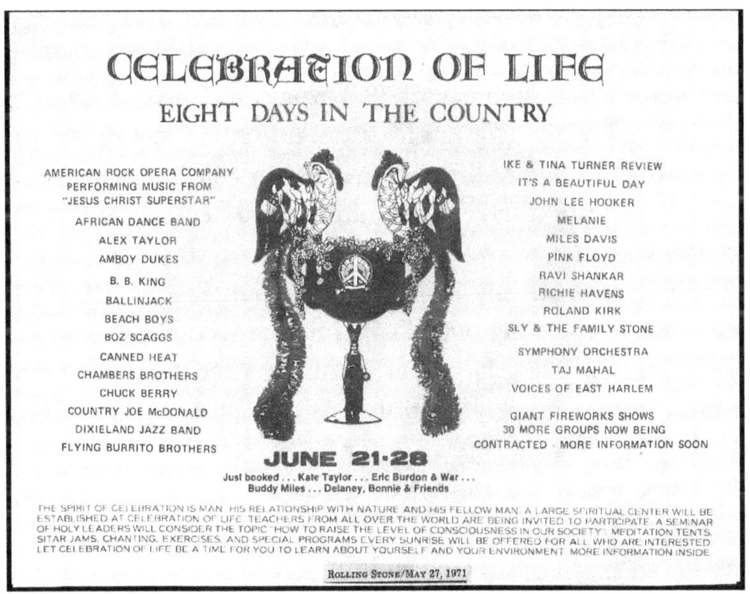

The poster that promised everything.

None of this really mattered to me. I was there in all my budding hippie glory, although the hitchhiking freak I picked up along the way had promptly stolen my stash of weed as soon as we arrived and disappeared into the sprawling, sweaty mass of hairy humanity. Drugs were in plentiful supply, however, and I soon replenished my stash. I spent most of my time down by the Atchafalaya, gloriously naked along with hundreds of other folks, wallowing in the mud created by the initial rainstorms, trying desperately to control my erection at the sight of so many naked women. One young woman was wandering naked around the festival in the middle of the day, probably tripping, and I noted that she would be suffering from a serious sunburn by evening. The music, such as it was, was great, as just about any music heard in the middle of a massive crowd of boogieing stoners tends to be. It wasn't Woodstock by any means, but it was the closest I was going to get, and I reveled in it.

And yet, as that summer of 1971 wore on, I was feeling the need to "go straight," or at least develop some sort of acceptable direction in my life. Going back to college seemed like the natural step to take. This fulfilled two needs. The first, of course, was that I now could claim direction and put to rest all the fears—both my own and my parents'—that I was on the verge of spinning out of control. The second was income. What seemed like a large pot of funds when I had returned from Vietnam quickly diminished, and enrolling in college would give me access to G.I. Bill money.

The original G.I. Bill (formally known as the Servicemen's Readjustment Act of 1944) had been signed into law after World War II. It provided military veterans with a variety of benefits, including no-interest, zero down payment home loans; a $20-a-week payment for fifty-two weeks after discharge; and an education benefit where the federal government paid directly to the institution a veteran's full college or training tuition, regardless of the amount or the institution. Elements of the Bill changed over time; for instance, after the Korean War, the direct payment of tuition was discontinued in favor of a monthly stipend paid directly to the veteran from which tuition, books, and other monthly expenses were supposed to be paid. By the time I became eligible for this education benefit, the monthly stipend was $175; in 1972, the amount was raised to $220. This, of course, was nowhere near sufficient to cover all costs associated with getting a college degree; neither did it take into account that books and tuition needed to be paid upfront.

In those days, tuition at state schools was somewhat manageable, however. I decided to attend Louisiana State University at New Orleans (LSUNO, or UNO, as it became known), and I paid a little over $500 in tuition and fees for an academic year. Initially, my housing cost me $90 a month for a studio apartment on Royal Street in the French Quarter (another bucket list check-off: to live in the Quarter), but I soon moved with two other students into an apartment on Amelia Street off St. Charles Ave. where we shared a monthly rent of $150. I picked up a part-time job pumping gas at a service station close to the campus, so I wasn't rolling in dough, but I had enough to pay my expenses, including a serviceable amount of recreational drugs each month.

A few weeks into my first semester at UNO, I spied a leaflet on a bulletin board that announced the formation of a chapter of Vietnam Veterans Against the War. I had been regretting not joining the demonstrations in D.C. earlier that year and saw this as my chance to get involved. My anti-war opinions were not particularly well formed at that time, consisting of such thoughts as "The war is bad. It should stop." Participation in anti-war activity seemed a necessary component of the hippie lifestyle I was attempting to adopt, and VVAW seemed the natural way for me to get started.

There was another reason for my attending this meeting. I was feeling distinctly alienated from most of my classmates. These were kids who were freshly graduated from high school, younger than me, and most definitely worlds apart from me in life experience. I didn't feel comfortable around them and didn't want to talk to them about what I had gone through and what I was going through as a result. Vietnam had turned me into an adrenaline junkie, and there were few fixes in everyday campus life that satisfied my craving. I took to doing things like sucking on razor blades during classes or leaning out the open door of a car and dragging my lengthening hair along the pavement as the car sped down the highway at sixty miles an hour. More than anything else, I was attracted to VVAW because I wanted to be around other vets who might possibly understand how I was feeling.

I showed up at the appointed time and place and found a room with about twenty people in it. The meeting was chaired by a guy named Don Donner, who identified himself as the regional coordinator for VVAW for Arkansas, Mississippi, and Louisiana. He had come down to New Orleans from Arkansas to try to stimulate veterans' anti-war activity in the Crescent City. He announced that our first action as a chapter would be to march in the annual Veterans Day Parade in New Orleans. The organizers of the parade—the traditional veterans' organizations such as the VFW and American Legion—had put out a call inviting all bona fide veterans groups to join the parade, and VVAW applied to march. The older veterans' groups were not enthused about this idea and initially rejected our application. Then some local lawyers got involved, and eventually we received a begrudging agreement.

Thirty-three of us showed up on the night of the parade at a designated location. We watched and waited as a parade of spangled high school bands and motley groups of older veterans, complacent in their hard-hearted patriotism, passed us by. Finally, we demanded to know when we would be allowed to march. The parade organizers then sprang on us the news that Congressman F. Edward Herbert, the Grand Marshall of the parade and recently selected as chairman of the House Armed Services Committee, had decreed that no anti-war groups were going to march in his parade. We tried to negotiate some sort of alternative, like marching down the sidewalk instead of the street, but we were told that if we marched anywhere that night, we would be arrested. Our response was, *Fuck it*! We marched and got busted for parading without a permit. The police held us overnight and then released us the following morning without bail. The case never went to court; the purpose of the arrest was to get us off the street so we wouldn't spoil F. Edward's parade. So, the first time in my life I was ever arrested was for trying to march in my first Veterans Day parade after I got back from Vietnam. It was not to be my last arrest.

After that, I threw myself into VVAW with an intensified commitment because of the injustice of the Veterans Day bust.

The city of New Orleans got some bad publicity for arresting veterans on Veterans Day, so they gave us permission to organize our own anti-war parade down Canal Street, then over to Jackson Square for a rally. It wasn't that much of a concession. The whole culture of New Orleans is based on parades; throwing another one into the mix barely raised an eyebrow. VVAW invited other anti-war groups to participate, and we managed to attract several hundred people. It was perhaps the only anti-war demonstration ever in New Orleans. I volunteered to speak at the rally, but halfway through my speech, in a surge of emotion, I began to choke up and couldn't continue. I wanted to deliver a coherent anti-war message like the vets in D.C. had the previous spring, but I was overcome by conflicting feelings of pride and shame for my military service—pride in surviving but shame in treating war as a means of personal aggrandizement. My credential for speaking was being a Vietnam veteran, but the war was an immoral undertaking. It was just too much for me to process.

Soon after, Don Donner appointed a vet named Al as the new Louisiana Regional Coordinator, then headed back to Arkansas. Al was an aspiring filmmaker, however, and soon left to pursue his aspirations in New York. I became VVAW's Louisiana Regional Coordinator pretty much by default. So, here I was again, a "leader" with little experience in leading, an "organizer" who had trouble keeping his own life organized. I quickly found that the Veterans Day bust and subsequent anti-war march a few weeks later were to be the high points of VVAW activity in Louisiana. In December of 1971, national VVAW organized a series of anti-war demonstrations around the country, the most visible of which was the occupation of the Statue of Liberty and the hanging of the American flag upside down from the statue in the universal signal of distress. Nothing happened in Louisiana. LSUNO was not exactly a hotbed of student activism, and the chapter meetings I tried to organize after Don and Al had left were more and more sparsely attended.

Two stalwarts who did show up were Karl Becker and Art Franz. Karl was a self-proclaimed libertarian, a red-haired, roly-poly eccentric who mostly hung out in the university cafeteria, drinking coffee and engaging in various political debates. He also liked to party and frequent the numerous strip clubs in and around New Orleans. Although Karl was not a vet, he was something of a movement gadfly who showed up for everything, so I never questioned his attendance at the VVAW meetings. I struck up a friendship with him, and we spent a number of nights drinking and trolling the clubs. He was one of my only non-vet friends, which gave him a status of importance in my life. Art said he was a Navy vet and was always willing to take on various mundane tasks like mimeographing leaflets, posting meeting notices, and the like. I welcomed his assistance since there were almost no other vets willing to take an active role in chapter work.

In February 1972, a meeting of VVAW's National Steering Committee took place in Denver, Colorado. As a regional coordinator, I was expected to attend, and I asked Becker to come with me. VVAW was going through some tough times at that point. The success of Dewey Canyon III had long since faded, and some serious fissures were developing between the more radical members of VVAW and the more moderate ones. John Kerry had resigned from the organization at the Kansas City steering committee meeting the previous November, ostensibly because of the growing radicalism of many of its members but also, frankly, because he was preparing to run for a congressional seat, which he subsequently lost because of his VVAW participation.

There was also a North/South fissure within the organization. VVAW had been launched in the Northeast, and the national leadership of the organization had remained in the hands of Northeasterners, much to the irritation of many of the Southern regional coordinators. Also, many of its members saw their anti-war journey as a rebellion against military authoritarianism. The streak of anti-authoritarianism ran deep, and they bristled under *any* authority that anyone tried to impose on them. Military officers, particularly former dumbass lieutenants like me, were viewed at best with suspicion, at worst with blatant hostility. I took to wearing my lieutenant's dress green jacket with no shirt underneath as a way of exhibiting my own anti-authoritarian chops. Coupled with all that was the usual ultra-democracy that reigned in such groups that recognized everyone's right to be heard regardless of whether the comments were on the topic at hand—not to mention the pervasive ingestion of a variety of legal and illegal substances, all of which made for an utterly chaotic meeting on the first day in Denver.

A significant amount of frustration had been building within the organization, especially among those who were serious about organizational issues. I stayed up most of that first night, trying to craft a series of compromise measures that could bridge some of the antagonisms, and then presented them to the group the next day. Many of them were voted through, but no one at the meeting was taking minutes, so none of them were ever seriously implemented. It did raise my profile within the group, however.

The second night, Al Hubbard showed up, a polarizing figure in the national office, a lightning rod for much of the anger directed at the national leadership. Al was from Brooklyn; he had joined the Air Force in 1952 and was medically discharged in 1966 after a back injury from a plane crash. He joined VVAW in 1969 and quickly rose to a leadership position through his superior organizing skills. He was also one of the few Blacks in a mostly all-White veterans group and, perhaps, chafed at the media embrace of John Kerry as the face of VVAW. Supremely confident in his own decision-making ability, more inclined to act than to try to build a consensus, he was one of the driving forces behind many of the most heralded VVAW protests. Of course, his manner could come off as arrogant, and he rubbed a lot of folks the wrong way. Then, in an interview on *Meet the Press* during the publicity for Dewey Canyon III, Hubbard, appearing together with John Kerry, claimed to have been a captain in the Air Force, which was later discovered to be untrue; he never rose above the rank of sergeant. Apparently, someone in the Nixon White House had tipped off several members of the press concerning this fact, and when confronted by Frank Jordan, Washington Bureau Chief for NBC News, Hubbard acknowledged he had lied and publicly admitted so on the *Today* show the following morning. Hubbard insisted, perhaps correctly, that he had claimed to be a captain because he didn't think anyone would listen to a Black enlisted man. The lie about his rank caused an uproar in VVAW. A key element of VVAW's success in attracting public attention to our anti-war message was our credibility, and Al's lie on one of the most prestigious news shows on national television did not sit well with most of the membership.

Al quickly deflected the ire directed at him by brandishing the first copy of *Winter Soldier*, a documentary of the Winter Soldier Investigation event the previous year. He said he had been late coming to the Steering Committee Meeting because he was waiting for the print of the movie to be finished. He assured everyone it was something we would want to see and suggested the proceedings be immediately halted so we could view it, which we did.

The star of the documentary—if you would want to call him that—was Scott Camil, the Florida Regional Coordinator. His stepfather, a cop and member of the John Birch Society, had regularly beat Scott and berated him for being too soft, someone who would never "be a man." Scott had joined the Marines three days after graduating from high school and went to Vietnam in 1966. Two weeks after he was in-country, the base camp where he was stationed was overrun by a Viet Cong force, and a number of Marines were killed, including Scott's first in-country friend. As Scott viewed the bodies of his friend and the other Marines, he reached several conclusions. First, he realized that war wasn't going to be as much fun as he had thought it would be. Second, he realized he was in a place where there were people whose job it was to kill him. Third, he decided that he wasn't going to divide the Vietnamese into "good guys" and "bad guys." They all became bad guys in his eyes, and he was determined to kill every Vietnamese he came into contact with, both as payback for the deaths of those Marines and as his personal survival strategy for the war. Twenty months later, after twice extending his tour in Vietnam, he returned home with a chest full of medals, a hardened soul, and an unrepentant heart.

After Scott got out of the Marines, he had no idea what he was going to do with his life. He applied to be a policeman but was rejected because, on a lie detector test, he admitted to smoking marijuana. Like me, he ultimately decided to go to school because the G.I. Bill provided a monthly income. The university exposed Scott to a whole new way of looking at the world and the war he had so recently returned from. He realized that he had been lied to by his government and that all the killing and dying he had been witness to and had participated in had been in furtherance of those lies.

At first, these realizations didn't move Scott to do anything. He was too busy immersing himself in the sex, drugs, and rock 'n roll that he saw as his reward for having survived Vietnam. That changed, however, when Jane Fonda gave a speech at the University of Florida, challenging Vietnam veterans to speak up and tell the truth about Vietnam and declaring that it was their patriotic duty to do so. Scott responded to this call and was given a plane ticket to Detroit. His testimony at the Winter Soldier Investigation, as captured in the film we were watching, was blunt, disturbing, and incredibly moving. You could literally see him changing on the screen as the weight of his own words sank in and opened his eyes. Scott Camil, the hard-hearted, merciless Marine, morphed into Scott Camil, the fervent anti-war activist.

But it was not necessarily a complete transformation. Scott had proposed at the previous National Steering Committee Meeting in Kansas City in November 1971 that VVAW assassinate pro-war senators, a proposal that supposedly hastened John Kerry's exit from the organization. Scott's rationale was that the lies these senators had promulgated had led directly to Scott's killing spree in Vietnam, so they deserved no less a fate than his in-country victims. Scott was an extreme example of the dilemma that many members of VVAW faced. Our power and credibility as an organization rested on our image as former men of violence who had turned to non-violence in our quest to end the war, but the violence of our recent past lurked just below the surface, threatening to burst out, providing ominous and menacing overtones to our presence.

When the meeting ended, Karl flew back to New Orleans. I had spent all my available funds on the plane ticket there, so I had no money for a return ticket. Camil and his entourage were driving back to Florida, and he offered to give me a lift as far as possible towards New Orleans, then I could hitchhike the rest of the way. I remember we had to stop for gas somewhere in Oklahoma, and some good ole boys hanging around the gas station began to make some noises about not wanting any longhairs around their town. Scott walked up to them smiling and said a few words to them that I didn't hear, but they quickly backed off and left us to gas up and get on our way.

Returning to New Orleans was a real downer for me after the energy and excitement of the National Steering Committee Meeting. Despite the sometimes chaotic nature of the event and the intense arguments over power and control, I had been surrounded by passionate, committed Vietnam veterans, and I had reveled in it. There was almost nothing happening back home. The Louisiana "chapter," for all intents and purposes, didn't exist. I think the Veterans Day bust was a bit more than some of the guys bargained for, and it was evident that they weren't interested in attending periodic meetings for the sake of meetings.

I did manage to get on television to answer an editorial about amnesty for draft resisters. In those days, when a local television station did an editorial, you could request equal time for an answer. One of the local stations ran an editorial coming out against amnesty, and I was able to make the case on air for granting amnesty. The television guy who taped the response complimented me on my presentation but commented that the way I looked—long hair and a beard—would keep most people from even listening to me. He was probably right.

In an effort to organize something that might bring guys back out to become active in the local chapter, I tried to plan a counter-demonstration to a "Young White People's March" being organized by David Duke, then a member of the Ku Klux Klan and a sometime student at LSU in Baton Rouge. Although not specifically an anti-war event, since racism was so much a part of the military's indoctrination techniques, it seemed that taking a stand against racism was appropriate for a chapter action. I relied heavily on Art Franz for the organization of this event, and it turned out to be a total failure. No one showed, and apparently, even if they had, the time that Art had scheduled for us to meet was an hour after Duke's march had already been completed.

Soon after I got back to New Orleans, Karl informed me on one of our barhopping jaunts that he had decided to go to New York to work as a volunteer in the National Office. That seemed a bit strange to me, but Karl always seemed to march to his own drum. He explained that after seeing all the tension and mistrust in the organization at the Denver meeting, he wanted to check out what was really going on up there. I didn't quite believe his explanation, but figured he was just looking for an excuse to take a trip to the Big Apple. Whatever his reason, I was sorry to see him go.

In early April 1972, the North Vietnamese launched their Easter Offensive, with three North Vietnamese divisions numbering between thirty and forty thousand men charging across the DMZ into South Vietnam. At that time, there were less than seventy thousand U.S. troops in the country, and the defensive positions along the DMZ were all manned by South Vietnamese troops. As had been predicted by many, the ARVN forces collapsed like a house of cards, and soon, tens of thousands of South Vietnamese soldiers and civilians were high-tailing it down Route 1—over the An Lo Bridge, which I had guarded during my tour—to Hue City, leaving the entire province of Quang-Tri in North Vietnamese hands.

That April, there was another National Steering Committee Meeting, this time in Houston, Texas. I couldn't wait to get on the road, out of comatose New Orleans and back among my activist brothers. VVAW, through its many contacts with active duty soldiers, was receiving reports from all over the country of major units being put on high alert, leaves being canceled, orders for deployment being issued, and troops already on the move. It had all the appearances of a possible reinsertion of substantial U.S. ground forces back into Vietnam to stem the North Vietnamese onslaught and perhaps preparations to suppress the inevitable anti-war backlash at home. It was also being done in total secrecy; none of it was being talked about in the national media. VVAW started issuing press releases detailing the plans being made and the specific units involved. None of these deployments ever came about. Perhaps the fact that VVAW exposed what was happening caused a change of plans. Perhaps the alerts were simply a contingency plan for what ultimately took place: a resumption of the bombing of North Vietnam and the mining of the North Vietnamese harbors.

Whatever the case, the whole issue hung like a black cloud over the Houston meeting as the Regional Coordinators again tried to grapple with the divisive internal organizational issues that had not been resolved at the previous meeting. That, and the undisguised provocative presence of the Houston police— blatantly monitoring the meeting and following participants with no effort at concealment—created a sense of unease and tension that was palpable. In addition, several of the Regional Coordinators had been busted on a variety of bogus drug charges. Scott Camil was also facing charges of kidnapping, in which the main piece of evidence against him was a receipt he allegedly signed for the ransom! If any of these charges stuck, then the guys were facing substantial jail time. As we hammered out a new leadership structure for the organization during the plenary sessions, contingency plans for jailbreaks, if necessary, were being discussed in hushed tones in the dark corners.

The Steering Committee agreed on a new structure for the National Office. Six National Coordinators would be elected from the regions, and would move to New York City to run the day-to-day operations of the organization. While many of the Regional Coordinators had been highly critical of the organizational leadership up to that point, few were actually ready to volunteer to move to New York City to change the situation.

I volunteered.

It was crazy. I had barely been in the organization for seven months and had not participated in any of the major events that had brought VVAW its national—and international—recognition. My "region" was a total bust, with nothing happening really since the Veterans Day arrests the previous November, and if I left, VVAW in Louisiana would be effectively dead. It was precisely for that reason, however, that I wanted to get away and get to a place where my fervor and commitment would be matched by many others. I wanted to feel the sense of higher purpose, of making a difference, that I had felt at these meetings, every day, and not just every couple of months. I also wanted to run away, to continue the pattern of leaving everything behind and starting anew somewhere else.

In some ways, I was the ideal "compromise" candidate for the National Office. I was considered a Southern Regional Coordinator, but I was originally from the North. Other Southern Coordinators like Camil, John Kniffen from Texas, and Bill Patterson from West Texas/New Mexico had developed a highly confrontational relationship with the National Office, and weren't particularly trusted by those from the North. Of course, none of them was interested in going to the National Office anyway. The Southern Coordinators trusted me, and the Northern Coordinators didn't mistrust me.

I was elected.

It had been a totally spur-of-the-moment decision for me. I had not gone to Houston with the intention of pulling up stakes in Louisiana and heading for greener pastures. I wasn't particularly prepared for the move, but also, my life was such that I didn't have many stakes to pull up. I dropped out of college and made arrangements with my two roommates. I had to get some serious mechanical work done on my VW van, and that took some time. Meanwhile, I heard through the grapevine that Karl Becker had been arrested in New York City for carrying a concealed weapon. Then, somewhat mysteriously, the charges were dropped, and he was let go the following day. Folks in New York were highly suspicious of these circumstances, and Becker soon left New York to return to New Orleans, but I didn't see him before I left.

None of this was of particular interest to me. I was headed to New York and whatever fate the future held for me. I never dreamed what awaited me.

Chapter 9

Veterans Day

November 11, 2021, another Veterans Day. I've "celebrated" nigh on fifty of them as a Vietnam veteran since that first one that ended in a jail cell in New Orleans. As a child, I remember watching my father march with his American Legion post in various Veterans Day parades. I didn't think much about it at the time; it was just another day of fun, of hanging out with my cousins at the picnic afterward, but I think it imbued in me a strong sense of duty, of unquestioned patriotism. I had always enjoyed the subject of history in school, and I fell in love with the amazing ideals of the country that I lived in, of the great and good America that I had learned about in the sanitized version of history taught to me in grade school and high school. I felt proud and privileged to live in such a great country and considered it my obligation to stand up and serve when it was my time, as others in my family had before me.

Veterans Day used to be called Armistice Day, commemorating the end of World War I, the "war to end all wars," marking the eleventh hour of the eleventh day of the eleventh month. In 1954, the national holiday was changed to Veterans Day, ostensibly to honor veterans of all wars, not just World War I. The reality was that Armistice Day celebrated peace, and Veterans Day quickly turned into a celebration of war.

I have always had somewhat conflicted feelings about

Veterans Day. It has been a constant and, I would say, unresolved personal struggle for those of us who consider ourselves "anti-war veterans." It is no easy task to maintain pride in one's service when one feels compelled to oppose and reject the cause in which that service was rendered. This ambivalence is compounded by others who seek to brand as "unpatriotic" those who question this country's use of military might, as if it is somehow injurious to this nation for citizens to exercise those rights of which we are so justly proud and for which so many have sacrificed so much to preserve. Such attacks do not bother me as much as they did before. I am a patriot. In a democracy, dissent is the highest form of patriotism.

Yet it has been a bitter, bitter pill for me to swallow, to watch this country again and again march off to engage in senseless foreign wars; to see how easily, again, we believe our government's lies; to watch, again, a country slowly wake to the nightmares we allow our leaders to foist upon us. And on this holiday, especially, I think of those who must bear the brunt of the consequences of these actions: the men and women we have sent to kill and die.

There is a fundamental pact made between a nation and its soldiers. The soldiers commit to protect the rest of us—to give up all or a portion of their rights, their freedom, their life, so the rest of us can enjoy our rights, our freedom, our lives. In return for this, the nation should commit to two things. First, if we ask our soldiers for the ultimate sacrifice, then we must guarantee that the sacrifice we ask of them is for something real, something important, something WORTH it. Second, when their service is completed, then we must take care of them and their families to the extent and for the duration that is necessary. This country has failed on both accounts.

I receive the requisite platitudes from friends and colleagues on Veterans Day: "Thank you for your service." My family knows better. I want to scream at the naïveté of such empty sentiments, but I don't. I understand they are given in good faith in the same way that we say "I'm sorry for your loss" at funerals, meaningless words that are considered "appropriate" when you do not know what else to say.

I wonder what exactly is the "service" I am being thanked for? My service as a soldier consisted of my going to a foreign land and killing as many non-White people as I could in order to prevent them from choosing the manner in which they govern themselves. I was the blunt instrument of a failed neo-colonialist foreign policy disguised as an anti-communist crusade. You cannot thank me for my service without implicitly supporting the mission I was sent to accomplish.

I don't say anything anymore, other than occasional rants on Facebook, which garner me a few "likes" from the choir I'm preaching to and a few incoherent retorts from right-wing family members I haven't yet unfriended.

History is a complicated issue. On the one hand, it seems that "history" as a scholastic subject in the United States is barely dealt with anymore. Not surprising, I suppose, since a dumbed-down population is essential for the current political elite to stay in power, and the less that people know about what happened in the past allows the same actions to be repeated over and over again with impunity. On the other hand, the "history" I was taught in grammar and high school was little more than propaganda—glorified myths, strategic elisions, and outright lies, which accomplished the same objective as not teaching it at all—a population ignorant of most of the causal events that got us to where we are now.

The history of the Vietnam War has been systematically contorted to try to fit this gross international interference into the internal affairs of another country into the America-is-always-the-good-guy rubric. So, the war was a "tragic mistake" instead of the conscious, colonialist-supporting foreign policy decision it actually was. America was trying to protect the freedom of the Vietnamese people rather than trying to assist the weak-kneed French to re-establish their illegitimate claim to colonial mastery of the place. America was fighting against the international communist conspiracy rather than suppressing the legitimate aspirations of a group of anti-colonial nationalists, some of whom were communists.

The central lesson we should have learned from Vietnam is that the U.S. should never send its sons and daughters to foreign lands to kill and be killed for reasons that have nothing to do with our country's national security. Instead, the lesson that has been carefully concocted and drummed into our collective American consciousness is that no matter what the mission is, we must support the troops. This clever and sinister rewrite of history has allowed succeeding presidents to send U.S. troops hither and yon, to satisfy macho urgings, to distract attention from domestic or personal failures, to replace diplomacy with brute force, and, of course, to fill the coffers of those who profit from these ventures. And the American people sit back and watch it all and dutifully support the troops, no matter what dubious enterprise they are sent out to accomplish.

I have a bumper sticker on my pick-up truck that I got from VVAW. It reads, "Honor the Warrior, Not the War." But why do we honor warriors?

What is it about warriors or ex-warriors that deserves such unquestioning adulation? Why do we not honor teachers, doctors, EMTs, research scientists, musicians, or poets in the same way? Why warriors?

Certainly, having served in the military gives no one a monopoly on "The Truth." On the contrary. Veterans in American society, after all, have traditionally played the role of cheerleaders for the next war, although I, for one, have always refused to pick up the pompoms. Where do the politicians go for a friendly audience for their latest militaristic adventure stories? Military and veteran audiences, of course. Actually, my stance as an anti-war veteran is made more special precisely because there are so few military or ex-military who stand for the same things as I do.

Yes, there are some outstanding individuals in the military. Sure, the ranks are filled with misguided patriotic youth, "ardent for some desperate glory," as Wilfred Owen wrote in his famous World War I poem (hey, I was one of them once), and economic draftees looking to learn a trade or escape the hood. Sure, the Guard is packed with ordinary Joes and Janes, trying to make a few bucks to support that mortgage, or make that car payment, or save for that kid's college. But there is also a plethora of careerists, boot-lickers, sadists, thugs, crooks, and mediocrities who populate this most reactionary of our national institutions. When I was in the Army, the highest praise—praise that was rather uncommon—heard for a "lifer" was "He could have made it on the outside."

So why do we honor warriors in the ways that we do? Is it not a reflection of the militaristic sub-text that has pervaded American life since WWII? Economic fortunes and political careers have been built on the myth of the great external threat. First communism, then terrorism. These "threats" keep us living in fear, unable to question, unable to offer an alternative point of view. If we are so "threatened," of course, then we need protectors. The glorification of the military and the adulation of the warrior are part and parcel of the myth used to keep us in our place and keep the American-flag-wrapped, pseudo-patriotic politicians in power. But wait; it gets better. Here it is: the Royal Scam. Create the climate of fear, foster adulation for the warriors who "protect" us, then use them to rape the rest of the world while we sit by and applaud their efforts.

Rape? Yes, does anyone question the connection between the macho, militaristic glorification of "the warrior" and the treatment of women in our society? Do the two not flow from the same source? Rape is a crime of violence, of power, of subjugation. Is it any wonder that a society that so celebrates the cult of the warrior would not also be so tolerant of the rapists who walk among us?

And what of us progressives? How many of us feel compelled to preface any anti-war remarks with "Of course, I support the troops, but ..."? Why? Because we have bought into the myth that supporting the troops, honoring the warriors, is a fundamental component of patriotism, and one cannot "patriotically" oppose a war unless one also supports the troops. But how do you support the troops without supporting the mission they are undertaking? How do you honor the warriors but not the war? And if, indeed, these cannot be separated—the troops from the mission, the warriors from the war—then why are we supporting and honoring those who are the instruments of the policies we oppose?

Well, I don't really know the answer to that question, at least not in the frame in which it is usually asked. I prefer to frame it differently.

Is not the education of our children a matter of national security? Is not the health of our citizens a matter of national security? Is not the financial well-being of our nation a matter of national security? Which is the better expenditure for national security, funds for education, health, and economic well-being, or funds for military hardware? Which is the better way to deal with national security issues: military force to bend other nations to our will or diplomacy to solve issues cooperatively? Is national security only about guns and bombs and soldiers, or is it something more?

So, what of "the troops"? Do we call them baby killers and spit on them when they come home (an urban myth from the Vietnam War)? Do we blame them for the failed policies of the government that sent them, as many did to the returning troops from Vietnam? I remember well the insinuation of the WWII vet at the VFW bar, "Well, we won OUR war." Do we forget about them and leave them to suffer in private with the physical and spiritual wounds they will come back with?

The sad reality of fighting in a war is that many, if not most, of those who survive return home with substantial problems. For some, those problems are physical—traumatic, life-altering wounds that will never heal and that will require treatment for the rest of their lifetime. In Vietnam, the life-saving procedures of getting severely wounded men from the front line to the operating room were perfected and have been implemented with improvements in Iraq and Afghanistan. Lives are saved, but men (and now women) who would have died on the battlefield in previous wars are given the "opportunity" to live armless, legless, sightless, brainless lives. Then there's the other "problems": PTSD, lost jobs, failed marriages, broken lives. As they say, in war, all wounds do not pierce the skin. They do, however, cost money. Who will pay?

Sure, we will all raise our hands now and demand proper treatment for the returning veterans, but what about ten or twenty years from now, when the latest war is a distant, painful memory, and all those brightly colored back-trunk decals are but fading pieces of refuse in some landfill? What will happen when there is real competition for where federal dollars will be spent, when some up-and-coming, budget-cutting politician frames the choice as your benefits or theirs? What will happen then to the invisible, powerless refuse from the long-forgotten war?

Happy Veterans Day.

Chapter 10

Fried Marbles

I left New Orleans behind, heading north to the city where I was born, my brief attempt at a normal life after Vietnam shattered by a surge of adrenaline-fueled idealism. All my life, I had wanted to make a difference, and this seemed to me to be my chance. I had quickly evolved from an aspiring hippie looking for veteran companionship to a full-time activist ready to sacrifice everything for the cause and the organization I had committed to. National Coordinator of Vietnam Veterans Against the War: I was scared, excited, and determined to fulfill my destiny.

When I reached New York City, I had little money and no place to live. Since I had dropped out of college (again), I stopped getting my monthly allotment from the G.I. Bill. I got $25 a week as a National Coordinator. I unrolled my sleeping bag in a closet in the VVAW office, and that's where I lived. I threw myself into VVAW work.

The VVAW office was located on West 26th Street, right next door to the U.S. Communist Party headquarters, a fact that some tried to make an issue out of, but it was simply an area for cheap office space. In addition to being the headquarters for the National VVAW, it also served as the office for the New York State VVAW. By the time I got there, most of the previous National Coordinators had already cleared out, with the exception of Al Hubbard, who provided the only link of continuity from the old regime to the new.

There was a rich mixture of New York City characters worthy of a Damon Runyon short story who flowed in and out of the office: Robby Dunne, Joe Hirsch, Brian Mattarese, Mark O'Connor, Frank Toner, Joe Treglio, Chris Soares, and Sheldon Ramsdell, among others. There was Eddie Damato—"The Chief"—a soft-spoken, laid-back vet who was the New York State Regional Coordinator. There was Jim Noonan, the fast-talking ex-Marine and Brooklyn VVAW Coordinator, who went on to become Senior Executive Vice President for Warner Brothers Entertainment. There was Jim Duffy, a gruff working-class vet who was intent on fomenting revolution. There was Robert Santos, a former platoon leader with the 101st Airborne Division in Vietnam, who earned two Silver Stars and two Bronze Stars for valor. There was Ann Hirschman, a nurse by training, who was quickly becoming a legend as one of the finest street medics in the anti-war movement.

There were the women of the Emma Goldman Brigade—named after the fiery radical anarchist of the early twentieth century—who had once managed to infiltrate a Republican Women's luncheon honoring Pat Nixon and release some white rats. One night, one of the Brigade, Jill, invited me to the apartment that she shared with another Brigade member, Coca Crystal. When I didn't seem to take the broad hint as to why I was there, Jill summarily threw me down on the bed to be less subtle about the message, all the while proclaiming, "This is not in my best interest!" She was right, but not in the way she imagined.

There was Danny Friedman, a former semi-pro football player with wild black hair and a scraggly beard that presaged Hagrid of Harry Potter fame. Danny was a man of massive strength with a heart as big as the borough of Brooklyn, where he was from. He could, at times, be irritatingly obnoxious in meetings—he would drive Jim Noonan crazy sometimes—

but in any action on the street, he was the man you wanted by your side. He quickly made it his personal mission in life to keep my naïve young ass out of trouble in the Big Apple. There was the time we were at an anti-war demonstration in Queens—not a strictly VVAW event, so we were mixed in with a whole crowd of rowdy rabble—when some guy threw something at a plainclothes policeman, then started running away through the crowd. The cop gave chase, and after the guy ran past me, I didn't make much effort to get out of the way of the cop. The cop pulled a blackjack from the pocket of his trench coat, whacked me on the side of the head, turned to a uniformed cop nearby and told him to arrest me, then charged off into the crowd. The uniformed cop started to approach me where I was lying on the ground, and Danny quickly stood in front of me, arms folded, and told the cop I hadn't done anything wrong and he was NOT going to arrest me. A group quickly formed around me behind Danny, all shouting at the cop that I had done nothing wrong. The cop took one long look at Danny, looked over his shoulder to see if the plain-clothes cop was still around, then turned and walked away.

A few weeks after I arrived in New York, on May 8, 1972, President Nixon announced the mining of the North Vietnamese harbors. VVAW denounced the action as the latest escalation in a war that was supposed to be winding down. A press conference was called by several New York City peace groups to announce plans to protest this escalation. I was chosen to be the VVAW spokesman at the press conference, and I announced on national television that unless the United Nations took the government of the United States into receivership until such time as a government representative of the people could be elected, then in seventy-two hours, VVAW was going to take over the United Nations.

Of course, we had neither the desire nor the capability to "take over" the United Nations, any more than the United Nations had the desire or capability to do anything about the U.S. government, but if VVAW had learned anything, it was the value of symbolic action.

On the day our ultimatum expired, the sidewalk in front of the United Nations building had a New York City cop standing at intervals of about every ten feet. We had separated our group into three teams. One team was able to get invited onto a regularly scheduled UN tour, and actually got into the building itself. A second team approached the main entrance gate and started to make a ruckus. As expected, the line of cops along the sidewalk immediately folded up and gravitated towards the commotion. A third team—of which I was a member—had been watching from an office building across the street from the UN. Once we saw the cops abandoning their posts, we ran across the street, pushed through the hedge, and scaled the low wall that separated the UN grounds from the street. All of us had chains wrapped around our bodies, with the intent to try to chain ourselves somewhere visible along the front of the building to symbolically "take over" the UN. We hadn't, however, accounted for how much the weight of the chains limited our mobility, and although we managed to get over the wall, we were all quickly subdued by UN security personnel—except Danny Friedman, who managed to elude the security and actually get inside the UN building. After a bit of roughing up by security, we were summarily ejected from the grounds. Danny managed to hook up with the team on the tour, who had barricaded themselves in the UN chapel for a brief period before they, too, were ejected from the premises. Although we hadn't succeeded in what we had planned, we got good local news coverage that evening, and one channel even had footage of the cops running to the ruckus and our team then running across the street and scaling the wall.

Our antics at the UN inspired a new possibility. The next

day, we received a call at the VVAW office from some students who attended Riverdale High School in the Bronx. They told us that the United Nations Association was holding a black-tie dinner in the high school's gym to honor George and Barbara Bush that evening, Bush being the U.S. ambassador to the United Nations at that time. The students suggested that if VVAW wanted to get into the dinner, they could arrange to meet us at a back door and let us in.

We devised a similar plan to the one executed at the UN. We broke into two teams. One team approached the front door of the school and started to chant anti-war slogans. Immediately, all the security for the place rushed to focus on these few. Meanwhile, the second team of five people—Danny Friedman, Brian Mattarese, Mark O'Connor, Ann Hirschman, and myself—met the students at the designated spot and got inside the building. The students led us through what seemed like a maze of corridors until we reached the door of the gym. We burst in on the tuxedoed and evening-gowned dignitaries seated at the tables, and Brian gave a short anti-war speech, the last line of which was "The blood of the Vietnamese people is on your hands." We then proceeded to throw balloons full of blood (actually, red clothing dye) at the assemblage and made our escape before any of the startled dignitaries could react. We all got away scot-free.

Now, as far as a "demonstration" goes, this was probably a total failure. The purpose of a demonstration is to attract as much attention as possible to the message you want to convey, usually by trying to get the media to cover it. No one knew about what happened in the Riverdale High School gym that night except those who were there. As one of the other national coordinators derisively dismissed it, it was pure adventurism, serving only to give a bunch of adrenaline junkies their latest fix. Yet, of all the various demonstrations I participated in during my lifetime, this one was somehow one of the most satisfying. Maybe it was the fact that we pulled it off and got away, but I think it was more than that. Most demonstrations make you feel powerless. You feel like you're beating your head against a stone wall, and those with the money and power sitting behind the wall are casually drinking their tea, blithely unconcerned with the rabble banging their bloody heads against the wall that protects those in power. This one time, they had to look us in the eyes, and, if only briefly, we got to disrupt their genteel indifference.

1972 was a presidential election year, and the political conventions of the two parties were natural magnets for major antiwar demonstrations. The Republican National Convention was originally scheduled to be held in San Diego, but Jack Anderson, a syndicated newspaper columnist, uncovered a memo dated June 25, 1971, written by Mrs. Dita D. Beard, a lobbyist for the International Telephone and Telegraph Corporation (ITT). The memo suggested that ITT pledge $400,000 toward the San Diego bid in return for the U.S. Department of Justice settling its antitrust case against ITT out of court. In fact, the Justice Department announced a month later, on July 31, that it had reached a settlement with ITT. Trying to avoid a scandal, the Republicans transferred the event to Miami Beach, the same city where the Democratic Convention had been scheduled. It was one of the few times that the conventions of the two political parties had been scheduled in the same city in the same year. For those of us planning the demonstrations, it somewhat simplified our plans.

Scott Camil and the Florida VVAW were at the forefront of the organization's planning for the conventions simply because they were "on the ground." There was no love lost between Scott and the other members of the National Office—Scott was one of the leaders of the regional rebellion against the previous National Office regime, and his proposal to assassinate senators caused many in the organization to view him as unpredictable, untrustworthy, and potentially dangerous. Nevertheless, the National Office reluctantly agreed that Scott's chapter should take the point, but they wanted to keep tabs on Scott. So when he organized a meeting in Gainesville for the last weekend in May to function as both a logistics meeting for the convention demonstrations and a Southern Regional Coordinators meeting, the National Office wanted someone there, and I was the natural candidate to attend. I didn't particularly share others' mistrust of Scott—I was somewhat in awe of him, and his support had been crucial to my election to the National Office—but I agreed that it was necessary for a National Coordinator to attend this meeting. I jumped in my trusty VW van and headed to Florida.

I arrived at Scott Camil's place in Gainesville late in the afternoon of Friday, May 26. The Texas contingent had already arrived. John Kniffen, the Texas Regional Coordinator, a short wiry ex-Marine with fiery eyes and a temperament to match, was there, along with his wife, Cathy. Wayne Beverly, another ex-Marine with a Hobbit-like look, was Kniffen's right-hand man. Bill Patterson, the West Texas and New Mexico Regional Coordinator—ruggedly handsome with piercing blue eyes—rounded out the group.

They had just returned from a nearby firing range owned by Scott's friend Emerson Poe, another vet and VVAW member. When I got there, all were sitting around Scott's living room, beginning to clean their weapons. I was a bit nonplussed by the scene but tried to stay cool. Even though I had become quite familiar with all sorts of guns while in the military, guns had never been a part of my upbringing, and I wasn't comfortable around them, but for good ole Southern boys, guns were as common as fishing poles. I accepted a shotgun from Scott and started cleaning it, trying to suppress my unease with a nonchalant pretense.

Shortly after that, Bill Lemmer, a former paratrooper trained in the Special Forces who had succeeded Don Donner as Arkansas-Oklahoma Regional Coordinator, arrived. I remember how his eyes absolutely lit up when he walked into the room and saw guns and vets strewn all over the furniture and floor. He said he had just come from a demonstration in Washington, D.C., and he was full of stories about sinister security personnel in black jumpsuits beating up on the demonstrators and implied that this is what awaited us in Miami Beach in the summer.

As the evening wore on, joints were passed, beers popped open, and things degenerated into what I came to call a macho show-and-tell session. John Kniffen had a crossbow, which he demonstrated to the group by shooting into the door of Scott's bedroom. Scott showed the assemblage a wrist-rocket slingshot, which he said could use steel ball bearings, or "fried marbles," as ammunition, which would shatter on impact. The advantage of both the crossbow and the slingshot, Scott explained, was that both were silent weapons, and there was no muzzle flash, so the location of the shooter could not be detected. Scott then demonstrated the effect of mixing potassium permanganate and glycerin, two drugstore chemicals. Scott put the chemicals separated from one another into a small plastic pill bottle and then shook the bottle to mix the chemicals. In a few seconds, the plastic pill bottle erupted in flame as the chemicals spontaneously combusted. Scott suggested that this could be dropped down a police car gas tank, which possibly could blow up the car, but he was unsure if this would work or not. All the while this was going on, Bill Lemmer was spinning increasingly wild and alarming scenarios: "What if the police do this, then what are we gonna do?"

Let's be clear. In the Spring of 1972, it was not uncommon for anti-war demonstrators to be discussing how they would react to a police riot. We had all seen or heard about the police riot at the Democratic Convention in Chicago in 1968, and, if anything, tensions were even higher in 1972. There were all sorts of rumors and conspiracy theories floating around, such

as the Miami police department having gotten a large shipment of M-16s in hand. And, as it came out later during the
investigations into the Watergate burglary, there were a number of actual discussions and proposed plans at the highest
levels of government about the use of all sorts of illegal tactics against the anti-war movement, including the kidnapping of its leaders before the convention demonstrations. It
did not seem out of the realm of possibility that the government might provoke a violent, perhaps deadly, confrontation
with anti-war demonstrators—a confrontation that many on
both sides would have welcomed—then use that as an excuse
for further oppressive measures including the declaration of
martial law and the canceling of the elections.

When Lemmer proposed a scenario involving the cops
closing off the bridges to Miami Beach and shooting the demonstrators, the assemblage of stoned veterans began imagining what would be an appropriate response to such an event.
The plan, if you wanted to call it that, was to send small
teams of vets to open the bridges and then disable them so
they couldn't be raised again. Other teams of vets we called
"fire teams" would start a series of diversionary tactics—fires,
explosions, non-lethal hit-and-run ambushes—meant to draw
police attention away from the other demonstrators so they
could escape over the bridges. In military terminology, a fire
team was a group that worked together, stayed together, and
had one another's back during an action or confrontation.
Other demonstrators called them "affinity groups," but we
used the military terminology with which we were the most
familiar.

Different people who participated in this discussion had
very different impressions of it. My own take was that it was
just an after-hours bullshit session, hypothetical responses to
hypothetical situations. Other anti-war groups—and many
within VVAW itself—tended to view the organization as the
anti-war movement's security forces. Indeed, VVAW had the

knowledge, experience, and discipline to perform this function probably better than anyone else. Certainly, VVAW took its role as movement protectors seriously, and I had no doubt we would do everything in our power to protect ourselves and other demonstrators should the situation arise. We just needed to come to terms with the difference between what we thought we could do and what we were actually capable of doing.

The next morning, a number of local Florida coordinators started to arrive, including Don Perdue from Fort Lauderdale and Alton Foss from Hialeah. A number of vets from the Gainesville area also showed up, including Emerson Poe and Stan Michelsen, a happy-go-lucky hippie who had spent twenty months in Vietnam attached to the Marines in a psychological warfare unit. We all convened in the attic of Scott's house, which seemingly provided an element of privacy and an entrance to the meeting that could be easily controlled. As I remember it, perhaps ninety percent of the meeting was taken up with all the mundane logistical concerns about organizing two large demonstrations in the same place within a month of each other. Do we have permission to camp in the park? Do we have parade permits? Will there be porto-sans? What are other demonstrators planning to do?

There was a lot of talk about security, how to protect ourselves from both the cops and from the other demonstrators. We all understood that VVAW's power as demonstrators lay in maintaining our unique identity as Vietnam veterans. We did not want to be mixed in with all the hippies, yippies, zippies, and other assorted groups and individuals who would be in the streets of Miami Beach during the conventions. We talked about "collective self-defense," stressing that VVAW was not there to start any trouble but that we would protect ourselves and other demonstrators should the situation require it. I remember the concept of fire teams being discussed at the meeting, but I don't remember any of the specific tactics that had been bandied about in the previous evening's bullshit session being discussed in this formal meeting.

About halfway through the meeting, we were told that Karl Becker and Art Franz had shown up from New Orleans and wanted to get into the meeting. Scott asked me if I could vouch for them. I wasn't sure about Becker; he was not a veteran, and he had not communicated with me since he had left for New York in February. Furthermore, I was pretty sure by then that Franz was an informer. Right before I headed north, he had set up a meeting for me with the head of the New Orleans Red Squad, a police intelligence unit that specialized in infiltrating political groups, ostensibly, he said, to improve relations between VVAW and local law enforcement. Franz did not participate in the meeting, but it quickly became evident that the meeting was an attempt to recruit me as an informer. Now, Becker and Franz showed up in Gainesville together unannounced and uninvited. I told Scott that I would not vouch for either of them, and they were not allowed entrance to the meeting. They left before the meeting was over.

Shortly after the meeting broke up, Scott pulled me aside and told me two things. One, he had received a call from Don Donner, the guy from Arkansas who had recruited me into VVAW in New Orleans. Don told Scott that Bill Lemmer was probably an informer. Scott had confronted Lemmer with this information, and Lemmer confirmed it but proposed that he could work as a double agent for VVAW. The second thing was that Alton Foss had relayed information that a right-wing Cuban group in Miami was making plans to attack anti-war demonstrators during the conventions. Scott was going to go down to Miami to try to make contact with the Cubans and head off trouble and asked if I wanted to go along. Of course, I immediately agreed. Strangely, to me anyway, Scott allowed Bill Lemmer to accompany us on this trip despite his then-known status as an informer. I never asked Scott why he did this. Perhaps he wanted to demonstrate to Lemmer our peaceful intentions; perhaps it was a matter of keeping your enemies closer.

Scott was able to set up a meeting with a man named Pablo Fernandez, who supposedly represented a radical group of Cubans named Alpha 66. Scott, Lemmer, and I met Fernandez in the evening on a street corner somewhere in Miami—Alton didn't attend the meeting. Scott explained to Fernandez that VVAW had no quarrel with Alpha 66 or any other Cuban group and that we did not want any violence at the conventions. Fernandez listened to Scott for a few minutes and then, out of the blue, offered that he could sell Scott a case of hand grenades for three hundred dollars. Scott, of course, declined the offer, and after a bit more small talk, the meeting ended. I didn't think much of it at the time—Scott and I just rolled our eyes as it seemed like just another pointless conversation— but its importance would later become clear. After attending another meeting with representatives of many of the various groups planning to demonstrate at the conventions—a meeting which underscored to me that VVAW must keep its distance from many of them—Scott and I headed back north. I dropped him off in Gainesville and drove back to New York City.

Things were happening at breakneck speed in the late spring of 1972. Shortly after I got back to New York, VVAW received an invitation to send a delegation of Vietnam veterans to Paris to meet with a delegation of North Vietnamese veterans. It would have been the first time that soldiers from opposing sides had met one another in peace off the battlefield while the war they fought in was still going on. I was chosen to be part of the delegation, as was Stan Michelsen whom I had met in Florida, and we were off to France.

Unfortunately, it turned out to be a total bust. The French government, probably under pressure from the U.S., refused at the last minute to grant visas to the North Vietnamese veterans, so we ended up meeting with members of the North Vietnamese and NLF delegations to the Paris peace talks. It was all very formal, sitting at a long table with us on one side and the delegation members along the other, sipping tea

VVAW delegation to Paris. Stan, with beard, standing fourth from left.

and exchanging mutual expressions of support. There was a brief flare-up when a woman—a member of the NLF delegation—stood up, said some angry words in Vietnamese, and then stalked out of the room. Her comrades told us that some of her family had been killed by American soldiers and that meeting us was just too much for her to bear.

The media, of course, had been alerted, and a number of journalists showed up but quickly lost interest when they saw no North Vietnamese veterans were there. There was a small game room adjacent to where we were meeting, and some Vietnamese and Americans started to play ping-pong. The hope was to provide a visual for the media that referenced "ping-pong diplomacy," as it had in April 1971 when the signal for improved relations with China came about when the American ping-pong team received an invitation from its Chinese colleagues for a trip to the People's Republic. From the media's perspective, however, there was no story, and most of them packed up and left, not bothering to stay around for the press conference to listen to the anti-American diatribes from the old French Socialists who had sponsored the event. Oh well, at least I got to see Paris.

We returned to New York only a few days before the start of the Democratic Convention, and I quickly jumped into preparations for heading back to Florida for the demonstrations. The National Office started to receive phone calls that a number of VVAW members had been subpoenaed to appear before a grand jury in Tallahassee, Florida. All the subpoenas demanded an appearance on the same day at the same time, Monday morning, July 10, at 9 a.m., day one of the Democratic convention. As I saw the names of those who had been subpoenaed, I had no doubt that there was one waiting for me somewhere. I shrugged, climbed into my VW van with a load of fellow demonstrators, and headed for Florida.

When we got to Gainesville, I hooked up with Scott, who, after a brief phone call with a local FBI agent, confirmed that I had been subpoenaed, along with about twenty-two other VVAW members, many of whom had attended the meeting in Gainesville at the end of May. I had a choice: I could continue to make myself scarce and head down to Miami Beach and wait for the Feds to find me and serve me with my subpoena, or Scott could let the local Feds know I was in town and make it easy for them. I decided to make my whereabouts known, preferring to head to Tallahassee with a group rather than alone.

The National Office contacted the Center for Constitutional Rights, an organization of lawyers that had started during the civil rights movement in the early sixties and had represented anti-war protesters who had been hauled before grand juries on several occasions. The Center agreed to send several lawyers down to Florida. They arrived in Gainesville on Sunday and had a preliminary meeting with a number of the subpoenaed vets. What they told us was not encouraging.

The grand jury in Tallahassee had been convened by Guy Goodwin, a Justice Department lawyer who had become a specialist in using the grand jury system against the anti-war movement. The attorneys explained some of the quirks of the grand jury. A witness was alone in the room with the prosecutor and the grand jurors; the witness was not allowed to have an attorney present with him. Once a witness answered one question, he would be required under penalty of contempt to answer all questions posed to him.

If a witness refused to answer any questions, the prosecutor could offer immunity. There were two types of immunity: transactional immunity and use immunity. We learned that transactional immunity, also known as "blanket" or "total" immunity, protected the witness completely from any prosecution related to the matter under investigation; this is what most people think of when they think of immunity. Use immunity, however, provided immunity from prosecution only based on the grand jury testimony of the individual. If the prosecutor were able to develop evidence independent of the testimony, then the person could be indicted based on that other evidence. Theoretically, a prosecutor could call two witnesses, give each one use immunity, ask them the same questions, and then indict each of them on the other's testimony. If a witness still refused to testify after receiving immunity, he could be jailed for contempt for the life of the grand jury. The lawyers strongly recommended that the best course for all would be to refuse to answer the very first question in the grand jury room and maintain that throughout. This was not citing the Fifth Amendment against self-incrimination; it was refusing to cooperate with an abuse of the grand jury system.

The hallway outside of the grand jury room was a chaotic scene on the morning of Monday, July 10, crowded with veterans milling around, playing cards, or speaking in low tones in small groups. It was unprecedented to subpoena so many witnesses to appear on the same day at the same time. Clearly, the grand jury could not possibly hear twenty-three witnesses in one week, much less one day. It amounted to a legal kidnapping of the leadership of VVAW that had been most involved in planning for the conventions. As we later found out, the kidnapping of anti-war leaders had been discussed by the likes of John Mitchell, Jeb Magruder, and G. Gordon Liddy when Liddy first presented his "Operation Gemstone" plan to then-Attorney General Mitchel in January 1972. What's more, as the day wore on, different vets approached the lawyers at different times, furtively whispering that they thought so-and-so was a government informer. To protect themselves and their clients, the lawyers had everyone who was willing sign a simple retainer form that designated the lawyers as representatives for purposes of the grand jury. The lawyers then went into court, and after some argument back and forth, the judge put Guy Goodwin on the stand under oath, and the names of all those who had signed retainers with the lawyers were read, and Goodwin was asked if any of them were agents or informers of the government. Goodwin swore that none of them was.

The grand jury process unfolded pretty much as the lawyers had predicted. A number of vets, myself included, were called before the grand jury, and each of us read a short statement given to us by the lawyers and refused to testify. The question I was asked would have been virtually impossible to answer even if I had wanted to. "Tell the grand jury everyplace you went, every meeting you attended, everyone you met at those meetings, and what was said by each person during the period of April, May, and June of 1972." Four vets—Wayne Beverly from Texas, and John Chambers, Jack Jennings, and Bruce Horton, all from Florida—were given use immunity. They continued to refuse to testify and were jailed for contempt. On July 13, the last day of the Democratic Convention, the rest of us were released from our subpoenas, most never even having been called before the grand jury, confirming our suspicions that one of the main goals of the subpoenas was to keep us from attending the demonstrations in Miami Beach. In the early evening of that Thursday, about an hour after VVAW was able to get a resolution on the floor of the Democratic Convention condemning the proceedings as an illegal and political use of the grand jury, six veterans were indicted for conspiracy to incite a riot at the Republican Convention, which was not scheduled to take place for another month. The indictment alleged that we planned to attack the convention using automatic weapons, hand grenades, firebombs, crossbows, fried marbles, and slingshots. I was one of those six, along with Scott Camil, John Kniffen, Don Purdue, Alton Foss, and Bill Patterson.

My apprehension by the FBI after the indictment was uneventful. The lawyers had rented rooms in a hotel near the courthouse, and we had just finished a wrap-up session with them, cautiously celebrating our release from the subpoenas but concerned about the four who had been hauled off to jail for contempt. As I remember it, the parking area for the hotel was located on the roof. After the meeting, I was heading to my van to drive to the house of the local VVAW guy named Frank, where many of us were staying. Two guys in suits approached me in the parking area and asked me my name. When I told them, they slapped handcuffs on me and told me I was under arrest. They escorted me downstairs and through the lobby of the hotel. I started shouting at the top of my lungs that I was being arrested, hoping somebody would hear me.

The attempted arrest of Scott Camil, apparently, was a bit more dramatic. After the meeting with the lawyers, most everyone was headed to Frank's house for dinner and perhaps a little party. Alton Foss needed to get back to Hialeah and Don Purdue to Fort Lauderdale, so they both got on the road immediately. By lucky chance, the others had to stop along the way to pick up some groceries and run a few other errands, so there were only a couple of vets, John Kniffen's wife, Cathy, and one or two other women at the house when about ten cars came roaring up the street in double file and screeched to a halt in front of the house. Dozens of men carrying shotguns and pistols, some in suits and ties and others in riot gear, jumped out of the cars and stormed into the house, brushing past one of the women, who demanded they show identification and a warrant. The men started ripping up the house, demanding to know where Scott Camil was. One of the vets there—a guy named Dave from Colorado—looked somewhat like Scott (wiry, long black hair, a black beard), and the men threw him up against a wall. Only after Dave was able to produce ID to prove he wasn't Scott did they let him go. These guys were looking for a fight—trying to provoke one, actually. If the house had been full of vets, they might very well have gotten their wish, and who knows what sort of violence might have ensued.

The next day, Camil and Kniffen turned themselves in to the authorities at the Tallahassee Court House. Alton Foss was arrested at home in Hialeah, and Don Purdue surrendered in Fort Lauderdale. Bill Patterson, after hearing the lawyers talk about how the government was abusing the grand jury system, had decided that he was not going to allow himself to be subjected to that abuse, and he fled and went into hiding before the grand jury proceedings got underway. He finally turned himself in to authorities in Austin, Texas.

Scott, John, and I were ensconced in the Leon County jail. For the first day or two, the three of us were put in a single cell together, isolated from the rest of the prison population. We passed the time playing chess with chessmen made from torn-up pieces of Styrofoam cups and scraping away at the mortar between the concrete blocks of the wall under our beds using the military dog tags we all still wore. While it was utterly futile to think that our scrapings would ever amount to anything, we couldn't just sit there passively; we needed to be actively involved in making some sort of effort to escape, if only to maintain our sanity. Finally, we were allowed to mingle in the common room with the other prisoners, where we took on a bit of a hero's image since our case had been prominently featured on the television news every night.

The government set bail at $25,000 cash each, at first not allowing the usual property bond or ten-percent bond. Through various efforts, we were able to raise bonds for five of the six defendants, and all but one of us was free in about a week's time. We decided that we would start to alternate time in jail until we raised the final bond—one of us would turn himself in, and the money would be used to bail the other guy out. I volunteered to be the first to go back in, but because we received some publicity for what we were planning to do, we raised the final bond before I had to re-enter the jail.

After our lawyers got the restriction to the Northern District of Florida rescinded, I decided to head back to New York City, but first, I drove over to New Orleans. I had hoped to find Karl Becker and maybe reestablish contact with him, but he was nowhere to be found. I had no phone number for him, and I did not even know where he lived. I dropped by the places that he had usually frequented but to no avail.

I was staying at the apartment of one of my old roommates, and on my last night in town, we decided to gather a few friends for a little party on the levee. We were standing around on the levee when we noticed a car with two men in the front seat parked about a hundred yards from where we were. Then, out of the blue, two teenagers walked up to us and offered to sell us some pot. It was a setup and a pretty ham-handed one at that. We pointed out to the two teenagers the two men sitting in the car and suggested to them that they might want to think twice about trying to sell drugs to total strangers.

As the two erstwhile drug dealers scurried away, the men got out of the car and approached us. As expected, they flashed their police IDs and proceeded with the usual hippie hassle. One of them got right up into my face and snarled, "Lemme see some ID, you mother-fuckin' long-haired freak!" I replied as calmly as I could, "You know, I think you're a real asshole for saying that." And so, they arrested me for reviling a police officer, restrained my hands behind my back using thumb cuffs—nasty little things with teeth on the inside that dug into your thumbs and cut off circulation—threw me into the back of their car, and drove off, leaving my flabbergasted friends gaping behind them.

On the drive to the station house, I struck up a conversation with the two cops, and it turned out the one who got up into my face was a Vietnam veteran. His whole manner changed when he found out I was a vet, too. We exchanged the usual unit and year info and were soon relating in-country yarns to one another as if we were in a VFW bar somewhere. I talked a little about respect and how I gave it to those who showed respect to me. The cop didn't say anything, but I think he got the point. I was starting to think that maybe they would just let me go, but at the station house, things seemed to go from bad to worse.

It was a chilly night, and I had borrowed a jacket from one of my friends. The cops started searching me and noticed small remnants of some agricultural products in one of the pockets. I explained the jacket wasn't mine, but the cops were like, "Yeah, right." Worse still, when they searched my wallet, they found a credit card that didn't have my name on it. I had totally forgotten about that. Some guy I didn't even know had given it to me before we left New York for Florida and told me I could use it to pay for repairs in case I broke down along the way. It looked old and dirty, but I just slipped it into my wallet without thinking, never really planning to use it. It turns out the credit card was stolen, as the cops gleefully informed me. I figured I was up shit creek with a drug bust and a stolen credit card bust about to be piled on the conspiracy bust. The cops kept me at the station all night.

Finally, at about four or five o'clock in the morning, the two cops who had originally arrested me came to my cell and asked me if I had ever used the credit card. I assured them

I hadn't and had never planned to. Shortly after that, they released me with no charges; I have always thought it was that brief connection with another Vietnam vet in the cop car that saved my ass. My friends, who had been sitting outside the station house all night, were waiting for me. They had phoned Doris Peterson, one of my lawyers, who had also stayed up all night. I called Doris and told her all that had happened. She breathed a sigh of relief, then exasperatedly asked if I could try to stay out of trouble so she could get some sleep.

My adventures on this trip were not quite finished. As I was driving back up to New York, I had to get on Interstate 65, which, in those days, started about thirty miles north of Mobile, Alabama. I had just gotten onto the interstate—a ribbon of relative safety from the hippie-hating, Nixon-loving rural South through which it wended—when my faithful VW van sputtered and died. I managed to pull it over onto the shoulder and climbed out to flag down a car. I was in serious hippie mode, hair down to here, driving in a Volkswagen van with psychedelic paint all over the interior, with visions of Easy Rider dancing in my head.

Sure enough, a classic pick-up truck with a rifle rack in the rear window pulled over, and I began to wonder whether I was merely going to lose my hair or lose my life. The guy got out of the truck and asked if I needed help. Although he was about my age, I called him *sir* several times and asked if he might be able to give me a lift to the next exit so I could find someone to tow me into a service station. He scratched his head and slowly drawled that there wasn't much of any-thing up at the next exit. He pulled a rope out of the back of his truck—was this gonna be a lynching?—and proceeded to hitch my van to the back of his pick-up. He then made a U-turn across the grass median on the interstate, hauled me back to the previous exit, and dropped me off at a service sta-tion about a mile from the exit.

The guys at the station looked at the van and figured out

the problem, but they needed a part to fix it. The only place that had VW van parts was a dealership down in Mobile, which closed at 5 p.m., thirty minutes off. The service station guy called the dealership, told them he was on his way, and asked them to stay open until he got there. The guy drove down to Mobile, got the part, came back, and fixed my van, and I was back on the road that evening. He only charged me for parts and labor.

So much for stereotypes.

Chapter 11

Standing Rock

On the way to Standing Rock.

In the fall of 2016, I had the privilege of watching my wonderful daughter perform in a student dance concert at the Baryshnikov Theatre in NYC. After all the post-concert hugs and kisses, and expressions of parental pride, I got on a plane and flew to the Standing Rock Indian Reservation, which straddles the border between North and South Dakota, with the likelihood that I could be beaten, tear-gassed, shot at with rubber bullets, and sprayed with water cannons in sub-freezing temperatures, all to support a group of Native Americans trying to keep their water from being poisoned by corporate greed and governmental complicity.

At issue was the Dakota Access Pipeline that begins in the Bakken oil fields in Northwest North Dakota and travels in a relatively straight line southeast through South Dakota and Iowa, ending at an oil terminal near Patoka, Illinois.

Routing the pipeline across the Missouri River near the city of Bismarck had been rejected because of the route's proximity to municipal water sources. The alternative route selected crossed underneath the Missouri River, half a mile from the Standing Rock Indian Reservation, and under Lake Oahe, the main water source for the reservation. An oil spill there could have major adverse effects on the waters that the reservation relied on, not to mention that the pipeline would be constructed through lands that the Dakota Sioux considered sacred. But, hey, when the choice is building a threat to White people's water or building a threat to Native Americans' water, well, we know how that decision is going to play out.

Energy Transfer Partners, the pipeline company, met with representatives of the Standing Rock Sioux, listened to the overwhelming opposition to the project, and, not surprisingly, completely ignored it. At first, they tried to use a permit process that treated the pipeline as a series of small construction sites, thus skirting the requirement for an environmental review mandated by the Clean Water Act and the National Environmental Policy Act. However, in March 2016, the Environmental Protection Agency and the Department of Interior asked the U.S. Army Corps of Engineers to conduct a formal Environmental Impact Assessment and issue an Environmental Impact Statement (EIS) for the project. This amounted to little more than bureaucratic window-dressing to try to legitimize a fait accompli, and, not surprisingly, in July, the U.S. Army Corps of Engineers issued an Environmental Assessment with a finding of "no significant impact."

The Standing Rock Sioux Tribe went into federal court trying to stop the pipeline and to get a preliminary injunction against further work until their case was heard. Most Native Americans are familiar with "White man's justice" and held out little hope that the federal courts would uphold Native American rights over the corporate interests of the White man. What started out as a handful of protesters at the pipeline construction site swelled to several thousand as the summer of 2016 wore on, gathering at what came to be called Sacred Stone Camp. In early September, the pipeline company brought in bulldozers and began to cut a two-mile, 150-foot-wide trench through an area containing possible burial sites and sacred artifacts. This area was specifically the subject of a pending injunction in the courts, and the company hired a private security firm that used pepper spray and dogs on the protesters when they tried to stop the work. The local cops from the Morton County Sheriff's Department watched it all from a nearby hill and did nothing to stop the brutality directed at the protesters.

On the contrary, they were itching to get in on the action and soon got their chance. In late October, Morton County Sheriff Kyle Kirchmeier assembled his own goon squad of several hundred men, including North Dakota state troopers, the National Guard, and various law enforcement officers from six surrounding states. The sheriff intoned piously, "I can't stress it enough; this is a public safety issue. We cannot have protesters blocking county roads, blocking state highways"—and, of course, the one thing that cops are so good at enforcing—"or trespassing on private property." Using armored personnel carriers, concussion grenades, mace, tasers, and batons, this modern-day Seventh Cavalry descended on the protest encampment and proceeded to wreak havoc on the peaceful protesters. Scores of protesters were arrested and taken to the Morton County jail, where some were held in what appeared to be dog kennels and had numbers written on their arms. The Morton County law enforcement officers also found it necessary to strip search many of those arrested, most particularly the female prisoners.

Although Sheriff Kirchmeier cited blockading state roads as one of the main reasons for the assault, in the immediate aftermath, the cops themselves blockaded the Backwater

Bridge on Highway 1806, thus effectively locking the protesters away from the pipeline route but also cutting off any emergency vehicles from reaching the reservation from the north. When the protesters tried to reopen the bridge in late November, the police launched an attack on them with water cannons in 28°F weather, along with teargas, rubber bullets, and concussion grenades, injuring hundreds.

So, what did all this have to do with me? I was a comfortable, somewhat complacent middle-class dad, safely ensconced in my easy chair, raging away as usual at current events as they flashed across my laptop screen. The country had just elected Donald Trump president. I had never thought we would so soon select a president more unfit for the job than George W Bush had been, but we had done so, and now we had to live with the consequences. People were demanding change, but the Democratic Party establishment did everything in its power—legal and illegal—to ensure that the candidate for progressive change—Bernie Sanders—would not win the nomination. Eight years earlier, Barack Obama had won the presidency on a promise of bringing "change you can believe in." What he ultimately provided was a healthy dose of "same old, same old," but he did it with class and dignity and rhetorical flourish, and not a hint of corruption. Still, "same old, same old" was not working for many people, so when the choice was between Hillary Clinton as the candidate of the status quo and Donald Trump, people voted for the only "change" available. In the old movement days, this would be called "heightening the contradictions."

I had not been to a protest demonstration in years. I had gone to a couple of anti-Iraq War demonstrations and even taken my two children along, but as the focus of my attention narrowed from trying to solve the problems of the world to trying to protect my own family from them, the activism of my youth faded from my life. It wasn't necessarily a conscious choice, although I had long since recognized that demonstrations seldom, if ever, accomplish anything more than an enhanced feeling of comradery among the participants. It's just that I was always doing other things, or so I told myself. When I started seeing messages on Facebook about a group of veterans who were planning to go to Standing Rock to provide "protection" for the demonstrators from the private security forces and the police, however, I snapped out of my middle-class reverie.

For better or worse, I am a member of a group—veterans—that can, at times, focus national attention on issues by our mere presence. I had no illusions about what could be accomplished by our presence at Standing Rock other than, perhaps, a blip of publicity for the issues there. The arrival of a couple of thousand veterans for a couple of days probably wouldn't change the course of the history unfolding at Standing Rock, but, for me, it was long past time for passive expressions of principles, for activism based on clicking "like" and "share" on Facebook. I wanted, for one more time in my life, to stand shoulder to shoulder with other veterans, to feel the passion and commitment of my youth, to try to make a difference even in the face of overwhelming odds. I went because I couldn't *not* go.

I flew from New York to Bismarck, North Dakota, and it quickly became apparent that this was not a well-planned operation. There was no organization like VVAW to coordinate events, just an ad hoc bunch of veterans with Facebook accounts, some looking to do good and some looking to look good for the cameras. I had dutifully sent my itinerary to the "organizers," expecting someone to meet me at the airport and transport me to the protest site, as they said they would. However, there was no one other than a bunch of other vets milling around the baggage claim area in the same situation as I was. I had hoped that I would meet up with some old comrades from VVAW days, but I saw no one I knew. This was a whole new generation of veterans. I hooked up with Neal, a burly, bearded bear of a man, former Army Ranger, now environmental consultant, and his wife Asta; Beth, a gruff-talking, sugar-sweet former MP from Kentucky; and Dani, an efficient, no-nonsense former Marine Corps nurse. They became my team for the duration of my stay.

We rented a car, found a motel for the night, and headed out to the protest site the next day. Neal and I were both itching for some action, but the orders for the day were to keep things cool. None of the dire predictions of potential police brutality that had been visited on the Native American "water protectors" before our arrival happened to us vets. The cops and security forces protecting the pipeline kept their distance, and the elders of the tribe asked the vets not to provoke them. We managed to muster a brief advance on the Backwater Bridge, but after a bit of verbal back-and-forth with the security folks on the other side of the barricades and some plaintive requests from the tribal elders, we backed off.

Later that afternoon, the Obama administration announced that they were putting a hold on the final permit for the section of the pipeline that would pass under the lake that provides all the drinking water for the Standing Rock reservation, stating the need to "explore alternate routes." While this was a small—but exceedingly sweet—victory, it did little other than kick the can down the road for the next administration to deal with. It did have the desired effect of taking the wind out of the presence of the vets, as most of the demonstrators immediately went into celebration mode. In my mind, there was nothing to celebrate, but there had been so little to celebrate for so long that folks went overboard on this.

On the third day we were there, we gathered at the events center of the Prairie Knights Casino in the morning, ostensibly for the tribal elders to thank us for our support. Unbeknownst to the mass of assembled veterans there, Wesley Clark Jr., son of the retired U.S. Army general who had campaigned unsuccessfully for the Democratic presidential nomination in 2004 and one of the two principal "organizers" of the veterans' protest, had a different agenda. He showed up decked out in dress blues complete with a dashing cavalry hat and—playing to the assembled media, who apparently had been notified in advance—gave the following brief speech: "We stole minerals from your sacred hills," Clark said as he knelt in front of a small group of Sioux spiritual leaders. "We didn't respect you. We polluted your Earth; we've hurt you in so many ways. ... We've come to say we're sorry." There was an audible sound of discontent that rippled through the gathered veterans. It wasn't that most might have agreed in some manner with the sentiments. It's that the apology was delivered ostensibly in our names, and we had never been consulted or informed about it.

As we were milling around and grumbling after this little speech, Mother Nature decided to remind all of us puny humans who the real boss was. She dumped a foot and a half of snow on us in less than eight hours with single-digit temperatures and fifty-mph winds. After that, the remnants of the protest became a mere scramble for survival against the elements.

By any reasonable measure, the Veterans Stand for Standing Rock action was nothing short of a fiasco. The number of veterans who responded to the call—five hundred were expected, and over four thousand showed up—totally overwhelmed the limited organizing capacity of those who initiated things, and this resulted in more chaos and confusion than positive action. What's more, a GoFundMe had been set up to accept donations, and it raised well over a million dollars. Since there was no non-profit organization behind the effort, most of that money was never fully accounted for. As many of us predicted, the "victory" was short-lived. The Obama administration just executed a brilliant bureaucratic end run, and the incoming Trump administration immediately overturned the hold and allowed the work on the pipeline to proceed. The whole thing, it seemed, had been an exercise in futility.

Yet, I am proud that I went to Standing Rock, and I am proud of my fellow veterans who joined me. I am proud of what we were able to accomplish and wish we could have done more. If our actions—our willingness to stand up and be unafraid in the face of massive corporate brutality and repression—can inspire others to do the same, to take action, to stand up for what's right—each in his own community, each in her own way—then perhaps we will have made a greater contribution to the effort to take back our country from the extremist minority about to plunge us all off the precipice. If we stick together, stick up for one another, and stick to our principles, then maybe—just maybe—we can stick it to those who want to put profits before people.

Sometimes, in life, you have to stand up and be counted. Sometimes you have to do what is right, even if it is not successful. Veterans Stand for Standing Rock was a failure, but I'm proud to have tried and failed rather than to have never tried at all.

Chapter 12

The Trial of the Gainesville Eight

In 1972, my whole life was about going to demonstrations. The biggest one was set for August at the Republican National Convention in Miami Beach. Our lawyers tried to convince us that none of the defendants should participate in the demonstrations when we were being accused of planning to incite a riot. If some sort of violent disturbance did occur, and we were present, then it could strengthen the case against us. I was determined, however, not to be intimidated by the government; I had to go.

Operation Last Patrol was the national VVAW's response to the Republican National Convention, an epic caravan of vehicles filled with Vietnam veterans and their supporters leaving for Miami Beach from a number of cities across the United States to demand an end to the Vietnam War and to protest Nixon's presidency. One caravan started in Boston. I joined it in New York City, and we snaked down the East Coast, picking up additional veterans and supporters along the way, growing to thirty or forty vehicles. In North Carolina, the entire caravan was pulled over into a rest area by state police for another typical hippie hassle. The cops didn't really do anything, didn't even check our licenses and registrations; they just wanted to hitch up their gun belts and show us who's boss.

The plan was for the three main caravans—from the East Coast, the West Coast, and the Midwest—to rendezvous somewhere north of Miami Beach and make our triumphant entry as one colossal last patrol of Vietnam veterans the Sunday before the opening of the Republican National Convention. It didn't quite work out that way. The East Coast and Midwest caravans reached Miami Beach on schedule, but the West Coast group was plagued with breakdowns and stragglers and didn't get there until the following day.

It didn't take long for VVAW to be confronted with its first crisis. On Sunday afternoon, as members were still in the process of setting up our campsite in Flamingo Park, a group of neo-Nazis strode into the park and commandeered the stage. Some accounts put their number at between thirteen and twenty, but photos show a number around six or seven. They then proceeded to strut around, giving Nazi salutes and shouting *Sieg Heil.* Their intent was clear: to provoke a violent confrontation with the demonstrators. The call immediately went up around the campsite: *Get the Vets!*

As scores of VVAW members rushed towards the commotion, the situation was quickly degenerating. More than a few of the other demonstrators were spoiling for a fight and were heading towards the stage with sticks, chains, ax handles, steel tent pegs, and anything else that could be weaponized in their hands. It could easily have turned into a shitstorm of carnage, but VVAW quickly took control of the situation. Without any real leader directing our actions, we linked arms and surrounded the stage, keeping the enraged demonstrators at bay, while a few guys tried to talk some sense into the Nazis and get them to leave the stage quietly. A fool's errand. You don't negotiate with Nazis. When that became clear, VVAW members rushed the stage, and after some brief hand-to-hand combat, the Nazis were bodily thrown out of the park.

At first, I was part of the group that linked arms, trying to heed our lawyers' advice not to get involved in anything that could be perceived as participating in a riot, but as the conflict with the Nazis ebbed and flowed in front of me, I soon found myself involved in the physical altercation with them. A group of us had surrounded a Nazi on the ground. I looked up and saw Scott grinning at me, then we picked the Nazi up and tossed him out of the park. So much for heeding the lawyers.

Some blood was spilled, to be sure—mostly Nazi blood— but it was no more than you would find in a schoolyard fist-fight. VVAW had efficiently de-escalated the confrontation and turned a situation that could have resulted in serious injury or even death into a few cuts, bruises, and nosebleeds. It also endeared us to the community of Jewish retirees living in the apartments adjacent to Flamingo Park. They showed their appreciation by bringing all sorts of tasty morsels to our campsite throughout the week.

VVAW storms the stage to eject Nazis from Flamingo Park.

On Monday, the West Coast caravan finally made it to Miami Beach, growing the VVAW contingent to over a thou-sand strong. We wanted to maintain our distance from the other non-delegates, many of whom were only there for sex, drugs, and rock 'n roll, not for serious anti-war protests, so we set up our campsite in the far corner of the park and established a well-patrolled perimeter to keep out the crazies.

On Tuesday, VVAW held what the gonzo writer Hunter S. Thompson called in his book *Fear and Loathing on the Campaign Trail* "the most impressive single performance during the three days of the GOP convention." It started out simply as a march to the Fontainebleau Hotel, where most of the GOP delegates were staying. As the march got underway, however, word spread quickly through the ranks: no talking, no chanting, no noise. It would be a silent march. We needed to say nothing; everything had been said. We would let the power of our presence speak for itself.

It did.

The silence of the march spread over the spectators as we passed. No one, anywhere, said a word. The only sound was the steady beat of our boots on the ground and occasional applause coming from the onlookers. It certainly ranked as one of the most impressive VVAW demonstrations—right up there with throwing medals at Congress and taking over the Statue of Liberty. Other than Hunter S. Thompson and a brief mention in a newspaper column by Mary McGrory, almost no media covered this powerful event. If a tree falls in the forest and no one hears it, does it make a sound? VVAW did not make a sound. And no one in power heard us.

Wednesday night was shaping up to be the night of reckoning. Nixon would be nominated, the crazies among the non-delegates were gearing up for mayhem in the streets, and the police were slapping their riot batons against their legs in anticipation of cracking some skulls. But the riots were minimal, and the arrests were few. A couple of vets in wheelchairs were able to gain access to the convention floor, but when they started shouting, "Stop the bombing, stop the war," they were drowned out by the delegates shouting, "Four more years, four more years!" The crowd's chant was an overestimation. The war would last another three years; Nixon wouldn't last that long. The vets were then unceremoniously hauled off the floor by security guards.

I was not present for any of this. In a curious coincidence of timing, where events associated with our indictment seemed to coincide with the political conventions, our arraignment on conspiracy charges was scheduled in Gainesville on Thursday morning at 9 a.m. So Scott, Kniffen, and I—the three defendants who chose to participate in the demonstrations—left Miami Beach early on Wednesday evening and drove all night to reach Gainesville in time for our court appearance. A state policeman stopped us during our journey, and Scott made sure the cop radioed in our identities to prove we were not in Miami Beach. While all this was happening, another drama was playing out, this one with more direct consequences for us. The FBI was trying to flip one of the defendants.

Alton Foss was the Miami-Dade chapter coordinator for VVAW, which had been infiltrated by two local police undercover agents, Sergeant Gerald Rudolph and his partner, Sergeant Harrison Crenshaw, nicknamed "Salt and Pepper" because Rudolph was White and Crenshaw was Black. Foss had grown up in Hialeah and attended Hialeah High School, where he starred on the basketball team. After graduation, he joined the Navy and became a corpsman (a Navy medic), assigned to a Marine unit in Vietnam. On one mission, he was shot in the leg and medevacked out. It was a relatively clean wound, but the hospital put his leg in traction. For over a week, Foss complained of the pain in his foot from the traction, but the medical personnel just kept feeding him painkillers. The doctors had not noticed that the traction had severed his Achilles tendon; Foss was doomed to spend the rest of his life in and out of VA hospitals, undergoing multiple unsuccessful operations to ease the pain in his foot and to deal with the severe addiction to painkilling drugs his condition had foisted on him.

Shortly after the indictment, Salt and Pepper had revealed themselves to Foss and started threatening him with a drug bust if he didn't agree to cooperate with the FBI. Foss initially refused, and true to their word, they busted him for possession of LSD and began leaning on him—*hard*—to provide evidence against his co-defendants. They isolated him and his girlfriend, Paula, in a motel room and subjected him to nonstop interrogation over several days. Salt and Pepper brought in an FBI agent, and Foss agreed to talk to him, thinking the agent could somehow get him out from under the drug and conspiracy charges. When the agent showed up with a formal confession for him to sign, however, Foss read it and realized there were things in there he never said. He refused to sign it.

Foss had called Scott and said he felt fucked over by VVAW, that he had put up his house as collateral for bail, and he was flat broke. He needed to look out for himself. Scott said no matter what happened, they were still brothers. At that point, Foss was on the verge of cutting a deal with the FBI. In fact, the FBI had encouraged him to call Scott in the first place, and they were taping the call, hoping Scott would say something incriminating. In what can only be described as a stunning act of bravery and trust, Foss made the decision to stand with his brothers rather than against them. When we saw him the morning of our arraignment in Gainesville, we all embraced him with no recriminations.

In what became a recurring pattern throughout the whole ordeal, there was a drawn-out argument among the defendants about whether we should stand as the judge entered the court or whether we should remain seated to demonstrate that we thought the proceedings deserved no respect. We could not agree on a course of action, so we decided that each would follow his own conscience and make an individual choice. When the judge entered the court, none of the defendants stood. In what would become another recurring pattern throughout the trial, we were fractious and belligerent with one another in private, but we remained united in public. The judge, David Middlebrooks, studiously ignored the seated defendants but had the marshals remove from the courtroom those spectators who had remained seated in solidarity with the defendants, most of whom had also traveled through the night from Miami Beach to show their support for us. When the judge asked each of the defendants, in turn, how we would plead to the charges, we each responded, "Guilty of war crimes against the people of Indo-China, but not guilty of these charges." Judge Middlebrooks was not amused. He muttered something about being a bomber pilot during World War II and that if he really believed we had committed war crimes, he would raise our bail, and then he directed the clerk to enter pleas of not guilty for all of us.

The next few days were a series of endless meetings as the lawyers tried to get some sense of what had actually happened at the Gainesville meeting; they found that there were as many versions of the event as there had been participants. We then tried to identify who we could expect to be witnesses for the prosecution. We pretty much assumed that anyone who had signed the lawyers' retainer forms during the grand jury was clean since we had the prosecutor's sworn testimony to that effect. We knew Lemmer was an informer, and we already knew about Salt and Pepper. There was also Art Franz from New Orleans, who had revealed his duplicitousness when he introduced me to the head of the New Orleans Red Squad. The other defendants were convinced that Becker was an informer. He had disappeared after showing up at the Gainesville meeting and had not been in contact with any of us since then. I continued to defend him in the face of others' doubts. He had been named in the indictment as an unindicted co-conspirator, and I thought he was just scared of getting tangled up in our mess and getting indicted himself.

We also needed to decide on who would be the legal team representing us during the trial. Several lawyers from the

Center for Constitutional Rights had represented us at various times during the grand jury and arraignment, but the two who had been constant throughout the process were Doris Peterson and Nancy Stearns. We wanted them to remain a part of the defense team, but neither had much trial experience. William Kunstler, the (in)famous lawyer from the Chicago Seven trial and who was associated with the Center, offered his services, but his reputation and flamboyant personality tended to obscure everything else. We were hoping to use the trial as a platform to further our anti-war message, so we declined his offer. Doris Peterson suggested Morty Stavis. Stavis was one of the founders of the Center for Constitutional Rights. He'd been counsel to Martin Luther King Jr., he represented Kunstler's appeal against charges of contempt from the Chicago Seven trial, and he defended Philip and Daniel Berrigan for their anti-war protests. Though not as well-known as Kunstler, he had comparable movement chops but without the extreme ego.

Also included at Kniffen's request were Cam Cunningham and Brady Coleman, two movement lawyers from Austin, Texas. When not representing clients getting screwed by the American judicial system, Brady would pick up his guitar, begin strumming, and then he and Cunningham would commence the Cam and Brady Show, an evening's entertainment of songs and jokes that rivaled the Smothers Brothers. Rounding out the legal team was Larry Turner, a whip-smart young local Gainesville lawyer who had defended Scott on a number of legal issues prior to the conspiracy charge. Larry was not a movement lawyer like the others—his primary practice was defending locals on drug charges—but he got involved because he saw himself as Scott's lawyer and felt his local reputation might take a hit if he didn't defend Scott on the biggest charge against him yet. He didn't know what he was getting himself into.

The final item on the agenda was determining which of the

defendants wanted to go "pro se," that is, defend themselves, a tactic that would allow them to make statements in court and cross-examine witnesses. It was something I dreamed of doing, but when Scott, Kniffen, and Patterson all declared their intentions to go "pro se," I decided that three loquacious defendants were probably more than any judge could stand, so I held back.

The fall of '72 brought more changes and surprises. In September, the four vets, the self-described Forgotten Four—Beverly, Chambers, Jennings, and Horton—who'd been jailed for refusing to testify before the grand jury, were finally released from prison after nearly two months of incarceration. The trial, which had been scheduled to begin in early October, was postponed indefinitely without explanation at first, though the reason became known soon after. The grand jury handed down a superseding indictment, adding two more defendants: Stan Michelsen, a Vietnam veteran from Gainesville, and John Briggs, a friend of Stan's who managed the Wang Dang Doodle hippie emporium in Gainesville. Briggs, the only non-vet among the defendants, had been called before the grand jury, refused to testify, and was then briefly jailed. Apparently, he had placed an order for a shipment of wrist-rocket slingshots to be delivered to the Wang Dang Doodle. So, now we were known as the Gainesville Eight.

A second arraignment of the Eight was scheduled for November 6, the day before Election Day. Richard Nixon—unsurprisingly—won the election in a landslide. In December, Judge Middlebrooks recused himself from the case, seemingly in response to a motion filed by defense attorneys. Since that was the only defense motion that he ever accepted, it came as something of a surprise and prompted some speculation of whether there was something else going on. Winston E. Arnow, a federal judge in Pensacola, was assigned to replace him. Arnow was no better or worse than Middlebrooks, but the possibility that the trial might take place in Pensacola—a military town—was troubling.

The Gainesville Eight. Standing from left: Briggs, Mahoney, Michelsen, Patterson, Perdue. Front row from left: Camil, Foss, Kniffen.

As I mentioned, Larry Turner was not a movement lawyer, and he tended to view the defendants' claims of surveillance and harassment by the government as just so much paranoia. In early December, however, he traveled to New York City for a lawyers' meeting. On the trip up, he was allowed to keep his briefcase with him on the plane. On the trip back, however, the stewardess told him that the briefcase was too big and had to be checked. Larry argued vociferously—he was, after all, a lawyer—but to no avail. An air marshal took his briefcase, and sure enough, when he got to Gainesville, his briefcase was "lost." It turned up two days later. Larry became a full-fledged believer in dirty tricks after that.

On a national level, the Watergate scandal was mushrooming. Despite the efforts of Bob Woodward and Carl Bernstein, the *Washington Post* reporters who were digging up evidence of the connection between Nixon's reelection campaign and the men caught trying to plant listening devices at the Democratic National Committee (DNC) headquarters in the Watergate complex, most of the major news media had passed it over completely. Ronald Ziegler, Nixon's press secretary, called it a "third-rate burglary" in the run-up to Nixon's victory.

It wasn't until March 23, 1973, when District Judge John Sirica read aloud a bombshell letter sent to the court by James McCord, one of the burglars and head of security for the Committee for the Re-election of the President (CREEP), that the mainstream media finally sat up and took notice. McCord wrote, "There was political pressure applied to the defendants to plead guilty and remain silent. ... Perjury occurred during the trial. ... Others involved in the Watergate operation were not identified."

As events unfolded, the connections between our case and the Watergate scandal started to multiply. First, there was the timing. The Gainesville meetings happened on the 26th and 27th of May. The first Watergate break-in happened on May 28; the second one, when they were caught, happened on June 17. The first explanation for their actions, which came out in late June, was that they had received information that the Democratic National Committee was cooperating with individuals who were planning to disrupt the Republican Convention. The grand jury that indicted us was convened on July 1, and the indictments were issued on July 13.

A former FBI agent named Alfred Baldwin, who had monitored the initial wiretaps and was supposed to act as a spotter for the burglars on June 17, said in a deposition that he had been recruited by E. Howard Hunt to infiltrate VVAW to "embarrass the Democrats." In a deposition taken by the Broward County State Attorney's office, a man with Cuban and Central Intelligence Agency ties, Vincent Hanard, said that he had been offered $1,500 a week in a telephone call from a man calling himself "Eduardo"—Hunt's code name—to infiltrate the VVAW and cause trouble. It turns out that the Cuban whom Scott and I had met on the street corner in Miami and who had offered to sell us hand grenades—Pablo Fernandez—was working as an undercover agent for the Miami Police.

Fernandez told the *Miami Herald* that one of the Watergate burglars, Eugenio Martinez, had offered him $700 a week to infiltrate protest groups at the Democratic convention and to embarrass Senator George McGovern "for the Republicans." He said that he had refused because he was already busy spying on VVAW for the FBI and the Miami police.

The most direct connection was made by one of the Watergate burglars himself—James McCord—who stated in his testimony before the Senate Committee investigating Watergate that information he had received in special briefings from the Internal Security Division of the Justice Department concerning VVAW had been a factor in the bugging of the Democratic National Committee offices. He specifically mentioned our subsequent indictment as proof of our violent intentions.

McCord apparently went to his grave convinced that VVAW was a terrorist organization and that his motivation for participating in the Watergate break-in—to expose a link between the Democratic Party and these violent Vietnam veterans— was real. According to a *Washington Post* article published in May 2019, McCord, two years before his death, left his family a PowerPoint presentation where he again tried to make a specific connection between the Gainesville Eight case and the Watergate break-in. He titled the PowerPoint "Watergate and the Gainesville 8 Terrorism."

In response to the information becoming public concerning the activities of the White House Plumbers unit and the flamboyantly illegal "Operation Gemstone" project proposed by G. Gordon Liddy that included plans to kidnap radical leaders who might disrupt the Republican Convention and hold them in Mexico until the convention was over, our lawyers filed an extensive pre-trial motion with Judge Arnow. In it, they delineated all the known connections to our case and requested a number of Watergate figures be subpoenaed to testify. We wanted to know about what other illegal activities may have been perpetrated by the government against VVAW and whether this illegal activity constituted sufficient justification to throw out the charges against us. Arnow, of course, did not want to hear about it and agreed with all motions to quash the subpoenas filed by the lawyers representing those potential witnesses, with one notable exception.

John Mitchell, the former attorney general who had become head of CREEP, was up to his eyeballs in legal trouble over the Watergate scandal. Arnow would have gladly quashed his subpoena, as he had all the others, but Mitchell's lawyers ignored the subpoena rather than responding to it. Apparently, this bristled Arnow's dignity—you didn't ignore a federal judge, at least not in those days—so he commanded Mitchell to show up in his courtroom in Pensacola, Florida. Of course, once Mitchell was there and under oath, Arnow was all obsequiously apologetic and sustained every objection raised by Mitchell's lawyers, ensuring that we could get nothing out of him other than his name and former positions, rendering the whole exercise a useless waste of time.

The pre-trial process seemed to move glacially, although it was probably the normal pace for such things. Our lawyers would file motions; usually there would be some sort of court hearing on them, and then the judge would deny whatever the lawyers wanted. The only motion granted—other than the motion for Judge Middlebrooks to recuse himself—was a motion to change the venue for the trial from Pensacola back to Gainesville. Pensacola was Arnow's home base; he would be sacrificing his personal comfort by moving the proceedings to Gainesville, but he did. This turned out to be one of the key decisions during the trial. Although the population of most of Northern Florida is staunchly conservative, Gainesville was a university town with a small but strong liberal community centered around the university. This gave us a potentially more diverse jury pool than we would have faced in Pensacola, with its heavy military presence centered around Eglin Air Force base. Moreover, Gainesville was home to Scott and Larry

Turner. Both were well known locally and had ample resources available to them there. This was of great help when we had five out-of-town defendants and five out-of-town lawyers to house and feed during the trial.

As the months dragged on, I was existing in a state of limbo. On the one hand, I was trying to maintain some semblance of a normal life. I had moved out of the closet in the VVAW office in New York City and moved into the apartment of my new girlfriend, Jill, in the East 50s. My friend Danny Friedman helped get me a job working twenty hours a week as a part-time cashier at Off-Track Betting. Of course, I failed to mention in my job application that I was currently under federal indictment, but at least I now had some small amount of income, which required a very small amount of my time to earn. On the other hand, I spent much of my time being a "professional defendant," which consisted of traveling around the Northeast doing speaking gigs and passing the hat to raise money for our defense. All the lawyers, including Larry Turner, were working pro bono, but there were still significant costs associated with preparing for the trial.

My status as a Gainesville Eight defendant made me something of a minor celebrity. I was rubbing shoulders with the likes of Jane Fonda, Donald Sutherland, Daniel Berrigan, and Ramsey Clark. When I made a speech, now, my words mattered, not because they were any different from what I had been saying before, but because somehow, who I had become gave the words I said greater weight. It was heady stuff, but all the while, there was the prospect hanging over my head of spending a significant portion of my near future in some federal prison. I dealt with this in the same way I dealt with the prospect of death in Vietnam: I simply refused to believe it would ever happen.

On one occasion, I was invited by the Boston area VVAW to do some speaking engagements around the city, culminating in a gathering of students and faculty in a hall at MIT. Also speaking on the program was Ramsey Clark, the former attorney general turned anti-war activist. In a show of hospitality, a couple of local vets shared some very excellent herb with me right before I went on stage. This was not an uncommon occurrence; in those days, I was pretty much stoned all day, every day. I was about halfway through my "stump speech"—the standard address I had developed from multiple deliveries over many months, the beginning of my career as a storyteller—when I looked out over this sea of several hundred of some of the smartest people in the United States, indeed, in the world—and I completely forgot what I was about to say, and, worse still, I forgot what I had just said. I just stood there and stared at the audience for what seemed like an eternity but was probably only a few seconds, and then I continued my speech with the first thing that came into my head. I don't even know if anybody noticed.

Finally, the trial was scheduled to start on July 31, 1973. The first phase of any trial is jury selection. Prospective jurors are put through the *voir dire* process, where both the prosecution and the defense ask the jurors a series of questions, and then each side can exercise two types of challenges: peremptory challenges, where no reason need be given for excluding a juror, and challenges for cause, where you try and convince the judge to exclude a prospective juror because he or she would not be impartial. Each side had three peremptory challenges and an unlimited number of challenges for cause, any of which may or may not be accepted by the judge.

Here is where the change of venue to Gainesville really paid off. Dr. Jay Schulman, a sociologist who had taught at Cornell University, and Dr. Richard Christie, a social psychologist at Columbia University, had offered their services to us for free. We intended to use their knowledge of social science to help us determine which jurors should be challenged. They had assisted in the jury selection for the trial of the Harrisburg Seven—another of the anti-war conspiracy trials—and had refined their techniques since then by creating a survey designed to draw out community attitudes. A random group of people was selected from the voter files and was asked the questions on the survey. Schulman and Christie then used their answers as the basis for a statistical analysis linking attitudes to things like age, sex, race, education, religion, job type, marital status, the section of town they lived in, and other parameters. Each parameter was given a point rating, which we could then apply to prospective jurors. The judge got wind of what we were doing and ordered that the actual jury pool for the trial would be kept confidential until the morning of the trial; usually this list is public knowledge.

Arnow's move was ineffective, however. The survey work had helped us develop a network of volunteers throughout the community. We created a telephone tree—each person in the tree having three other people to call—and although we only received the names on the jury pool list at 9 a.m. on the first morning of the trial, by noon that day, we had first-hand information about every prospective juror on the list—this long before Google searches became the norm. This allowed us to identify a young female student who fit the profile of an ideal juror for us and had scored high on the profile developed from the survey. We got first-hand information, however, that someone had heard her speak disparagingly of anti-war demonstrators while watching the demonstrations on TV. In a calculated gamble, we pretended that she was someone we wanted on the jury and tricked the prosecution into using one of their peremptory challenges to remove her.

The final jury seated consisted of seven women and five men, most of them young and well-educated. There were three Black people on the jury, one of them a Vietnam veteran. I remember seeing the face of Jack Carrouth, the local prosecutor who had been brought in to try the case, when the final jury was seated. He looked like he had found coal in his stocking at Christmas. He realized we had ended up with a jury that would be sympathetic to the defense.

The court adjourned late in the afternoon of the first day, and members of the defense team crammed into a small office across from the courtroom provided to us by the judge for meetings and consultations. Jay Schulman was speaking about what we had accomplished during this first day of jury selection and what we should look forward to the next day. I was standing at the back and glanced down to see what seemed to be an air vent with light shining through it and some flickering shadows. I pointed this out to the man standing next to me, Arthur Egendorf, a VVAW member from New York City with a Ph.D. in psychology from Harvard who was a part of Schulman's team. We bent down to look through the vent. Two men in suits were in the "broom closet" next door, standing in front of a circuit box containing telephone Centrex terminals, systematically touching terminals in the switch box with wires from an electronic gizmo in their hands. We quickly alerted the federal marshals, who took the two men into custody. The two turned out to be FBI agents, who claimed to the judge that they were "checking the FBI lines." We immediately responded by saying that the telephone line to our office also ran through that switchbox and that a simple wire connection from the terminals to our phone would make it possible for the FBI to monitor our calls. Of course, Arnow overruled most of our questions about what the FBI was doing and even admonished our lawyers for "making mountains out of molehills."

The vent to the broom closet was blocked, and the room was sealed.

The government's case against us consisted almost exclusively of the testimony of informers. Day after day, we were subjected to a stream of former friends, associates, and colleagues taking the stand for the prosecution, admitting that they had been paid government informers, and testifying against us. The first witness, though, was Scott Camil's landlord, Charles R. Marshall Jr., who was not a paid informer but testified that he was a Marine veteran of the Korean War and a small arms expert and that Scott had shown him a stash of M-16 automatic weapons at his apartment. Larry Turner, on cross-examination, held up an M-16 in the courtroom and asked the witness if this was what Scott had shown him. When he answered in the affirmative, Larry pulled the trigger on the plastic toy, the clicking sound barely audible above the laughter that erupted in the courtroom.

So much for the prosecution's small-arms expert.

The prosecution then put on two inconsequential witnesses in quick succession, who offered nothing to build the prosecution's case. They were a prelude for a procession of five informers and a police sergeant whose testimony made up the heart of the prosecutor's case.

First up was Bill Lemmer, the erstwhile Arkansas Regional Coordinator for VVAW. Lemmer was pretty much a known quantity to us. Before the Gainesville meeting had even taken place, Lemmer confessed to giving false information to the FBI on eight hours of tape to two members of the Arkansas VVAW chapter. This became the basis for "The Confession of an FBI Informer," a *Harper's Magazine* cover story in December 1972 by Frank Donner, a civil liberties lawyer and director of the ACLU's Project on Political Surveillance at Yale Law School. We also had ten hours of taped conversations between him and Richard O'Connell, his FBI handler in Fayetteville, Arkansas.

Lemmer's testimony was a Grade-B movie of fact and fiction, starring himself as the action hero, risking it all for love of country. In fact, he admitted to sometimes wearing a red cape and carrying a bullwhip in high-laced boots. Arnow protected him from answering any questions put by the defense concerning his drug use, his documented mental health problems, and his penchant for pushing others to commit crimes and then dropping a dime on them when they did. Nevertheless, we thought the jury saw him for what he was: a seriously disturbed young man devoid of loyalty who lived in his own feverish fantasy world.

The next witness called by the prosecution was Charles Henry Becker, my friend Karl from New Orleans. His long red hair had been cut short and neat, and his straggly red beard had been shaved off. He identified himself as an FBI informer, an "intelligence operative" for the New Orleans Police Department, and an "undercover security agent" for a "New Orleans department store specializing in liquor" whose job was to catch shoplifters. My co-defendants were already convinced that he was an informer. It cut me to the quick to find out how wrong I had been when I had defended him.

Not only did Karl testify for the prosecution, but he also out-and-out lied in his testimony. To understand why he would lie, you must understand the situation of an informer. The government is paying him to become your friend and to report on the bad things you are doing. If the informer continues to come back to his handler and reports that you are doing nothing wrong, then most likely, his paycheck is going to end. It is in the informer's financial interest to report that you are doing bad things or to try to stimulate you to do bad things if you are not. Most of the other informers in our trial generally stayed near the truth, bending it and stretching it as needed to whet the FBI's appetite and, when testifying, to fit the prosecution narrative. But Karl just flat-out lied. We started calling him the "Prosecution Garbage Man." There was so much garbage in the indictment against us for which the prosecution had not a shred of evidence. It was put there to try to make us look as dangerous and violent as possible. Karl apparently was willing to testify to anything and everything the prosecution had no other evidence for: meetings that never took place, conversations that never happened, and actions that had never been undertaken. He was trying to make us look as dangerous and violent as possible, and it appeared he couldn't care less.

His most egregious lie, at least for me, was his testimony that after the Gainesville meeting, I told him that I had decided that to end the bigger problem in Vietnam, it was necessary to commit violence, and I was prepared to do it. He cited the incident of throwing blood at Bush at the black-tie dinner as proof of my violent tendencies. He also testified that I told him I wanted to be "a hero of the New Left." He tried to tie Stan Michelsen and John Briggs into the conspiracy by testifying that Scott took him and Art Franz to John and Stan's house to buy wrist rocket slingshots. On cross-examination, he admitted that he could remember no details about the inside of the house but that he was sure that the house was painted an off-white color. This was a direct lie he was caught in since the house had been painted its off-white color long after the Gainesville meeting took place.

Becker studiously avoided any eye contact with the defense table during his testimony, but as Brady Coleman began the cross-examination, I went over and stood behind Brady, staring intently at Becker. He still refused to look at me. After a brief recess, Arnow instructed me to sit back down at the defense table since the witness had complained that I was trying to intimidate him. I guess when you betray a friend, having to look him in the eye must seem like a form of intimidation.

After that first day of testimony from Karl, I was feeling like crap, not just because of his utter betrayal of me but also because I was stupid enough to have ever considered him a friend to begin with. We were on our way back to the defense house for one of the endless lawyer/defendant meetings to go over the current day's proceedings and plan for the next day. When you have seven lawyers and eight defendants, coming to a consensus can be a long and arduous process. In preparation for that evening's anticipated marathon, we stopped by a local pizza parlor to grab a couple of pies. The guy behind the counter looked like a classic redneck: T-shirt, crew cut, beer belly, an American flag on the wall behind him. His manner was gruff and seemingly inhospitable as he took our order. Needless to say, my fellow defendants and I were rather well known in those parts in those days, and our bearded, pony-tailed, anti-war-buttoned appearance contrasted rather starkly with our pizza parlor host. As we were waiting for the pies, the man continually scowled at us in what seemed to be a particularly disapproving way; I was honestly worried he might jump over the counter and assault us or maybe just refuse to sell us pizza.

I was wrong.

When the pies came, the man scowled at us again, then gave us a big smile. He handed us the pies, shook each of our hands, and wished us all good luck. He also refused to take payment for our food.

I needed that.

Up after Becker finished the next day was a rather nondescript witness named Louis Anchill, who described himself as a "source of information" for the Florida Department of Law Enforcement. He testified that he had posed as a member of the Florida People's Coalition in a meeting with Scott, and Scott had confided to him that VVAW was stockpiling rifles and grenades that had been ripped off from the military by disgruntled soldiers. Leaving aside the fact that Scott did not even remember ever having met Anchill, it strained credulity to think that Scott would have shared such information with a total stranger even if they had met. Anchill was just filler, however, as it seemed the prosecution needed a little more time before presenting their next witness.

If Karl Becker had been a shock—at least to me—the next witness utterly gobsmacked Scott Camil. Emerson Poe, VVAW's Florida Deputy Regional Coordinator, took the stand and announced he was an FBI informer. Carrouth could not suppress a smirk of triumph as he called Poe to the stand, and he seemed to take special delight in seeing the effect this craven betrayal of trust had on Scott. I had never seen Scott so nonplussed. The friendship between Scott and Poe had been on a whole different level from my friendship with Karl. While Karl and I had hung out together, done a little barhopping, and talked politics, Scott and his girlfriend, Nancy, had helped to take care of Poe's family when his wife was in the hospital. Poe and his wife had thrown Nancy a surprise birthday party. Scott and Nancy had been on hand to comfort Poe's wife after she had a miscarriage, the two couples had played bridge together, Nancy had ridden horses on their farm, and Scott and Nancy even helped to decorate Poe's Christmas tree.

Moreover, Poe had signed a retainer form with the lawyers during the grand jury process, and Guy Goodwin had sworn, under oath, that none of those who had signed retainers were agents or informers of the government. Poe had been a trusted member of our defense committee up until the day he testified. He sat in on many defendant/lawyer meetings and routinely picked up the mail from the VVAW mailbox, which was occasionally used by the lawyers to transmit confidential legal information.

Of course, our lawyers were apoplectic at the brazen and patently illegal invasion of the defense camp and immediately called for a mistrial. Arnow sent out the jury and conducted a day and a half of hearings on the matter. Claude Meadows, Poe's local FBI handler, testified that he had instructed Poe not to tell him anything he heard in the defense meetings, although Poe testified that he had reported "every conversation" with Scott since the indictment. Arnow—in the tradition of Mizaru, the first of the three famous monkeys—could see no evil in any of this, denying the motion for a mistrial and allowing Poe to testify.

Scott Camil, Don Perdue, and Alton Foss demonstrate Judge Arnow's approach to government misconduct.

I don't know whether he did it on purpose, but Poe's testimony ultimately was more helpful to the defense than the prosecution. In one of the more bizarre factoids about the case, Poe testified that a key piece of evidence the prosecution was using against us—a leaflet put out by the Florida chapter that stated, if necessary, VVAW would defend itself and other demonstrators from police violence—had actually been reproduced using the FBI's copy machine. Under cross-examination, Poe testified that he had never heard Scott planning violence at the convention, that the only plans he ever heard were peaceful ones, that he had never seen or heard of Scott trading "dope for guns" as alleged in the indictment, and that he had never heard of Scott planning to take weapons to Miami.

In perhaps the most dramatic moment of the trial, Scott,

acting as his own lawyer, stood to cross-examine Poe. Unlike Becker, who was able to get the judge to keep him from having to look me in the eye, Poe had to look Scott in the eye and answer his questions.

"Would you say we were good friends?" Scott asked Poe.

Poe looked away as he answered, "No, I don't consider myself a friend."

Up next was Pablo Fernandez, who had tried to sell us hand grenades when Scott, Lemmer, and I met him on a street corner in Miami. Fernandez testified that he was wearing a wire during the meeting. "Great," we said, "where is the transcript?" because we knew that a transcript of the meeting would show that we firmly and specifically rejected his offer. Fernandez testified that, unfortunately, the wire did not work, so there was no transcript.

Tsk, tsk.

After a number of other inconsequential witnesses, mostly informers—including Harrison Crenshaw, Pepper of the Salt and Pepper team—the prosecution abruptly rested their case. This was somewhat surprising since their pre-trial declaration had indicated they had around forty witnesses, and they had only called about twenty-five. It also posed a dilemma for the defense team. We all agreed that the prosecution had not come close to proving their case. They had not even bothered to align the informers' testimony so there was a coherent storyline for the jury to follow. The "evidence" against us was a mish-mash of wild accusations and often-contradictory stories, related by a bunch of unsavory individuals for whom lying and betrayal were a way of life. A few times, they even managed to testify against one another.

The practical legal strategy for the defense, at this point, was to present no witnesses and rest our case. All the lawyers were strongly in favor of this approach. This offered two advantages for us. The judge, citing an inordinate amount of publicity, had ordered the jury sequestered from the beginning of the trial. They had been living in hotel rooms for four weeks, with little contact with the outside world. There was, of course, no Internet in those days, they were not allowed to watch TV, and the newspapers they were given were so cut up by censorship that they barely had more than sports stories and real estate ads to read. In the second week of the trial, the jury had sent a note to the judge, reporting "three-fourths of our home telephone numbers have been acting strangely," that they've heard "strange clickings, cut-offs, anonymous phone calls inquiring as to name and number, and hollow sounds as if someone were perhaps monitoring ..." (The defendants thought, *Welcome to our world.*) Judge Arnow's only response was to ask the jurors to let him know of any other telephone issues. He took no other action.

Informing the jury that we were not going to prolong their imprisonment by presenting an unnecessary defense could certainly be a point or two in our favor when it came to a verdict. The second advantage would be that if we presented no defense, then the prosecution would not be able to present any rebuttal. It seemed clear that the prosecutors had held back some of their forty witnesses for rebuttal purposes. We could eliminate that testimony from the mix.

There was, however, a very strong argument—not a legal one, but a political one—for putting on a defense. We were being put through this ordeal for our beliefs and our activism. The public attention the trial received provided an opportunity for us to make our beliefs known to a wider audience than would be possible otherwise. In and of itself, a "not guilty" verdict would get us out of harm's way but would do little to advance the anti-war cause that we espoused. If we wanted the trial to be about more than just us as victims of government skullduggery, if we wanted to use the trial as a platform to proclaim our message, then we needed to put on a defense where our voices could be heard.

At first, I was strongly attracted to this argument, but two things worried me. Arnow had been ruthless in keeping the defense under his thumb and had repeatedly prevented us from making any political statements in front of the jury. While we had good intentions to make our anti-war beliefs the center of our defense, Arnow would do everything he could to keep us from proclaiming them in his courtroom. The second, more disturbing concern was that I just did not know what some of my co-defendants might say. At least one had suggested that our defense should be to plead guilty to everything because we were revolutionaries. That was not a defense; that was a ticket to jail. We argued long and hard and passionately about the issue. Finally, we took a vote among the defendants. The vote was six to two in favor of not putting on a defense.

The lawyers suggested we call one witness: Dr. Steven Stellman, a chemistry professor from the University of Colorado. In addition to the conspiracy charge, only Scott was charged with possession and teaching the use of a firebomb. Stellman testified that potassium permanganate and glycerin, the two substances Scott had demonstrated could spontaneously combust, were available over the counter in drugstores, were "not an explosive at all," and did not constitute a firebomb under the law. If Scott had put the concoction into a police car's gas tank, it would have been "very unlikely" to have caused an explosion. In fact, Stellman testified he always carried a bottle of glycerin in his briefcase to soften his hands.

We rested our case.

After closing statements by both sides and instructions from the judge, the jury retired to deliberate at about 11 a.m. on Friday, August 31, 1973. The trial had lasted exactly one month. There was a picture of me in *The Washington Post* the next day, playing Frisbee outside the courthouse while awaiting the verdict, implying a sense of relaxed confidence. In reality, I was shittin' bricks. No matter how much I told myself the government had failed miserably in proving its case against us, I could still feel the specter of five years in prison hanging over my head.

*This photo appeared in the Washington Post on September 1 1973.
The caption read: "Gainesville 8 defendant Peter Mahoney plays
frisbee as he waits for the verdict to come in. All were acquitted."*

Three and a half hours later, the jury announced they were ready to render a verdict. The courtroom was packed with the forceful presence of fourteen U.S. Marshals strategically placed around the room. The tension among us dissipated when we saw the jurors come into the courtroom with big smiles on their faces.

The first verdict read out was, "We find the defendant Donald Perdue not guilty." John Kifner, a reporter for *The New York Times*, who had covered the trial from the beginning, reported:

One defendant, Peter P. Mahoney, put his hand lightly on the T-shirted shoulder of Mr. Perdue, a former Marine with short hair ... who carried books on ecology to court each day. As the list continued, another defendant, Stanley K. Michelson, began to walk about the table, throwing his arms around each man found not guilty.

The defendants and their lawyers stood in a long row, arms on shoulders, as Federal District Judge Winston E. Arnow formally dismissed the charges and bail bonds.

As members of the prosecution team skulked out a side door, the smiling jurors, the defendants, and the lawyers all fell into each other's arms by the jury box, laughter and tears in abundance.

It was over.

Several jurors dropped by the raucous victory party afterward, where we discovered that they had been ready to acquit after only an hour of deliberation, but Northern Godbolt, the one Vietnam veteran on the jury, suggested that if they waited a little longer, they could get one more free meal on the government. Another juror, Gerald E. Bennett, a thirty-three-year-old crewcut lineman for the county, came to the victory party with his wife, but they decided to stay outside by his car, judging, correctly, that there were probably some illegal intoxicants being consumed inside.

"They had nothin' on you boys," he drawled. "They said you had guns. Hell, I have guns." Then he opened the glove compartment of his car to prove his point.

VVAW put out a statement:

The government needed, first of all, to defuse the anti-war issue in the 1972 presidential campaign. What better way to do this was there than by portraying a leading anti-war group as a bunch of vicious killers? With the public outcry caused by the Watergate scandal, a secondary purpose for the trial can be found: an attempt to partially divert attention away from the Watergate affair by fabricating a phony 'threat to national security.' James McCord specifically named VVAW/WSO [Winter Soldier Organization] as the chief villain in this 'threat to national security' and as a justification for their actions.

The next day, I left Gainesville. The whole affair had left a bittersweet taste in my mouth. Yes, we had been acquitted, but the government had beaten us even without getting a guilty verdict from the jury. We never really got to use the trial as a platform for our anti-war views. The defendants, as well as VVAW, had spent enormous amounts of time, energy, and organizational resources fighting against the indictments rather than fighting to end the war. VVAW, to its credit, had our backs and strongly supported us by publicizing the trial, helping us raise money, and organizing demonstrations on our behalf. But there were at least some within the organization who would have preferred VVAW disavow the Gainesville Eight and cut ties with us. Most of the defendants prior to the trial had been hard-core activists in VVAW. After the trial, we were all exhausted, and none of the defendants stayed active in VVAW, although I stayed a member in New York.

After this brief Warholian fling with fame, I quickly faded into obscurity in the bowels of New York City. I did have the sum-up sound bite that was used by all the major media that covered the trial, including a week-in-review article in *The New York Times* and a scathing editorial in the pre-Murdoch *New York Post:*

"In spite of all this joy and elation, I can't forget that the government put me through fourteen months of hell."

Chapter 13

Getting Old

I love to dance.

Granted, these days, after one or two full-tilt boogies, I'm stumbling towards my chair, gasping for breath, sweat dripping from my eyebrows, my legs feeling like melting chocolate. But for that brief five or so minutes, I am me again, my body feeling as young as my mind. And as for those staid and stationary scolds standing on the sidelines tsk-tsking at the old fossil who forgot his age, I say kiss my gyrating ass.

To dance is to live, to attach yourself to the rhythms of the universe, and go for a ride. I am mostly a solo dancer, although the protocols of the dance floor usually require a "partner" of sorts somewhere nearby. Natasha is always available and generously fulfills this requirement while giving me all the space I need to do my thing. I don't do steps, which require the mind to tell the body what to do. For me, dancing is a direct visceral connection between the music and my body. I want the music to shove the mind aside, to show it to its seat where it can watch in rapt admiration as the music makes love to me and takes me on a magical adventure across the floor.

It wasn't always that way, of course. For much of my adolescence, my innate shyness had combined with my strict Catholic upbringing to relegate me to wallflower status once the music started, shriveling into a sniveling mass of self-doubt at the least comment or glance of disapproval. What will the neighbors think? Somewhere along the line— perhaps it coincided with my increased intake of cannabis—I discovered, to my surprise, that I was a good dancer. A few beers and a joint or two at a party, and the inhibitions that had kept me glued to the wall faded like a safe chameleon's hues. The brownstones of Brooklyn were pulsing with house parties on weekends in the middle seventies, and my room-mate, Danny, seemed to know about every one and dragged me out of the apartment on many Saturday nights, away from the couch potato, TV sports addiction I was comfortable with. It also helped that the social decorum of that time didn't nec-essarily require me to approach a female first in order to get on the dance floor. This wasn't couples' dancing; it was just— dancing. Fueled by various stimulants, I somehow found a way to eliminate my mind as a filter for my movement and allowed my body to connect directly with the music. When my mind stopped worrying about how I looked and what oth-ers thought, my body amazed me with what it could create on its own.

As the years have passed, dancing has become even more important to me, the last vestige of the physical me I was in my youth. I used to dunk a basketball, but now I can barely even reach the bottom of a basketball net. I used to stride along the streets of New York City, my lanky, confident gait outpacing everyone else on the sidewalks. Nowadays, I trudge wearily along, a slight limp that used to be occasional but has become chronic slowing me down to an old man's shuffle. I used to be a skinny sapling of a thing who, after work, would often down a roast beef sandwich with a half-pound of potato salad, then top it off with a full Entenmann's apple pie and a gallon of butter pecan ice cream. I never gained a pound, much to the envious chagrin of Danny, who could just look at food and gain twenty pounds. Now the ribs I used to be so ashamed of showing on the beach have long since disappeared beneath the pear-shaped folds of a body whose metabolism has faded but whose appetite hasn't.

The inevitable physical deterioration has brought on another dilemma I must face in my old age: the need to visit and talk to doctors. Doctors are only one or two steps above politicians on my trust scale. In a for-profit medical system, I am constantly wondering whether what the doctor is recommending is good for my health or good for his wealth. Many doctors like to hide behind a veneer of omniscience and get highly offended if you question their judgment. I asked a doctor once if he had any treatment recommendation for my high cholesterol that didn't involve me having to take a pill for the rest of my life, and he told me no. I told him I wasn't particularly interested in becoming an income stream for some pharmaceutical company, so we probably didn't have anything else to talk about.

If you have a good medical insurance plan—and I have been fortunate in most of my work life to have had one—then you might find yourself undergoing an MRI, a costly medical procedure, every time the doctor isn't sure of the diagnosis, which is often. One of my ailments is hearing loss, and I had seen an ear doctor, who put me through the usual beeping sound tests to determine the extent of the loss and then recommended an MRI. I asked him why I needed an MRI, and he said that there was a maybe fourteen percent chance that there was something else wrong with my hearing that the beep tests couldn't detect. When I mentioned to him that it seemed that the MRI had become much more prevalent as a diagnostic tool since the non-profit health organization he worked for had been bought up by a for-profit outfit the year before, he was indignant. How dare I question his medical integrity? I did the MRI, it found nothing, and I never saw that doctor again.

When I was young, I didn't need doctors. Other than some occasional stitches here and there—and I was fortunate never to have broken a bone—it seemed there was no injury or illness that my body couldn't cure on its own. I would just crawl into bed and let the healing begin. Now, all the things that used to heal have become chronic: the ankle, the shoulder, the knees, the back. Now, instead of trying to eliminate my ailments, I try to live with them, and I visit doctors so they can tell me there's nothing they can do.

There was a time, not so very long ago, when I was sure I could regain the physical prowess of my youth and that I was still capable of doing the things I could do when I was young. I just needed to "get in shape." Slap on the sneakers, hitch up the gym shorts, get out there, and feel the burn, and I would be my old self in no time. But then, each effort to "get in shape" produced a result that wasn't anything near what I used to do; indeed, most times, I couldn't even get the results I had achieved the last time I tried to "get in shape." The pattern stayed pretty consistent. I would crank up the willpower and start an exercise regime. I would start slowly, telling myself I needed to work my way up to get back to where I was. I'd follow the regime for a time, maybe two weeks, maybe three, then something would happen—an injury, an illness, a change in my schedule—and the regime would fall by the wayside, and I would sink into my chair, and succumb to the creak and ache of age. Then, at some point, I would crank up the willpower again and start slow again, but this time slower than the last time, further away from the self-deluded goal of regaining my youthful form, and the pattern would play itself out again. I still follow the pattern but have finally laid the self-delusion to rest. Slowly, painfully, a recognition of reality has set in: I will never dunk a basketball again, I will never run a 10.5 second hundred-yard dash again, I will never long-jump twenty-two feet again.

What I hold out hope for is that there might be some physical accomplishment that I still could attain that I have never achieved before. I've never completed a marathon. I've never competed in a triathlon. I've never hiked the Appalachian Trail. These are things that still seem doable, that seem realistic to strive for. I just got to "get in shape."

Chapter 14

Resurrection

The decade of the seventies was basically lost to me. I bounced from place to place, from relationship to relationship, from school to school, from interest to interest. I tried to cling to the counter-culture trappings of the radical revolutionary that I perceived myself to be, even as the world around me shucked off the last vestiges of the sixties and got on with it. However, I was not so ready to give up.

Jill and I were married about a month after the end of the trial, a beautiful hippie wedding in the backyard of her mother's palatial home in New Jersey. We found a radical Catholic priest willing to participate in a ceremony that we had written; my parents thought, well, at least it's a Catholic priest. However, the marriage lasted little more than a year, as it became clear that once there was no anti-war movement to occupy our mutual time, we had little else in common.

Ever present in my life during this time were drugs—mostly marijuana, but occasional forays into cocaine, speed, LSD, hash, or whatever. I never got to heroin, although I probably would have tried it if it had been put in front of me. As unbelievable as it may seem to me now, I was basically stoned all day, every day, for about ten years. I would wake up to a triple-C breakfast—caffeine, cannabis, and vitamin C.

I returned to my job as a part-time pari-mutuel clerk for

Off Track Betting, a conveniently innocuous job that required about twenty hours of my time each week. It paid, along with the money I got from the G.I. Bill, for my expenses and left me plenty of time to pursue all the "interests" that were more important but paid me no money. I worked the Manhattan pool; each morning, I would call in at a particular time, and I would be sent to an office that needed me, where a regular had called in sick or was on vacation. I worked all over Manhattan: from the dank and crowded Chinatown branch, where waiters came in and made hundred dollar bets with one-dollar bills, to the 14th Street and First Avenue branch filled with junkies and drug addicts to the chichi branches on the upper east side.

Although I continued to work in Manhattan, once my marriage was over, I headed out to Brooklyn to live. It was cheaper and more neighborhood-y than Manhattan. I settled into Park Slope, sharing an apartment with my best friend, Danny. Park Slope in the middle to late seventies was not the yuppie, upper-middle class bastion it later became. It was also much more well-defined: Flatbush to Ninth Street and Prospect Park West to Fourth Avenue. Yes, at that time, there were still remnants of Brooklyn upper-class living in luxury brownstones along PPW and Eighth Avenue, but the lower part of the Slope was a disaster area. Fifth Avenue was a long stretch of boarded-up storefronts and abandoned brown-stones, with addicts and rip-off artists lurking on every cor-ner. There were several retail drug stores along Fifth Avenue, too. No, not pharmacies, but rather places where you could go in, slip some bills through a slot in the wall, and buy pot or, perhaps, other drugs, although I never tried to get anything more from them than pot. Mean-looking Rastafarians hung out around the front door and peered through the slit in the wall. Scoring pot there was always a bit of an adventure, and one best avoided if other, more savory vendors were available.

My "interests" were all over the map. Although by then I was already in my mid-twenties, I still was going to college, primarily because it was an income source for me from the G.I. Bill, mostly attending SUNY-Old Westbury out on Long Island. The commute from Brooklyn to Old Westbury was difficult—sometimes by car, sometimes by Long Island Railroad—but I usually managed to group my classes on two or three days to lessen the burden. The attraction, for me, of this school was that in the midst of a flatulent suburban curriculum, there was a small core of radical professors in the American Studies department, among them Barbara Ehrenreich; her husband, John: Diedre English; Paul Lauter; and Florence Howe, who had founded *The Feminist Press* on campus in 1970.

I heard through the grapevine that Jan Barry, a Vietnam veteran and founding member of VVAW, was planning a sequel to *Winning Hearts and Minds*, his first anthology of poems by Vietnam veterans, which he had edited with Larry Rottman and Basil Paquet and which had been well-received and highly praised. I had dabbled a bit with poetry, but it never amounted to much, mostly secret scribblings in private journals, but the news of this new anthology spurred me to try my hand more seriously. I would wander out into the woods surrounding SUNY-Old Westbury in a break between classes, sit down under a tree, smoke a joint, and wait for the words to come. They did. Over the course of three weeks, I wrote seven poems, four of which were accepted for publication in the anthology *Demilitarized Zones: Veterans After Vietnam*, edited by Barry and W.D. Ehrhart, a Marine Corps veteran who's been called "the dean of Vietnam War poetry." Sitting in those woods, it wasn't as if I was creating the poems. It was like the poems already existed, and I was merely the instrument pulling them from the universe. I've never quite had a writing experience like that before or since.

I got involved in a political street theater group called Mass Transit. I had always been attracted to theater and acting but never really pursued it. This was perhaps the lowest rung of theater available, but, hey, at least I had stepped onto the ladder.

My biggest "interest" was starting a community newspaper for the Park Slope neighborhood. Several of my friends and acquaintances also had a similar idea or became enthused when I pitched my idea to them. We first put out a one-page broadsheet announcing our plans and looking to attract advertising from local businesses. I wrote the lead article:

The meeting starts late: they always do. People straggle in, in twos and threes, chatting among themselves and flopping on the assorted sofas and chairs in the front room. Inevitably, all the conversations drift towards the same subject—the newspaper—and the meeting begins by spontaneous combustion.

Many of the eleven people seem physically tired; it is evening, and they have spent the day at their jobs. The discussion, however, is lively. People's ideas and comments are charged with enthusiasm. Robert's Rules of Order are constantly broken, but no one minds. A natural courtesy prevails.

It has not always been this way. The first few meetings, when they had grappled with the idea of starting a community newspaper, had been marked by ego clashes, overreaction, and unwillingness to compromise. Tempers still flare occasionally, but these are highly opinionated people. Their control is remarkable, especially since many had never met before the newspaper project brought them together.

The common bond of the group is activism. All are young; all have experience in the movements and struggles of their generation—students' rights, civil rights, women's rights, the anti-war movement. They are involved in the newspaper because their experience is involvement.

Some have previous newspaper experience; many do not. All seem eager to learn new skills.

Some feel a creative void that they hope to fill by writing for the newspaper. They talk of essays and poetry and short stories. Others see the newspaper as a political tool for organizing the community. They talk of investigative reporting, political analysis, and community issues.

All agree that Park Slope, the community they live in, needs a good newspaper, one where people can read about what their neighbors are doing and learn what they are thinking.

The discussion turns to money, always the stumbling block to any good idea. Creative energy in this society means nothing, unfortunately, unless there is money to pay the energy bills. The first issue will cost three hundred dollars—sixteen pages, two thousand copies. They must sell advertising to cover the cost.

There is much discussion about this, whether they should sell advertising, whether they could sell advertising, whether the paper can be financed another way. They agree to try it, and several people volunteer to approach local merchants. Thirty ads for ten dollars is all they need. There is confidence that what they are doing is worthwhile and that the people of the community will support their efforts.

The meeting ends with the group still undecided about a name. This has become the major bone of contention; no name has excited a majority of the people. As the meeting breaks up, several people continue to throw names back and forth, free-associating. Someone yells out Up the Slope, and it catches. There is the hint of a Brooklyn sneer in it, the hope of a clenched fist chant. The people scurry out into the frigid Brooklyn night.

Up the Slope lasted for about two years. We put out a monthly edition covering local issues like redlining and police brutality, as well as a healthy dose of celebration of our community. We were able to attract enough advertising from local merchants to pay for production costs but never enough to pay a staff, so we had to keep it up on a volunteer basis. Eventually, the energy ran out. I was long gone before that happened.

My time in Park Slope in the mid-seventies was the closest I ever got to being the person I thought I wanted to be, to embodying the self-image I had in my head: warrior for peace, poet-activist, radical artist who changed the world simply by my incandescent presence in it. It didn't last.

As 1977 was coming to an end and 1978 loomed in front

of me, I was confronted with a dreaded milestone—my thirtieth birthday. Thirty is a natural summing-up age, a time when one reflects upon what has been accomplished in the early stages of one's life. As I began to mull over this milestone, I found myself to be long on experience but short on accomplishments. Sure, I was living the ultra post-hippie life, supposedly being who I wanted to be, but there was that little voice in the back of my head, measuring me against the suburban, middle-class standards I had been raised on. I looked around at my contemporaries, up to their eyeballs in careers and jobs and families, and I had nothing but a pocketful of stories and last week's paycheck. I woke up one morning, packed a few things in a bag, took the sixty-something dollars I had to my name, and bought a bus ticket for New Orleans.

New Orleans! The city I always seemed to run to. I found a job as a busboy at the Caribbean Room of the Pontchartrain Hotel. "Causes" were now a thing of the past. I wanted to make money, and working in a restaurant seemed as good a place as any to start.

The Pontchartrain Hotel was owned by Mr. E. Lysle Aschaffenburg, "Mr. Lysle" to his employees. He built it in 1927, managed to hold on to it through bankruptcy and the Depression years, and turned it into one of the finest, most elegant hotels in New Orleans, the hotel of choice for many celebrities, including Charles Laughton, Walt Disney, Mary Martin, and Richard Burton. It was originally designed as a residential hotel, and a few rich old ladies were still in residence, like Edith Stern, heiress to the Sears & Roebuck fortune, as well as Mr. Lysle and his wife. It's said that Tennessee Williams wrote part of *A Streetcar Named Desire* while living there.

The Caribbean Room of the Pontchartrain was one of the premier restaurants in the city, with several distinctive dishes on the menu, including oysters Caribbean, crabmeat Remick, turtle soup Amontillado, and its most famous dessert, Mile-High Pie. In 1969, Mr. Lysle won the Gold Plate Award given by the International Food Service Manufacturers Association, which designated him as the finest food service operator in the United States.

By the time I got there in late 1977, the Caribbean Room had dropped a notch or two. The day-to-day operations of the hotel had passed to Lysle's son, Albert, who was never able to generate the same passion for it that his father had. After a few months as a busboy, I was promoted to room service waiter. An old Black man named Eddie had been the room service waiter for many years, but he was running both the day and night shifts by himself, and it was getting to be too much for him. So, I accepted the job as a room service waiter on the night shift in return for a position as a waiter in the Caribbean Room for lunch.

The good thing about being a waiter is that you always have ready cash in hand. The problem was getting off work at midnight or 1 a.m. with a wad of cash stuffed in your pocket and a fair amount of adrenaline coursing through your veins in a city that offered sparkling entertainment twenty-four hours a day. Many a morning, that wad of cash from the night before had been seriously depleted by the time I crawled into bed at 6 or 7 a.m.

I was making money but not making any headway. The fact was I was still running from myself, and when you run from yourself, you can never get away.

After two years in New Orleans, I packed up and headed back north. Serendipitously, the guy who moved into the apartment with Danny after I left was moving out, and after a bit of hesitation on Danny's part—I had, after all, left him in the lurch two years earlier—I moved back in.

I scuffled for money, at first, working for a second-rate Brooklyn catering joint, then selling orange juice from a cart on the streets of Manhattan. For a while, I was a waiter at a restaurant on the ground floor of the Empire State Building, but it didn't last long. I started doing volunteer work at the Vietnam Veterans Ensemble Theatre Company (VETCO), an off-off Broadway theater company made up of Vietnam veterans. I was trying my hand at writing a play and figured if I helped out in the office, it might increase my chances of someone showing some interest in it.

Several members of VETCO worked as waiters at O'Neal's Baloon, a restaurant owned by two brothers, Michael and Patrick O'Neal, across the street from Lincoln Center, and they got me a job there. It was said that when the brothers applied for their liquor license for a place named O'Neal's Saloon, the State Liquor Authority said that it would not license a saloon. There was no formal law banning saloons, but a regulation dating back to the end of Prohibition had halted the practice. Michael's wife came up with the idea of changing the "S" to a "B." Eventually, a law was passed permitting the state to license saloons, but the O'Neals had gotten so much publicity over the incident—Patrick, an actor of some renown, is said to have remarked it was the most press he had ever received—they just kept the name "Baloon" as a little joke. The final scene of Woody Allen's *Annie Hall* was filmed at the Baloon.

I quickly settled back into my old New York City lifestyle, a pay-the-rent job with sufficient flexibility to pursue other "interests," this time as a budding playwright rather than a budding poet/journalist, stoned every waking hour, flitting through all the pseudo-artistic parties, where everyone, when asked, was an actor, or a dancer, or a painter or a sculptor or a writer. I liked to ask a second question after the what-do-you-do question: "What do you do for a living?" It was an impertinent question, one you weren't supposed to ask because it forced people out of their party role-playing and back into the real world: I'm a waiter, a secretary, a data entry clerk; I sell perfume at Macy's.

It was an appealing and comfortable existence, with lots of fun, lots of sex, and little responsibility. But I was not happy. The activism of the sixties and seventies had faded. There was an occasional demonstration, but the Boomer generation had moved on from making trouble to making money, re-adapting to the consumer mentality we had shunned in our youth.

I certainly wanted to get in on the moneymaking frenzy, but I wasn't ready to surrender all my ideals. No one was interested in the play I had written, and I got fired from O'Neal's for writing in a $2.00 tip on the credit card receipt of a guy who had stiffed me. I seemed to be tumbling backward.

There was another change that was happening in the early eighties: the attitude of America toward its Vietnam veterans. For the first time, the U.S. had lost a war in Vietnam, and the country could not really come to terms with it. We had always been the good guys, and we had always won, but in Vietnam, we didn't win, and there was this nagging feeling that maybe we hadn't been the good guys in that war after all. The country, in its collective guilt over Vietnam and the political divisions it had caused, had come to put the blame for the war on the veterans as a way to avoid shouldering the national responsibility for the fiasco. There developed the iconic image of the drug-addicted psycho baby-killer Vietnam vet. In virtually any movie or TV show that required an out-of-control, irrationally violent character, they made him a Vietnam vet, and no further explanation of his actions or motivation was necessary. Any newspaper article about an individual who had done something violent or crazy would be sure to identify him as a Vietnam vet in the headline or the first paragraph if that were the case. Many Vietnam veterans who came back to professional careers of one sort or another found it prudent to hide their Vietnam service from their employers and co-workers in fear that being branded a Vietnam veteran could hurt their career advancement.

Things started to change at the beginning of the Reagan presidency with the return of the hostages from Iran. As parades and accolades were bestowed on the returning hostages, some people began to wonder why such treatment hadn't been given to returning Vietnam veterans. There was, of course, something of an ulterior motive for this belated recognition: the Reagan administration was gearing up for another potentially disastrous military incursion, this time into Central America, and "honoring the vets" was a key component of the strategy to cure the American populace of the "Vietnam Syndrome"—the aversion to foreign military intervention that permeated the country post-Vietnam. It took another ten years for the Syndrome to be fully expunged during the first Gulf War, but once it was, the U.S. government was again able to impose its will through military might with impunity.

For many Vietnam veterans, the motivation for this recognition was irrelevant. For most of us, service in Vietnam was and would be the single most formative event in our lives. Yes, the war sucked, and being a soldier sucked, but we had *done* it, and no matter one's feelings about the war, most of us felt a certain pride that we had done it, while most others of our generation had not. For years, each of us had nursed that pride in solitary silence, but the "honor the vets" movement of the early eighties allowed us to pull it from under the bushel basket and let it shine.

After the 1982 dedication of the Vietnam Veterans Memorial in Washington, D.C., many other localities began to form their own plans for building a Vietnam Veterans Memorial; New York City was one of the first to take action. Mayor Ed Koch, himself a World War II veteran, established the New York Vietnam Veterans Memorial Commission and tasked one hundred city citizens—fifty of them being Vietnam veterans—

to raise a million dollars from private donors, half of which would fund the memorial, and the other half would fund a jobs program for Vietnam veterans—a so-called living memorial—since unemployment among Vietnam veterans at that time was rampant. An executive committee was organized, as well as several other committees, each co-chaired by a Vietnam veteran and a non-veteran. The two overall co-chairs of the Commission were F. Scott Higgins, a Vietnam veteran and Wall Street investment banker, and Donald Trump, then a local real estate developer.

Most of the work of the Memorial Commission was carried out by volunteers, but it was agreed to hire an Executive Director to coordinate the work. I interviewed for the job, but that position was given to Jim Hebron, a well-known figure in the Vietnam veterans community in New York City who had served as a Marine in Vietnam during the battle of Ke Sanh. It seems I sufficiently impressed the interview committee that they decided to create a Deputy Director position and offered it to me. It probably helped that two of those making the decision—Jim Noonan and Robert Santos—had been members of VVAW whom I had met back in the old anti-war days. Noonan, a former VVAW coordinator for Brooklyn, had worked for a small public relations firm that was hired by CBS News to handle public relations during the trial when William Westmoreland sued *60 Minutes* for defamation of character. Once the trial was finished, CBS News hired Jim for their in-house communications staff. He was a good friend of mine who lived in the same Park Slope neighborhood I did. Santos was one of the most decorated New York Vietnam veterans, having served as a platoon leader in Vietnam, and had risen quickly in the New York City bureaucracy to become Deputy Commissioner of Parks. I think my hiring was something of giving a chance to an old comrade down on his luck, but whatever. I was in, and I was cranked. I had a "cause," and they were actually going to fuckin' pay me to pursue it.

The whole Commission thing was a proving ground for me.

I had pretty much lost the decade of the seventies to the con-sequences of the trial and returning from Vietnam. Vietnam had made me feel on the fringe, out of the mainstream. The trial, with the betrayals and the branding as a radical, only cemented these feelings. I embraced the fringe, reveled in my placement there, using drugs to distort and distance myself from reality. When I finally decided to reel myself back in, I was way behind many of my contemporaries.

When I got the Commission job, I was surrounded by these enormously successful Vietnam veterans: investment bankers, lawyers, city commissioners, CPAs, advertising exec-utives, corporate communications specialists. And I quickly realized that in spite of all my adventures and experiences, I was basically a nobody. I hadn't done anything as far as what "anything" meant in the real world. "Former political pris-oner" was *not* an "anything."

The members of the Executive Committee of the Memorial Commission were all highly successful professionals before they ever got to the Commission; indeed, their previous suc-cess was why they were there in the first place. I desperately wanted to prove—to them and to myself—that I belonged in their company. Every little accomplishment I achieved was something I wanted to be recognized for. When I wrote an op-ed about the work of the Commission for the *New York Herald Tribune*, I was proud because it would show everyone that I could write. I was blown away by the response, which was that the op-ed should have Scott Higgins' name on it. But I *wrote* it, I protested. Yeah, but I was just a low-level staff guy; my job was to make the big boys look good. I wasn't really ready to accept that role. At least they didn't put Donald Trump's name on it.

The thing is, in retrospect, I didn't feel like I belonged with them. As much as I wanted to, I didn't really "make things happen" in the way they did. It was an illusion for me. Because they worked through me, it seemed to me like I was the one making things happen, when in reality, I was merely the tool they used to accomplish things. I was a good tool, to be sure, but the accomplishments were much more theirs than mine.

I suppose we accomplished it together, though, and I was accepted as part of the group, the inner circle that pulled off the New York Vietnam Veterans Memorial. I suppose one of the proudest pieces of my history is the plaque embedded in the ground at Vietnam Veterans Memorial Park in New York City, with my name alongside the names of Scott Higgins, Jim Noonan, Robert Santos, Ed Vick, Robert Patterson, Steve Mersereau, Catherine Saxton, Patrick FX Mulhearn, Bob Ptachik, and Jim Hebron.

Things started slowly. Higgins and Trump each put in an initial donation of $10,000 to get the fundraising going. Ed Vick, a Vietnam veteran and highly successful advertising executive, created a fundraising blurb and got it placed gratis in a few publications, and soon, small donations started to dribble in. New York City agreed to donate a park called Jeanette Park, next to 55 Water Street in the financial district, to be renamed Vietnam Veterans Plaza, as the site for the memorial. We also got two rooms in a city-owned building to function as an office.

It was clear from the start that we would not reach our fundraising goal based strictly on the small donations we were receiving. Thus, the main topic of conversation at the first meeting of the Commission's Executive Committee was about organizing a major fundraising event—dubbed the Red White and Blue Gala, the brainchild of Catherine Saxton, a public relations specialist on the Committee. Needless to say, I was not enamored of the pseudo-patriotic overtones of the title, but I was in no position to make my feelings known.

There was one distinguished-looking gentleman who attended that first meeting. He sat silently at first, listening to the back and forth of the other participants. He was much older than the others, who were all in their middle thirties, and perhaps he felt a little out of place. When the conversation turned to getting an A-list of names and addresses to invite to the Gala, he tentatively raised his hand and offered that he could help with that.

The old gentleman was Robert Patterson Jr., son of Harry Truman's Secretary of War. Patterson Jr. had served in the Army Air Corp during World War II and afterward had become a lawyer and joined the prestigious New York law firm of Patterson, Belknap, Webb & Tyler, founded by his father. Bob became one of the rocks of the Commission's work. He was always the voice of reason in the sometimes spirited discussions that took place during Executive Committee meetings, but he always deferred to the younger Vietnam vets on the Committee. He understood that the Memorial Commission was their passion; for him, it was a civic duty. In 1988, he was appointed as a federal judge by Ronald Reagan.

Jim Hebron, the Executive Director, was a consummate glad-hander and backslapper; everybody liked Jim. In a full-blown organization, external relations and board relations are a central part of an Executive Director's job. But in a three-person operation—we had added a secretary position—the lofty titles of Executive Director and Deputy Director were just fluff, and we were all grunts who needed to roll up our sleeves to get the work done. Jim preferred, for the most part, to keep his sleeves unrolled, concentrating his efforts on meetings, lunches, dinners and phone calls, leaving me to do most of the unglamorous grunt work.

I gritted my teeth, but threw myself into it, routinely working twelve to eighteen hours a day. I had left Brooklyn, and moved in with my latest girlfriend, a modern dancer who had a loft on lower Broadway, so it was a five-minute walk from where I lived to the office.

First, we organized a design competition to choose the design for the memorial. The jury for the competition, consisting of design professionals and Vietnam veterans, met over a Saturday and Sunday to view the submissions. Generally, they were underwhelming. Many were designs that had been submitted earlier for the national memorial in Washington,

D.C. Many were simply inappropriate or unattainable. At the end of two days, we had gone through 572 submissions, and nothing stood out. Then, during a lunch break, William Broyles, Jr., a former First Lieutenant in the Marine Corps, then the editor-in-chief of *Newsweek*, began to sift back through the submissions and pulled out one that had not been seriously considered the first time around. Looking over his shoulder was Andy Phelan, a former medic with the 101st Airborne Division, then dean of academic affairs at Pratt Institute. The design was simple—a seventy-foot-long, fourteen-foot-high glass block wall, illuminated from within—which was why the design-oriented jury had paid it little attention at first. But there was a second element to the submission: etched on the glass block wall would be actual letters that had been mailed to and from Vietnam. It was Broyles and Phelan who recognized the potential power of the words in these letters, pulled the submission out of the discard stack, and re-presented it to the jury. We had our winner.

The design had been submitted by two young architects, Peter Wormser and William Fellows. They had added a third member to their team, Joseph Ferrandino, a writer and Vietnam veteran, who, in their conception, would gather and choose the letters to be etched on the memorial. Robert Santos, however, wanted the key element of the choice of the letters to remain under the control of the Commission, and he unceremoniously rejected Ferrandino as a member of the winning team.

We announced our winner on May 29, 1984.

We chose May 7, 1985, the tenth anniversary of the official end of the war, as the day to dedicate the memorial and throw a ticker tape parade for Vietnam veterans. We had a little less than a year to collect and choose the letters, build the memorial, and plan the dedication ceremonies. I began the dogged effort to collect the letters by preparing a poster and sending it out to various Vietnam veterans groups, logging in the letters, and collecting the permissions necessary for their use.

By October, we had barely collected one hundred letters. I remembered that David Dunlap, the City Hall reporter from *The New York Times* who had covered the announcement of the winning design, had expressed an interest in seeing some of the letters we had collected. I gathered together a collection of about ten or twelve of the best letters we had received and sent them along to Dunlap. He got the *Times* to print the letters verbatim over half of page B1, with another half-page inside the B section. What's more, the article was referred to by a picture of one of the letter-writers on the front page situated—as Ed Vick admiringly told me—"above the fold," in advertising terms, the most desirable positioning you could ask for. The best thing was that Dunlap, in the brief introduction he wrote for the article, printed the address to which others could send their letters.

The story went out on the *New York Times* wire service, and the result was a tsunami of submissions. Within a week of the *New York Times* publication, we had offers to publish a book of the letters from five publishers. *Newsweek* called, asking to use some of the letters in an article. Anticipation had been slowly building in the country towards the tenth anniversary of the end of the war, and we caught the perfect wave. Letters started pouring into the little Commission office literally from all over the world. Suddenly, we had jumped from a relatively obscure New York City effort to a national media sensation. At the final count, we received over three thousand letters from forty-six states and six foreign countries.

Meanwhile, I was reading every letter we received and spending long hours recording the letter writer's name, rank, age, unit, and dates of service. It was also my job to clear permissions to publish them. No matter who received the letters, permission to publish them only rested with the people who signed the letters or their next of kin, which meant tracking down the writers because most of the letters were sent to us by people who *received* them, not *wrote* them. If, as was often the case, the letter writer had been killed in Vietnam, I needed to verify the date of death.

Most of this work was done through cold calling on the telephone, an incredibly sensitive and draining experience. I would work alone after hours, searching for phone numbers and making the calls. Of the vets I spoke to, some had difficulty with the details and had to pause to remember or ask me to wait while they consulted their files. The mothers of dead soldiers always knew everything off the top of their heads. The hard part for them was having to relive the experience all over again when I wanted to know when their son was killed and how old he was at the time.

In some cases, however, I simply could not locate the letter writers or their next of kin. One such letter was written by "Johnny Boy," a Marine who had sent a letter to Mrs. Perko, the mother of one of his deceased comrades. Mrs. Perko sent the letter to us, but we needed permission from Johnny Boy to publish it:

Dear Mrs. Perko,

I'm sorry for not writing sooner, I received your letter when I was discharged from the hospital 29 April, then went straight to Saigon for a week or so.

What can I say to fill the void? I know flowers and letters are appropriate, but it's hardly enough. I'm Johnny Boy, and I'm sick both physically and mentally. I smoke too much, am constantly coughing, never eat, and always sit around in a daze. All of us are in this general condition. We all are afraid to die and all we can do is count the days till we go home.

We're all in desperate need of love. When we go to Saigon, we spend all our money on women and beer. Some nights I don't sleep. I can't stand being alone at night. The guns don't bother me—I can't hear them anymore. I want to hold my head between my hands and run screaming away from here. I cry too, not much, just when I touch the sore spots.

I'm hollow, Mrs. Perko. I'm a shell, and when I'm scared, I rattle. I'm no one to tell you about your son. I can't. I'm sorry.
Johnny Boy

One late afternoon, I took a call at the office from a man who had seen the design competition poster that featured a famous photograph of the 173rd Airborne Brigade, but he would not give his name. He would only identify himself as a Vietnam veteran. He had served in the 173rd and had called to thank us for using the photograph and, perhaps, because it stirred up memories he had long been suppressing. He had been a part of the operation the day the picture was taken, and he knew the names of the men in the photo. We talked for a while, swapping war stories, and somehow in the course of our conversation, I mentioned the trouble I was having locating some of the letter writers. He asked me if I could tell him whom I was trying to find and any other pertinent information; he said he worked in D.C. and might be able to help me. Clearly, he did not want to reveal his sources and methods, but I figured it was worth a shot. I came to call him "Deep Vet" and gave him the names of the men I couldn't find. A few days later, he called again and gave me phone numbers for several of them, including "Johnny Boy." I asked if I could contact him again if I needed any more help. He said he would be glad to help, and he would call me periodically.

Whoever he was, wherever he was, Deep Vet was a real help to me. Of the many letter writers later etched into the glass, there was only one guy he couldn't find. Charles Dawson was a medic in the First Calvary Division in 1968, and he sent a letter to the mother of Richard Carlson, a fellow medic in his company, after Carlson had been killed in battle. Mrs. Carlson sent the letter to us. Deep Vet was able to track Dawson to the projects in New Orleans, but the phone number he found for him was no longer in service. The trail went cold after that. Dawson's letter is the only one on the memorial that we didn't have permission to use.

The process of getting the signed permission slips and verifying the facts made me privy to all kinds of personal information about the men and women who had written and received the letters. I knew about the soldier whose father moved in with his wife while his son was fighting in Vietnam. I knew about the POW who committed suicide six months after being released from North Vietnam. I knew about the gay infantryman and the drug-abusing officer. I met the father of George Olsen, 75th Ranger Regiment, one of the most articulate letter-writers we had. After Olsen graduated from St. John's University, he immediately volunteered to become an Army Ranger and undergo what was perhaps the most grueling training regimen in the most elite fighting force in the military. He probably could have avoided military service altogether had he chosen to do so. His father showed up at the Memorial Commission office one day to return the permission form in person. He was a quintessential New York City blue-collar guy; he reminded me of my own father. It is always difficult to know what to say to the parent of a slain soldier. I awkwardly murmured that he must be proud of his son. He gave me such a look filled with pain and anger and loss and said to me, "My son is dead. What is there to be proud of?" And I suddenly saw the anguish of a working-class father whose dreams of seeing his college-educated son succeed in life in ways he never could had been snuffed out in the rice paddies of Vietnam.

In the early eighties, the raw political divisions from the sixties still lingered just below the surface, ready to break out and ruin the slim veneer of harmony we had tenuously achieved. Those divisions ran deep on the Commission's Executive Committee. Santos, Noonan, and I had all cut our teeth in VVAW, while others on the Executive Committee held much more conservative political views. It is a tribute to the men and women on the Committee that they were able mostly to put those differences aside and work together to achieve the common goal without letting the things we disagreed on interfere with accomplishing the things that we agreed on. Politics did finally rear its head near the end, but that was after we had accomplished what we set out to do. We held it together until the work was done.

The place I was most concerned about politics was in the ultimate selection of the letters to be etched on the memorial. Certainly, we had enough material that could have allowed us to make a strong political statement either for or against the war. My position was that we just needed to tell the truth, to represent the complexity of the emotions and politics of the era through the material we chose. I was firmly convinced that "The Truth" itself was inherently anti-war and that the political message I wished to convey would be well represented if truth were our goal.

Santos handpicked the small group that chose the material for the memorial. His choices reflected a desire for an unpolitical, even-handed approach. I was the most overtly and outspokenly political of the group and, by the criteria that Santos seemed to have used, perhaps didn't even belong there, but my unparalleled familiarity with the letters and the writers made me indispensable to the process.

Participating in choosing the letters for the memorial was, without a doubt, one of the most extraordinary experiences of my life. The members of that group showed a commitment to put aside our individual beliefs to make choices that represented the whole of the city of which we were citizens. Over the course of three weeks, we differed, we argued, we struggled in a passionately principled way to shape the material into something that we could be proud of and that our city could be proud of as well. It wasn't easy by any means. Each of us developed attachments to particular letters and fought hard for their inclusion. Beyond simply choosing what would be included, we also had to decide the arrangement, the juxtaposition of one letter to another and to the historical news reports we decided to include to provide the larger context of what else was happening in the country while the war in Vietnam was raging—the civil rights movement, the walk on the moon, the shootings at Kent State. There were also the choices to be made of which letters to give prominence, which less so. Some of the most interesting letters are buried in small type below the shelf on the memorial. They are difficult to read because of their size and placement. One has to really want to know what they say, but a person could be well rewarded for the effort.

Choosing the letters for the memorial. Robert Santos with hands on hips. Bernie Edelman kneeling and writing on board.

The memorial we created, I think, is as complex and as nuanced as the era we were trying to reflect. That is both the beauty and the flaw of the memorial. Most people don't do nuance. They want their history in simplified soundbites, summed up in ten words or less. They want their memorials to elicit a single, overpowering emotion, preferably one of

Anastasia Mahoney reading the letters under the shelf.

heroism and glorification of the soldier. This memorial does not answer questions; it stimulates them. It does not glorify soldiers; it highlights the ordinariness of the individuals called upon to endure extraordinary circumstances in war.

One day, Mary, our secretary, answered the phone, then looked at me a little frantically and said, "Peter, it's Mike Wallace, asking for you."

"Mike Wallace? *The* Mike Wallace of *60 Minutes*?"

Mary nodded her head, "Yes, I think so."

I took a deep breath and picked up the phone. I heard the voice so familiar from the television on the other end. He started asking me about one of the vets whose letter we were considering for the memorial. I had spoken to this vet on the phone on several occasions. It seemed he was not doing so well, and he needed someone to talk to. He kept me on the phone for a couple of hours at a shot. Playing pseudo-therapist for down-on-their-luck vets had become part of my job description. At that point, we were in the middle of making the final cuts on the material that would ultimately be etched on the memorial, and this guy's letter was one of the ones that was currently in the design. The guy sounded so depressed, and I didn't know what to say, so I told him that his letter was going to be on the memorial, and it really seemed to cheer him up. Unfortunately, the next day, during the deliberations on the final cut for the material for the memorial, his letter was taken out. I then had to go back and tell him that his letter was not going to be on the memorial. Trying to be helpful, I just made things worse.

It turned out that this guy's sister worked for *60 Minutes*, and she went to Mike Wallace to enlist his assistance. That's why he called me. I explained it all to him and admitted I had made a mistake telling the vet his letter was on the memorial before the final cut was made. All the while, I had visions of myself sitting sweaty and uncomfortable while being grilled by Wallace in front of a national TV audience on *60 Minutes*. When I was finished, Wallace just sort of sighed and asked if there was anything that could be done. I told him it wasn't my decision alone; I was part of a group, and it seemed that the group decision had already been made. He thanked me for my time and hung up.

In addition to collecting the letters, building the memorial, and planning the dedication, we also had to pull together a book and have it published by May 7, 1985. We chose a publisher, and Santos chose Bernie Edelman, a freelance writer and photographer who had co-curated the first Vietnam art exhibit in New York City, to be the editor for the book. Bernie was a Vietnam veteran and a good friend of Santos. I was disappointed, to be sure, because it was a job I really wanted. I was so wrapped up in the collection of the letters at that point and literally knew more about them than anyone. I had read every one of them, I'd had extensive conversations with those who had written and received the letters, and I saw it as my chance to really blossom and show everyone what I could do. But it was also true that I had a load of other day-to-day responsibilities for the Commission, and it probably made better sense to give the editing job to someone else.

I stayed involved with the book project, however. I was still the one who received, recorded, and filed the letters and was still the main point of contact for the letter-senders. I collected all of the background information on the letter-writers. When it was decided that a glossary of terms was needed for the book, I dutifully put the whole thing together. When Bernie came up with the first draft of the manuscript, I worked with him to refine it and further shape it. As we were nearing the final manuscript, Santos had me work long hours with Bernie to make the final cuts and edits. I had hoped that my efforts might lead to my being designated as a co-editor with Bernie, but it was not to be. The book, titled *Dear America: Letters Home from Vietnam*, was well received and ultimately was turned into an award-winning documentary about the Vietnam War. Working with Bernie on shaping the final manuscript was some of the most rewarding and pleasurable work I have ever done, but you need to go to the second page of the acknowledgments in the book to find out that I was even involved in the project. The acknowledgments—written by Santos—described me as "the administrator" of the project. For a very long time, I was bitterly disappointed over the lack of public recognition for my efforts on this book, but over the years, that need for recognition has dissipated. I now look at the volume of *Dear America* on my bookshelf, and I do not need my name on the cover to feel the surge of tremendous pride that I have for my involvement in its creation.

As mentioned, Donald Trump was a member of the Executive Committee, but we only saw him at one meeting. He sashayed in unannounced, trailed by a young, rumpled-looking man who sat in the corner and said nothing. Everyone in the room sort of deferred to Mr. Trump; would he actually get personally involved in our work? It turns out the rumpled young man in the corner was William E. Geist, a reporter from

The New York Times, who was doing a puff piece on Trump for the magazine, so "the Donald" was performing for him. All we ever got from Trump was his money—begrudgingly, to be sure, but, in the end, substantial. The story went that he got involved in the Commission because he was looking for some quid pro quo from the city on one of his real estate ventures, and when he didn't get it, he had little interest in the Commission after that. He dutifully cut a check for $10,000 early on and bought a $10,000 table at each of the two fund-raising dinners the Commission held, but for him, that was like tossing a dime on the table. Worse, as the co-Chair of the Commission, his ten grand became the standard for the maximum donation for a very long time. Finally, near the end, when all the hard work had been done, and the Memorial Commission had already caught the wave of the ten-year anniversary of the end of the war, Trump agreed to the "Trump Challenge"—actually the brainchild of Pat Mulhearn, the sharp, savvy young counsel to Mayor Koch, who sat in on all the Executive Committee meetings to ensure the Mayor's interests were protected—where Trump pledged a million dollar donation if the Commission could raise a million by the dedication. Well, we met that goal, and Trump kicked in his part.

For much of the day on May 7, 1985, I was roaming the streets of New York City with a million-dollar check from Donald Trump in my pocket since Steve Mersereau, the Commission's treasurer, had given it to me the night before to deposit in our account. In the ticker tape parade on May 7 to honor Vietnam veterans, Donald Trump was in the first line marching down the street, although he never came close to ever setting foot in Vietnam or even soiling his suit in the military. All the other non-veterans who had done so much work to make the memorial happen understood that the parade was for the vets and didn't ask to participate. But like everything else in his life, I guess Donald bought his way to the front of the parade.

Steve Mersereau hands me the check from Donald Trump
for one million dollars.

This idea of holding a ticker tape parade ten years after the war was over, of wrapping up the whole Vietnam fiasco with a red, white, and blue bow and turning what had been a national tragedy into some kind of patriotic celebration, was not exactly something I wanted to spend my time doing. The parade was the one element of the Memorial Commission effort that I spent almost no time on.

In retrospect, the parade itself was a wonderful event. It was not so important for the veterans themselves because most of us had already come to terms with our service and gotten on with our lives in one way or another. It was, perhaps, more important for the ordinary people who stood and cheered us as we marched by, who felt bad at the way Vietnam veterans had been treated and never had a chance to say "Thank you" for what we had endured in their name.

Yet the reality of what I feared had come to pass. The true lessons of Vietnam—the lessons of the waste and futility of

In the Canyon of Heroes. From left: Jim Noonan, Peter Mahoney, Steve Mersereau, Ed Vick.

sending American soldiers to fight and die in a foreign country for no reason other than the political posturing of micro-penised politicians—were never learned. So American soldiers are still sent to kill and be killed in remote countries all over the world on the whim of whichever politician is in charge and needs his gonads massaged, and we all stand and cheer as they march off and then ignore them when they come home with broken bodies and crushed spirits. Oh, they will get their parades and monuments—we are so good at parades and monuments—but they will never get back what they have lost.

And neither will we.

Chapter 15

Old Friends

I have a little game I play when I get bored. I think of the name of someone from my past that I haven't seen or heard from for a long time, and then I Google the name to see if I can find any recent information. I've done this with childhood friends, high school buddies, and even adulthood friends that I had lost contact with. I've actually located a few people this way.

Once, I remembered the name of a guy I met in the Army. We were in the same OCS company down at Fort Benning, Georgia. I was part of a group of candidates who decided to publish a company newsletter. We were probably hoping to earn a few brownie points with the Tac Officers, showing initiative and all that. We had a little extra space in one of the issues, and I published a poem, which I find to be an embarrassing piece of work when I read it today. Shortly thereafter, another guy in the company approached me, told me he enjoyed my poem, and said he also wrote poetry and showed me some of his stuff. It was an immediate and solid connection between the two of us, an intertwining of spirits that I had seldom felt before or since, two aspiring poets caught up in the macho, militarized swirl of the Vietnamized sixties.

My newfound friend soon dropped out of OCS and was sent to dog-handler training, which was also located at Fort Benning. Since I was stationed at Benning after OCS, we got to hang out together for a little while. The Army frowned on what they called "fraternization" between officers and enlisted men, but we just laughed at their bullshit. My friend would occasionally call me "sir" just to bust my balls. Eventually, as so often happens, the Army sent us in different directions, and we lost contact after that brief, intense connection.

Years later, I decided to Google his name to see if there was anything there. I figured I had a decent shot at finding something since he had a rather distinctive name—Lamont B. Steptoe. This is what I found:

Lamont Steptoe is a poet, photographer, journalist, and activist based in Philadelphia, PA. His most recent collection of poems, A Long Movie of Shadows, was just awarded a 2005 American Book Award.

Peter and Lamont.

Lamont is the founder/publisher of Whirlwind Press. He was a Combat Army Sergeant in Vietnam and was decorated with the Bronze Star. Among other awards and grants, Lamont has won:

- *The 1999 Literary Fellow for the Pennsylvania Council on the Arts*

- *The 2002 Kuntu Writers Workshop Lifetime Achievement Award in Poetry from founders Rob Penny and August Wilson*

- *Discipline Winner in the Literature Category of the Pen Fellowship Program in Philadelphia*

- *Twice nominated for the Pushcart Award.*

He has read his poetry in Paris, France, Den Haag, Holland, and Managua, Nicaragua. In the United States, he has read at the Etheridge Knight Festival, the Library of Congress in Washington, D.C., the Geraldine R. Dodge Festival, the Schomburg Center for Black Literature, and the Annual Black Writers Conferences in Philadelphia, PA.

Of his many, many books and other works, the most well-known are Mad Minute, In the Kitchens of Masters, Catfish, and Neckbone Jazz. Lamont Steptoe is widely considered to be one of the most accomplished and important poets in the U.S.

Whoa! My Army buddy from decades ago actually BECAME a poet, as opposed to me, who only aspired to be one. I found an email address and made contact with him, prefacing my communication with the usual "I don't know if you remember me, but ..." Not only did he remember me, he actually remembered the title of the poem I had published in that newsletter. He agreed to come up to NYC from Philly to meet me the next time I was in the city. I met him outside of Penn Station, and the old connection was as immediate and as intense as it had been all those years ago. We were both inveterate storytellers, and we each now had a rapt audience who had never heard any of our oft-repeated yarns and was eager to hear them all. We spent a magical afternoon together. We sat for about six hours in Fanelli's Cafe in SoHo, totally oblivious to the artsy crowd around us. We made sure to tip the waitress well since we monopolized one of her tables for her entire shift. My sense was she didn't seem to mind and enjoyed overhearing bits and pieces of our conversation, two old soldiers—one

Black, one White—reminiscing about the shared experience of our youth.

I recently went to see my old friend and roommate, Danny. The wild man of VVAW days had settled into a comfortable urban middle-class lifestyle. He finally met a good woman, married her, and bought a small, single-family home in Brooklyn. He traded in his Hagrid look for a more Bruce Willis look: shaved head, goatee whiskers. He worked for years as a veterans' counselor for the Department of Labor and was a stalwart of the Brooklyn Vietnam Veterans of America (VVA) chapter.

Peter and Danny.

Danny was in the hospital, having just had hip replacement surgery the day before. He was doing well under the circumstances. That is the mantra of the boomers these days: doing well under the circumstances. The last time I had seen Danny was the year before. He was again in the hospital, this time for open-heart surgery. His wife jokingly calls him "the Bionic Man"; every year, he gets a new body part.

I spent a couple of hours with him, catching up and reminiscing. Danny hadn't been asleep in more than twenty-four hours, and the heavy-duty painkillers he was taking caused him to wander about in the conversation a bit, but that was okay. We don't get to see one another very often these days, and in a lifetime where I can count the number of true friends on the fingers of one hand, Danny is the index finger.

Later on that same day, I met Armand in the East Village. I hadn't seen him in about thirty years. We were briefly in the VVAW chapter in New Orleans together—he was known as Al back then—but he soon left, searching for fame and fortune as a filmmaker. His name had come up in a conversation with Don Donner and Nancy Saunders, some other old VVAW folks I had seen a few months earlier. Don had been the VVAW coordinator for Arkansas, who had come down to New Orleans to get VVAW things going, and he recruited Armand and me into VVAW. Don and I had both been invited to a conference on student organizing in the South, and over beers after the conference, we got to the inevitable "Whatever happened to …?" stage, and the question of "Whatever happened to Al?" came up. I later Googled his name, found his website and email address, and discovered he was living in NYC.

We met on a street corner in the East Village. I thought it a bit strange that Armand had not just given me his home address, but when I saw him, I understood that perhaps there was something about where he lived that he preferred not to share with me. The years didn't seem to have been good to him. He looked old, of course, because we all *are* old, but he had a look about him of someone worn out by life. He had been eking out an existence in the East Village as a fringe artist for decades, and his dreams of fame as a filmmaker were long behind him. He was full of plans, of course, as he always had been, but there was an air of tired defeat in the way he related them, as if he had long since stopped believing that any of them would ever come to pass. I recognized the feeling.

I suggested we catch up over lunch, and he reluctantly agreed to it. When the waitress came, he ordered only coffee, and I realized that he may not have had enough money for anything else. Not wanting to embarrass him, I did the same. We talked for a while about what each of us had been doing—it's amazing how thirty years of life can be summed up in ten minutes or less—then, with little else to talk about, we spent the usual time talking about physical ailments. I remember that when I was young and we would go to some family gathering of one sort or another, it always amazed me how the adults could sit around for hours talking about their ailments. Now I know.

We parted on the street corner, promising each other that now that we had reconnected, we'd continue to be in touch. I never saw or heard from Armand again.

At the end of August 2023, Natasha and I boarded a plane for a long weekend in Florida. This was no run-of-the-mill end-of-summer vacation. Florida had never been high on my list of places to visit with its oppressive summer weather and even more oppressive politics, not to mention my own personal history with the state. But we were headed back to Gainesville for the fiftieth anniversary of the acquittal of the Gainesville Eight.

This was the third reunion around the case; we had gotten together for the thirtieth and fortieth anniversaries. Each time, the number of participants dwindled. John Kniffen died from cancer in 2002, most likely from exposure to Agent Orange in Vietnam. His wife, Cathy, died shortly thereafter. Bill Patterson also succumbed to cancer in 2003. Alton Foss had continued to battle his Vietnam demons. After numerous operations on his damaged foot, it was finally amputated, but he was never able fully to overcome his addiction to painkillers. He died in 2020.

The Gainesville Eight, fifty years later. From left: John Briggs, Peter Mahoney Scott Camil, Stan Michelsen, and Don Perdue.

Of the lawyers, only Larry Turner made it to the fiftieth reunion. Doris Peterson, Morty Stavis, and Cam Cunningham had all died: Doris in 2017, Morty in 1992, and Cam in 2012. Brady Coleman, who quit law in 1989 to become an actor—he played Jack Black's lawyer in the movie "Bernie"—was suffering from the effects of long COVID and didn't make it. Neither did Nancy Stearns, who gave up her law career in 2001 for a second career as a cabaret singer in New York City. Nancy was just not physically up for a trip back to Gainesville, but she did call and speak to her five former clients during the weekend.

The first night, Natasha and I went to dinner with Stan Michelsen and John Briggs. Stan and I had reconnected at the thirtieth reunion, and we had stayed in touch over the years. Stan's still happy-go-lucky demeanor belied a fierce determination to express himself creatively. He had written and produced several music CDs, as well as a couple of books. He was still good friends with John—they had been roommates before the trial—but I barely knew Briggs. John was very quiet during the trial. He always seemed somewhat overwhelmed by the whole thing, yet he was perhaps the most remarkable of the defendants. He was not a veteran nor an activist. He could have easily testified before the grand jury and walked away unscathed. Instead, he had stood by his friend Stan, refused to testify against him, was thrown in jail, and then indicted along with these seven slightly crazy, unpredictable Vietnam veterans. It was an act of moral courage that few could match. He hadn't attended either of the previous reunions—he, like many others, did not like to be around Scott—but Stan had convinced him to attend this one. I enjoyed getting to know him and his wife Roseanna a bit better at dinner—he had worked for many years as a regional distributor of musical instruments—even if it was fifty years too late.

Most of the weekend was laid back and informal. Folks sat around Scott Camil's living room catching up and telling stories, more reminiscent of a common room in an old folks home than a bunch of radicals planning a revolution. The five surviving defendants were there, along with John Chambers, one of the Forgotten Four. Scott Camil's girlfriend from that time, Nancy, showed up, despite the fact that she and Scott had gone their separate ways years before, along with Alton's ex-wife Paula and his daughter. Donna Ing, who had been one of the jurors, also came by.

Carol Gordon, one of the unsung, behind-the-scenes heroes of the Gainesville Eight case, was omnipresent. During the trial, she had been indefatigable, working as a legal secretary for the lawyers, ready to take on any task, no matter how menial or difficult, to assist in the effort. She may very well have saved the whole case. The night before the trial was to begin, we had just finished one of our long, contentious lawyer/defendant meetings, and Carol was driving two of the lawyers, John Kniffen, and myself back to where we were staying. As was our habit after such tedious and tire-some events, someone lit up a joint, and we were passing it around to unwind a bit before bedtime. Suddenly, we saw a blue-flashing cop light behind us. As Carol pulled the car over to the curb, we quickly opened the windows in an attempt to dissipate the marijuana smell before the cop reached the car. Carol was cool as a cucumber. As the cop was walking up to the car, she quickly grabbed the baggy of marijuana and stuffed it down the front of her pants. She smiled up at the cop through the driver's side window and asked him sweetly, "What's wrong, Officer?" The cop was on the verge of the bust of his life, collaring two of the Gainesville Eight defendants and two of our lawyers on a drug possession charge the night before the beginning of the trial. It would have been sensa-tional, to say the least. It seemed one of the tail lights was not working, and Carol assured the policeman in a voice that somehow managed to be both respectful and flirtatious at the same time that she would take care of it first thing in the morning. The cop—unaware of his brush with fame—let us go with a warning.

Don Perdue was at the reunion, as he had been at the other two. I could never quite figure Don out. On the surface, he seemed so different from the other defendants. Certainly, he was as passionate and committed about his anti-war beliefs as the rest of us, but he was a straight arrow in appearance during the trial. His hair was well groomed, unlike his hirsute co-de-fendants, and he always wore a tie to the courtroom. Some wag once remarked that the iconic photo of the Gainesville Eight looked more like the Gainesville Seven and the arresting offi-cer. He didn't drink, smoke, or do drugs of any sort, and he'd gone on to a distinguished career in the Hollywood, Florida, fire department. He was always one of the reluctant ones whenever we discussed any type of courtroom demonstration, but he always went along with whatever was decided. Perhaps, for me, one of the seemingly most out-of-character things he did during the trial was to vote, along with Scott, to put on a defense despite the advice from the lawyers that the practical legal strategy was to rest our case without calling any witnesses. In retrospect, it seems his behavior could be summed up rather simply. Don Perdue was a Marine, and Marines do not walk away from a fight nor abandon their brothers.

Scott Camil, of course, was the ringmaster of the reunion, in the same way he had been the ringleader of the conspiracy. There were few things in life that Scott participated in where he was not the center of attention. He was the one defendant who never gave up his activism, becoming a fixture in Gainesville at any peace or anti-war demonstration. He took to organizing political campaigns for local progressive candidates. His continued activism was not without its consequences. Larry Turner told the story of how, in 1975, Scott had been shot in the back by two DEA agents during a drug bust sting. The feds sent in a female undercover agent—they had, at last, found Scott's weak point—who quickly jumped in bed with Scott and then introduced him to the two DEA agents. Scott survived the attack but was put on trial again in Gainesville, this time for possession with intent to sell marijuana and cocaine, as well as resisting arrest. There was the physical evidence of the pound of marijuana and the two and a half ounces of cocaine, but Larry, again defending Scott at trial, ignored the drugs and concentrated on Scott being set up by an informer and being shot in the back. He was again found not guilty.

Despite the high-school reunion air about the event, there was a palpable sense of pride among the participants of having shared in a piece of history. We had all gone in a thousand different directions after the trial, but there was a bond among us from the experience that would never be broken. The one formal activity of the weekend was for the five remaining defendants to go down to the federal courthouse in town and recreate the picture of us standing by the federal seal on the front of the building. As we were posing for the picture, the mayor of Gainesville showed up and read the following proclamation:

City of Gainesville, Florida
Office of Mayor Harvey L. Ward, Jr.
Proclamation

WHEREAS, peace activists John Briggs, Scott Camil, Alton Foss, John Kniffen, Peter Mahoney, Stanley Michelsen, William Patterson, and Don Purdue, collectively known as The Gainesville Eight, occupy an important and special place in the history of our community and our nation; and

WHEREAS, the Gainesville Eight were accused and indicted on charges of conspiracy to disrupt the 1972 Republican National Convention held in Miami Beach, Florida, but were acquitted and cleared of charges under representation of the Honorable Larry Gibbs Turner; and

WHEREAS, seven members of the Gainesville Eight were veterans of military service in the Vietnam War and had become active in the Vietnam Veterans Against the War (VVAW) and were passionate about ending the war; and

WHEREAS, following the historic acquittal, Scott Camil was quoted as saying, "We had no conspiracy to disrupt the convention. Our conspiracy, if you want to call it that, was to go down to the convention and exercise our Constitutional rights as citizens and to defend those rights against anybody who tried to take away those rights, whether it be the government or anyone else. And the jury sided with us," and Peter Mahoney was quoted as saying, "In spite of all this joy and elation, I can't forget that the government put me through fourteen months of hell;" and

WHEREAS, in the years since the acquittal members of the Gainesville Eight have been dedicated to the cause of peace both in the United States and abroad, including service in the Veterans for Peace movement, and continued to prove themselves as true heroes and patriots in the daily life of the Gainesville community and other communities; and

WHEREAS, the surviving members of the Gainesville Eight and many of their supporters and colleagues are now gathering to commemorate and celebrate the historic significance of their trial and acquittal after fifty years;
NOW, THEREFORE, I, Harvey L. Ward, Jr., by the authority vested in me as Mayor of the City of Gainesville, do hereby proclaim August 31, 2023, as

Gainesville Eight Day

in the City of Gainesville and invite all our neighbors to join me in commemorating the 50th anniversary of the end of the trial of the Gainesville Eight, and invite all our neighbors to celebrate with them and with me their shining example of commitment to constitutional freedoms and to the cause of peace.

IN WITNESS WHEREOF, I have hereunto set my hand and caused to be affixed the official seal of the City of Gainesville, Florida, this 25th day of August, A.D., 2023.

Harvey L. Ward, Jr.,
Mayor

Gainesville Eight Day! It's not often in life you get to be labeled a political pariah and a community treasure for the same deeds.

Chapter 16

The Wounds of Two Wars

When the Memorial Commission finished its work in 1985, I was determined that it would be the end of "Vietnam veteran" as my primary identification. I had played that role almost exclusively for over fourteen years, and I needed to put that part of my life in its place. I was offered the job of Veterans Coordinator for the City of New York, but it was the last thing I wanted to do. Beyond primary identification, I just didn't want to become a professional veteran, one who makes his living by being a veteran.

The Memorial Commission had given me contacts for all sorts of job possibilities for the future. One of our fundraising strategies was to identify a Vietnam veteran in a particular company and then try to cultivate him as a conduit to whatever corporate donations might be available. A lot of vets were working in the financial sector, and one of my contacts said he could get me an interview for an investment banking position. *Sure, what the hell?* I thought; it would give me a chance to practice my interview techniques. I knew I wouldn't get the job, so I was totally laid back when I found myself at E.F. Hutton. Ironically, the company was started by the same man who had founded the Bath and Tennis Club in Palm Beach, where I had lived and worked as a busboy twenty years earlier.

Even more astounding, E.F. Hutton made me an offer to work on Wall Street.

I had one final hurdle: a lie detector test. I knew one of the questions would be about drug use. I figured, well, I'm dead in the water on that one. I called my prospective new boss and asked him to meet me for a drink. I told him my whole history: Vietnam, Gainesville, drug use, the years of living an alternative lifestyle. I said I didn't think I could pass muster on a lie detector test. He looked at me with a mixture of awe and confusion—what I had described was so far removed from his own experience—then he told me whatever they asked me, just tell the truth, and he would take care of the rest.

I told the truth, and they hired me. My transformation from radical revolutionary to corporate cog was now seemingly complete.

I was surrounded by men and women with prestigious MBAs in Brooks Brothers suits. My friend Jim Noonan once told me that no matter how successful he became, he could never quite get over the feeling that he was faking it. I was faking it big time on Wall Street. The Brooks Brothers suit was the easy part. I never pretended to have an MBA; I was just expected to perform as well as those who did.

The two fundamental aspects of investment banking are the numbers and client relations. I was a low-level associate, so my focus was mostly on the numbers. I didn't have the finance background of my peers, but I tried to make up for it with on-the-job training. The hours I had spent with Steve Mersereau, the Memorial Commission's treasurer, on preparing the monthly financial reports had given me some facility with spreadsheets, but that was rudimentary compared to what was required for this job. I routinely spent twelve to fifteen hours a day running numbers, manipulating spreadsheets, and wending my way toward conclusions through a healthy dose of trial and error, mostly error. However, through hard work and perseverance, I eventually got good at the numbers.

I was not good at client relations, though. Investment banking is a highly competitive, cutthroat business, where almost every opportunity had multiple companies jockeying for the work. Success was not just having the best financing plans but also required a significant amount of schmoozing and salesmanship, neither of which I was particularly adept at. It wasn't an issue at first. My boss was brilliant at both, and as long as I kept pumping out the numbers, he took care of the client relations. But as I got into my second year on Wall Street, I needed to show my client relations chops in order to fill out my banker skill set. It was touch and go whether I would make the grade.

I never got the chance.

On October 19, 1987—Black Monday—the stock market crashed. The boom-boom, greed-fueled eighties came to an ignominious halt, and with it came the end of my Wall Street career. E.F. Hutton was hit hard—fatally so—and started jettisoning personnel trying to survive. I was in the first wave of firings, along with my boss, who had worked there for nearly twelve years. We each got a month of severance pay for every year that we had worked there. A month later, Hutton finally bit the dust, and the remnants were sold to American Express. My colleagues who had survived the first wave got the axe in the second wave; their severance package was a week's pay for every year worked.

I was back out on the street at the age of thirty-nine. The severance gave me a small cushion to look for a new job. At least I now had a résumé that consisted of a little more than "former political prisoner," although if I could sense the political leanings of an interviewer, I found that mentioning that little factoid could sometimes elicit a favorable response.

I had sent a résumé to John Mroz, the founder and president of a foreign policy think tank called the Institute for East-West Security Studies. I had met Mroz through my Wall

Street boss. The Institute had just released a report titled "How Should America Respond to Gorbachev's Challenge?" The document itself was a rather bland rehash of potential policy options, most of which broke no new ground in East-West relations. The significance of the document lay not so much in the content but in the forty-five foreign policy heavyweights from across the political spectrum that Mroz convinced to endorse it. The Institute held a conference in Minneapolis to publicize the document, and my boss volunteered to help with the publicity. He then turned and told me to get it done. Through E.F. Hutton (unbeknownst to anyone, of course), I bought a list of the addresses of the top two hundred newspapers in the U.S., drafted a press release about the report, and made copies using the Hutton copy machine, then sent the press release out to the list through the Hutton mail room. The result of this was a massive amount of national publicity for the report, more than the Institute had ever garnered for any of its previous efforts. So, Hutton, before its inglorious demise, made a significant contribution to East-West relations. It also helped get me my next job.

A few days after I sent him my résumé, Mroz called (actually, he had his secretary call) and asked me to come by about 5 p.m.. I was there at 5, and Mroz was overbooked and running late—as I came to find out was very usual—and at about 5:45, he rushed out of his office, apologized, and said that he had an appointment in Darien, Connecticut, at seven and didn't have time to talk. He barked at his secretary to get him a car. I said I had my car there and could drive him to his appointment.

Mroz and I had a very pleasant conversation on the drive to Darien. I sensed he was someone I could relate my Gainesville Eight story to, so I gave him the full beyond-the-résumé account. I wasn't really looking for a job from Mroz. He was a man with a huge amount of contacts in government, in academia, in business, and in the philanthropic world. I had asked him in my cover letter if he could forward my résumé to some of his contacts who might be interested. I got him to his appointment in Darien on time, a fact that impressed him since it was the height of rush hour traffic leaving the city.

I thought that was that. A few days later, however, I got a call from Mroz himself, and he offered me the job of Director of Administration for his Institute. Less than three weeks after I had been fired from Wall Street, I had a new job. As previously, it was one that I had never held before, with only the vaguest idea of what needed to be done. Nevertheless, I threw myself into the work, trying to make up with enthusiasm what I lacked in experience.

A few months later, I got a call from a woman named Diana Glasgow, who worked for an organization called the Earthstewards Network, an international nonprofit organization located in Washington State. She explained that her organization was working with the Foundation for Social Inventions, a group in the Soviet Union trying to help its nation's grassroots organizations operate independently of government control. Earthstewards had sponsored several groups of American professionals to travel to the Soviet Union to meet with counterpart professionals from there, a process they called citizen diplomacy. On one of those trips, they were approached by some Soviet veterans of their Afghanistan War, asking if Earthstewards could sponsor a group of Vietnam veterans who were professionals. The Soviet Afghanistan veterans were facing many of the same problems returning from their war that Vietnam veterans were facing in the U.S.; they were hoping to learn from Vietnam veterans in America how to transition to ordinary life. One group of American veteran professionals comprised mostly of specialists in veteran readjustment problems—psychologists, prosthetists, and wheelchair specialists—had already made the trip. Earthstewards now wanted to organize a second trip, and I had been recommended to her. I agreed to go without hesitation.

We assembled in Copenhagen before flying on to Moscow.

This group was much more diverse than the first one, with lawyers, graphic artists, linguists, mental health workers, writers, administrators of nonprofit organizations, juvenile probation officers, political professionals, alcohol rehabilitation counselors, small-business owners, and a television news director. And then there was Mike, a "lifer" noncommissioned officer in the Army who did twenty-three years and retired. He had just completed his undergraduate degree in psychology at Evergreen State College in Olympia, Washington. We roomed together the first night in Copenhagen. Mike told me that he felt left out. He had been a professional soldier who had done his duty then and would do it again if his country asked. He felt we were justified to be in Vietnam, and no apologies or second thoughts were warranted. In his local vets center, the names of Jane Fonda and Tom Hayden could stir feelings of anger and rage. In the initial introductions, when one of the group announced that he had worked for Tom Hayden for ten years, Mike looked around the room and saw everyone nod approvingly. He realized then that in this group of veterans, he was a distinct minority.

In Moscow, we were met at the airport by about twenty Afghanistan veterans. They offered enthusiastic greetings and great bear hugs for us, all except one. He remained sullen and separate from the proceedings. One from our group went over to him and tried to shake his hand. He pulled up his shirt and showed a jagged scar on his rib cage.

"You see this?" he snarled. "This was caused by an American-made M-16 round in Afghanistan."

The Vietnam veteran quickly pulled up his own shirt.

"You see this?" he said. "This was caused by a Soviet-made AK-47 bullet in Vietnam."

The two men looked at one another, then fell into one another's arms in a crushing brotherly hug.

The next day, the Afghanistan veterans took us to visit their memorial. It was not yet a monument, merely an irregular four-foot stone square set on a base with a plaque on it. It sat in the middle of a field in Friendship Park, stark and solitary on that windswept Moscow morning. The Afghantsi—the name the Soviet veterans had given themselves—had been getting the runaround from the bureaucracy for three years concerning their request for land on which to build their memorial. Finally, a group of them simply went out and "liberated" this field, galvanizing public support for the project. The Afghantsi told us they planned to build a larger monument soon and had already raised money from all over the country to pay for it. But that didn't matter to us. This unpretentious stone—so different from the other, massive war memorials of the Soviet Union—had a power that belied its size, imbued with the pain and pride of those who visit it.

At the Afghantsi memorial.

We formed a ragged column of twos and threes—Vietnam veterans and Afghanistan veterans, arm in arm—and trudged toward the modest Afghantsi marker.

Sasha and Nikolai, two of the Afghantsi, handed each of us

a red carnation, which we placed at the base of the memorial. We stood around the stone in the snow holding one another, middle-aged Vietnam War veterans and youthful Afghanistan veterans, separated by a chasm of age, politics, and culture yet bonded together in a brotherhood of experience. Several in the group around the memorial were moved to speak, the words pouring from them. It mattered little if the speaker was a Vietnam veteran or an Afghanistan veteran; the sentiments were the same: we must honor those who died, we must serve those who survived, we must swear to one another that our sons will never go through what we did.

I took my Vietnam Service Medal out of my pocket and placed it on the memorial. I had not taken part in the iconic VVAW medal-throwing demonstration back in D.C. I was not ready then, but I was ready now. Seventeen years later, I would leave my medals all over the Soviet Union to make my own small anti-war statement. Then I cried on the shoulder of one of the Afghantsi, and he held me.

The night after our visit to the Afghantsi memorial, we left Moscow for Alma-Ata, the capital of the Central Asian Republic of Kazakhstan. The six-hour-long red-eye flight to Alma-Ata turned into a fourteen-hour marathon as the plane was diverted to Tashkent because of fog, and we were forced to sit around the airport for eight hours, isolated by airline officials from the rest of the passengers on our plane. Finally, we got into Alma-Ata, exhausted, unshaven, and short-tempered.

We were welcomed at the airport by Afghantsi, dressed in their military uniforms. Their welcome was high-energy, all flowers and handshakes and songs, and there was an official film crew taking pictures. The welcome helped to melt some of our exhaustion and edginess, but something didn't seem quite right.

Later that evening, after a quick shower and shave, there

was a formal reception with the Afghantsi and their wives at the hotel where we were staying. Here, we learned that these men, unlike the Afghantsi we had met in Moscow, had been carefully chosen by the local Komsomol—the youth wing of the Communist Party—whose officials hovered at the fringes of the proceedings.

I spoke with an Afghantsi named Beslan and his wife, Tanya. They were very friendly but too much like "Ozzie and Harriet," too unwilling to share more than mundane experiences. We drank wine, I showed them pictures of my wedding, I gave him a copy of the book *Dear America: Letters Home From Vietnam*, and I gave her an *I Love New York* button. It was all very cordial but not very deep when contrasted with the immediate bond we felt with the Afghantsi in Moscow. I told myself that maybe I was expecting too much in the first meeting. They invited me to their home for a dinner to be held several days later. Beslan introduced me to a friend of his who was not an Afghantsi and told me his friend would join us for dinner. I asked Beslan who his friend was. He was an official of Komsomol.

With Beslan and Tanya.

Two days later, after visiting Alma-Ata's tourist spots and landmarks, we were scheduled to go to a cemetery with the mothers of slain Afghantsi to lay flowers on the graves of their sons. As we climbed into the bus that would take us to the cemetery, the Komsomol officials, talking rapidly in hushed tones, were clearly getting nervous. I later learned that they feared they were losing control and that there would be an embarrassing incident at the cemetery. At the last minute, after everyone was seated on the bus, the officials made excuses and said it was not possible to go to the cemetery. There was haggling back and forth, then finally Baikal, a tall, strapping Afghantsi, ripped his jacket off in front of a Komsomol official, stood menacingly in his face, and told him we were going to the cemetery and there wasn't anything he could do to stop us. The official backed down. Later in the trip, the Komsomol again tried to assert their control. They got one of the local organizers of the trip—a filmmaker who was perhaps dependent on the good graces of the government to stay in business—to throw them a political bone. He handed the group a letter to Prime Minister Benazir Bhutto of Pakistan to be signed by the Vietnamsi (as we had begun calling ourselves) and Afghantsi, asking her to release Soviet prisoners of war. The Afghantsi, though they had not been consulted beforehand on the letter, thought it was a good idea. Prisoners of war, after all, were as emotional an issue for them as they were for many Vietnam veterans.

The Vietnamsi, some of whom saw only the healing aspects of the trip and some its political ramifications, were divided over signing the letter. The Healees, as they were half-jokingly called, wanted to sign the letter as a gesture of goodwill toward the Afghantsi. The politicians were acutely aware—almost self-consciously so—of the potential propaganda value of seemingly innocent documents signed in good faith. They wanted to avoid signing this letter at any cost. Mistrust raged briefly through the group. Accusations were hurled back and forth, and tempers rose. How fragile our newfound friendships suddenly seemed when manipulated by skilled propagandists. However, the moment of our estrangement quickly becomes the moment of the reaffirmation of our brotherhood. After airing our views, Afghantsi and Vietnamsi alike realized that our friendship was more important than any letter. It remained unsigned, and we remained friends.

At the cemetery, we wandered from grave to grave of young men—nineteen or twenty years old—killed in Afghanistan. At each grave, the mother of an Afghantsi told the story of the boy who was buried there. It was an emotional blowout. I remember Greg—a gentle giant of a man from Missoula, Montana, whose rib-crushing, eyeglass-popping hugs became legendary on the trip, a Navy SEAL who could not speak of his experience in Vietnam without great heaving sobs—standing with his arms around the father of a dead Afghantsi, trying to come to terms with his feelings as a son and as the father of two young sons himself. I remember Victor, a stolid, severe man—once a political officer in Afghanistan, now a local official—launching into an eloquent, passionate, anti-war speech, condemning the Soviet government for sending men to die in a useless war and for hiding the truth from the Soviet people for so many years.

Most of all, I remember the Mother. She told of getting a letter from her son that said he was on his way home and telling her to cook something sweet for him because he never had anything sweet in Afghanistan. Shortly after that letter arrived, he was killed, and for months, all she did was cook sweet things. Her neighbors asked her why she was cooking so much food, and she said that her son was coming home and he wanted sweet food.

That day, she shed no tears. She said quietly, almost matter-of-factly, that there was no pain in the world that surpassed the pain of a mother who had lost her child. She didn't care about life anymore, she said. Day was the same as night to her, all meaningless.

Just then, an Afghantsi named Sergei came up and looked long and hard into her eyes. She returned his stare. Sergei reached into his pocket and gave her a folded photograph. The woman looked at the picture. It showed her son lying in a coffin. "I have something more than most mothers, now," she said to Sergei. "At least I know for sure my son is dead."

I had met Sergei the night before. He spoke quietly about the soldier in the photograph, a friend who had been killed in Afghanistan. He told us he went to visit his friend's mother, and she locked the door behind him and wouldn't let him leave. "You must be my son now," she demanded. He ran from her house.

During our conversation, I asked Sergei about *glasnost*. All Afghantsi support *glasnost*, Sergei said. For six years, the Soviet people had not known the war in Afghanistan was going on. "We wrote letters home, telling our parents we were planting trees and building schools," he said. "When boys were killed, they were sent home in sealed zinc coffins. The parents were not allowed to open the coffins; they were not allowed to put on the gravestone that their sons had died in a war. When Afghantsi came home, people did not respect us because they didn't know we had been to war. Older veterans from the Great Patriotic War ripped the medals from the uniforms of Afghantsi, saying how dare we wear medals we had never won. We support *glasnost* because *glasnost* will keep these things from ever happening again."

Sergei ran a small business. He had some land under a new government lend-lease program. He was farming it and selling the produce for his own profit. He had a car, a VCR, and a cooperative apartment. He was definitely in the then-burgeoning Soviet middle class. He intimated that he was mortgaged up to his eyeballs but liked the fact that the harder he worked, the more money he made.

As we continued talking about the wars in Afghanistan and Vietnam, we betrayed our ignorance of each other's experience. Slowly, the stories came out, though. Each time, Sergei responded to a Vietnam story of mine with a parallel story of his own: about drugs, about wanting revenge on the enemy, about not being able to tell the enemy from the local population, and beginning to regard everyone as the enemy. It was as we expected. Their war was our war, their experience our experience.

We had poured out our grief at the cemetery. After such a cathartic memorialization of the dead, we needed a celebration of life. The party lasted for two days—food, music, laughter, toasts of vodka and cognac. Stamping dances of male prowess. Hugs, kisses, backslaps, handshakes. My new friend Beslan was there—Ozzie transformed into Zorba—now a man of huge appetites. My glass did not stay empty long, nor was my plate bare with Beslan nearby.

The next day there was a picnic at a local park, a feast of freshly killed antelope shish kabob, called *shashlik* in Russian. The Afghantsi challenged us to some games—soccer and American football. The fortyish, past-prime, out-of-shape Vietnamsi took one look at the ripple-muscled, tight-end physiques of the Afghantsi and made two quick strategic decisions. The first was to play on mixed teams rather than national teams. The second was that when we showed them how to play American football, we declined to teach them about blocking.

That night, we went to Beslan's house for another feast. Tanya, who had been cooking all day, chided Beslan for having already stuffed me with food at the picnic. Beslan assured her we would eat everything she had prepared. I was blissfully ignorant of the gastronomic marathon to which he had just committed us. Tanya spread a tablecloth on the living room floor, and we sat around it on cushions. Although not religious, this household adhered to Muslim traditions—the men sat and feasted while the women served the food. After each course—there were seven—the men retired to another room to smoke and drink while the women cleared the remains and readied the next round of food. By my hazy calculation, seven of us consumed nine bottles of vodka, two bottles of wine, and a bottle of cognac during the meal.

I mentioned to Beslan that Tanya had not sat with us during the meal. He said this is so; it was traditional and appropriate. In a marriage, there could be only one person in charge of the family, and that was the man. The man was the head, he proclaimed loudly; it has always been so. Tanya, scurrying in with another bowl of food, sassed him good-naturedly. Yes, the man is the head, but the woman is the neck. Whichever way the neck turns, the head must go.

Karat, the Russian interpreter, had a hard time translating as the alcohol thickened our tongues and dulled his brain. We all laughed at his dilemma, words being only a small part of the exchanges taking place. Even Beslan's Komsomol friend turned out to be a man of good humor and easygoing manner.

Little was said through the evening of the two wars that brought us together. Only once did the subject intrude, in a ceremony that would be repeated many times during this trip—the Third Toast. Russian toasts tended to be long and bombastic, with a great flourish of clinking glasses at the end. The Third Toast was always for comrades who had died in war. There was no speech or clinking of glasses. Each man raised his glass silently and remembered a friend's moment of death or a shared moment of life. You looked around the room during the Third Toast at the eyes of the other men. The eyes said it all.

With our Alma-Ata goodbyes shared, we returned to Moscow. Most of us never saw one another again. Nonetheless, we were brothers forever. It had been a special time, indelibly etched in all our memories. Because of it, none of us, neither Vietnamsi nor Afghantsi, would ever be the same.

Back in Moscow, my new friend Sasha invited me for a visit to see his friend Amir. Amir was a young man, twenty-one years old, with an angelic face, a reflection of the strength of character that got him through each day. I first set eyes on him as he sat on a bench in the visitor's room of the hospital, talking animatedly with Nadia, a dark-eyed, witty journalism student from Moscow State University. Sitting together, they seemed like an ideal couple—handsome, obviously fond of one another, engaging in a serious yet friendly debate about some intellectual topic or another. In the budding Moscow spring of 1988, such couples were as common as red stars and pictures of Lenin. The only distinguishing feature of this couple was the light blue hospital garb Amir was wearing.

He had been in the hospital for a year since shortly after a radio-detonated land mine had exploded beneath the personnel carrier he was riding in, sending Amir, as he cheerfully described it, "flying through the air like some great big bird." I didn't notice the effects of that explosion at first. It only became apparent later when Amir tried to stand, balancing himself precariously on two canes and two grotesquely fitting prosthetic devices, which substituted for the legs he left in Afghanistan.

Amir had met Nadia several months after he got to the hospital. She had visited his ward to do a newspaper story. She offered to get him some water, and he refused, turning away from her on his bed. Later, he got her telephone number from a nurse and called her at home, saying he didn't mean to be impolite, that he just didn't want to be treated like a cripple. "Look," she said, "It's your water! If you want it, you can have it. I just offered to get it for you." Amir asked if he could call her again. She said yes and began to visit him every day.

We sat around a small card table next to Amir's bed as Nadia poured tea and cut fruit and salami for guests who'd gathered. There were three other Afghantsi there, one of whom had served with Amir in Afghanistan. This man brought his recent bride with him. Nadia was clearly the hostess of this amputee ward tea party, but she never sank to the role of servant. She maintained a friendly running feud with Sasha over which of them was more qualified to be my interpreter. She argued passionately about politics with Alexei. She chided Sergei for his off-color jokes, then told one of her own. All the while, Amir sat there beaming with pride as he watched her in action.

Several times during our brief visit, a man in a wheelchair rushed into the room, stayed for several minutes, and then hurried away in a mad dash down the corridor. Formerly a captain in Afghanistan, Valera had been in the hospital for three years. His chest and arms were massive, a once extraordinary specimen of a man whose magnificent body now ended just below his hips. His two prostheses stood idle against the wall near his bed. He hadn't accepted it; perhaps he never would. He spent his days drinking vodka and watching television, occasionally putting on an X-rated video when the hospital staff wasn't around. Amir shook his head sadly. Valera spoke often of suicide, he said. I invited him to join us, but he said he didn't like tea. Each of the visiting Afghantsi took a turn talking to Valera, trying to reach him, trying to break through. Valera's face never softened.

After leaving the hospital, Sasha, Nadia, and I walked together to the Metro station. We had been talking about Amir, about his progress and his prospects for the future. Nadia was intense, laying out a rehabilitation program for Amir in a manner that sounded like my old drill sergeant, repeating each word twice for emphasis. Physical therapy, physical therapy, study, study, work, work, struggle, struggle. I mentioned to her the difference between Amir and Valera, and she suddenly grabbed my arm and lost her confident demeanor.

She knew that she was the reason for the difference.

She asked me impossible questions about whether Amir could really make it in ordinary life, whether he could really ever expect to leave the hospital. It's too hard, she said. It's too hard.

Amir had asked Nadia to marry him. Nadia said maybe. Amir thought maybe meant yes if only he could prove to her he had the strength to succeed in his rehabilitation.

Sasha was wiser.

Maybe means no, he said sadly. She just can't bring herself to say it.

Three Vietnam veterans, along with Sasha's friend Igor, were invited to Sasha's home. It was clear that Sasha was stretching himself to the limit to offer his hospitality to us. The apartment was minuscule, with a small living room dominated by an overstocked bookshelf, a tiny kitchen, and a bedroom. Sasha lived there with his wife and child.

As we sat crowded around the kitchen table to the meager meal of weak fish soup, rice, beets, potatoes, some canned mystery meat, Sasha's prized tin of Olympic mackerel—a memento from the 1980 games—and his only bottle of champagne, we talked about the possibility of an international veterans organization dedicated to working for peace. The Vietnam veterans were wary, not because it wasn't a good idea, but because of the challenges of logistics, agreeing on an agenda, control, and the potential for being co-opted.

Sasha wouldn't listen to our objections. He was passionate that we should band together to work for peace. The Afghantsi reminded me so much of Vietnam veterans from years ago—zealous, fearless, unwilling to accept no for an answer, determined to change the world that had put us through such pain. Seeing that determination again briefly rekindled these old feelings in me. Maybe we could make a difference.

Alas, it was all only an illusion. The Afghantsi were soon fighting among themselves and then killing one another over control of the benefits that the government had given their organizations. And the children and grandchildren of the Vietnamsi became Afghantsi, as the cycle of death and destruction we so wanted to end continued unabated.

For me, however, the trip completely changed the course of my life.

Chapter 17

Death be not Proud

It seemed my mother would outlive us all, with the East European gene pool she drew from having longevity as one of its major attributes. Her mother lived to ninety-two, her father ninety-nine. Her mother's father lived into his late nineties, and her father's father might have lived as long had he not committed suicide when the market crashed in 1928. My mom made it to ninety-five.

We had celebrated her ninety-fifth birthday in June of 2019 with a gathering of over forty family members on my mountain in Vermont. My mother didn't quite get there. Her mobility had severely decreased in the previous few years, and she mostly made her way around with a walker or a wheelchair. She had flown up from Texas, where she lived with my brother Joe, and met my older sister and her husband at Kennedy Airport in New York. The plan was for her to visit her sister Justine in a nursing home on Long Island, then visit my father's grave, also on Long Island, and then drive up for the party. Shortly after arriving, she slipped trying to get into a car and broke her leg. So, while we all gathered to celebrate her birthday in Vermont, she was lying in a bed in a rehabilitation facility in New York. Through yeoman's work by my son, Dan, we were able to set up a remote connection so we could all sing "Happy Birthday" to her as she stared out at us from a computer screen, a bittersweet moment but the best that could be accomplished under the circumstances.

The Mahoney boys celebrate their mother's 95th birthday. From left: Tim, Brian, Joe, Henry, Peter.

After six weeks, she was finally ready to head home. All five of her sons showed up to check her out of the hospital—Joe and Brian from Texas, Henry and me from Vermont, and Tim from New Hampshire. When my brother Henry and I approached the front desk, the nurse on duty nodded knowingly, "I know where you boys are going!" We must have been an amazing sight, five strapping six-footers fawning over this bedraggled old lady in a wheelchair and jumping to her every command or wish. My mom made the most of the moment, showing off in front of the staff who had befriended her during her stay. They loved it.

The first thing we did when we got her out was to visit my father's gravesite. There, we quietly shared a few yarns about him, and we boys all downed a shot of Irish whiskey and left the bottle at the graveside. As we were leaving, my mother turned in her wheelchair and called back to the grave, "I'll be joining you shortly, Joe." We all pooh-poohed it, told her she was going to live to a hundred and that we'd be celebrating her hundredth birthday with her.

That night, we all stayed together at a rental house. It was a magical night. The Mahoney boys were in fine form, downing shots and smoking herb, something we had always done around the corner or in the other room when our mom was around. This night, we just let it all hang out, a bunch of aging reprobates masquerading as upstanding middle-class citizens, swapping stories of our youthful misadventures and brushes with the law, as she sat there soaking it all in with a knowing smile on her face. She had, after all, bailed almost every one of us out of jail at least once, and she knew way more about many of the things we thought we had kept secret from her than we ever expected. Most of all, it seemed, she was just damned proud of her five boys—proud of who we had become, proud that we had all showed up—and savoring this one final night together with all of us.

She left for Texas the next day, but it became evident soon after that going back to her original living arrangement with my brother Joe was not going to work. The limited mobility she had before the broken leg was gone; she required assistance getting from the bed to the wheelchair or the wheelchair to the toilet. My brother worked at night and slept through most of the day. After my mother spent several hours on the bathroom floor because she couldn't wake Joe, who slept at the far end of the mobile home they shared, we seven children made the painful and difficult decision to move her into an assisted living facility, something our mother had dreaded and resisted for years. At first, she seemed to adapt to it quite nicely. In my final phone conversation with her, she sounded enthusiastic about the increase in social contact with others, something she lacked in the relative isolation of my brother's mobile home. Soon, however, her body just started breaking down, and she was in and out of the hospital with a variety of ailments, soon accompanied by hallucinations and bouts of uncontrolled anger.

She died on the morning of March 7, 2020, just as the COVID pandemic was ramping up in the United States. Her seven children were spread out all over the country, from Maine to California, from Texas to Vermont. Natasha and I were in the Bahamas and at the beginning of our annual get-away-from-the-snow-and-find-a-warm-beach vacation. To complicate matters even more, she had died in Texas but was to be buried with our father at Calverton Cemetery on Long Island, then fast becoming part of the metropolitan New York epicenter for the virus. As can be expected, the funeral did not go well. My two sisters were unable to attend because of the dangers of travel. We tried to get the funeral home to delay the wake until the epidemic quieted down, but they did not have the capacity to hold her body for that long. They told us they would be burying her on a particular day whether anyone showed up or not. The Church canceled her funeral mass, a cruel irony for a woman who had steadfastly adhered to the strictures of her religion her whole life. In the end, we five brothers, along with assorted cousins and uncles, braved the infection risk to attend the funeral. The funeral home agreed to let us hold a one-day wake, but it was sparsely attended. The brothers and some of their family members were there, and a handful of relatives who lived nearby showed up. It wasn't nearly the kind of Mahoney family send-off that our mother deserved.

We tried to rectify that a year later. My older sister, Kathy, organized a memorial event that included a church service, a visit to the cemetery, and an extended family gathering afterward. We flirted with COVID infection again—one person at the gathering tested positive a few days later, but no one else was affected—but it was something that we had to do. We, the seven Mahoney kids, needed to get together to provide a proper send-off for our mother.

It turned out to be the last time the seven of us were together.

A few weeks after the memorial service, my brother Joe—the fifth of the seven—died of cancer. He had been diagnosed with stage four cancer, terminal, but the doctors had told him with treatment, he could live another four or five years. He barely lasted three months. He had just finished chemo before the memorial, and with great effort and in great pain, he managed to attend. He actually looked pretty good and seemed in good spirits. He was a few months short of his sixty-sixth birthday and was counting the days to his retirement. He never made it.

Joe was a proud, gentle, and compassionate free spirit who worked hard and partied harder. He was always ready to lend a helping hand to anyone who needed it. He was the primary caregiver to each of our parents in their final days. He cherished his daughter and doted on his grandchildren. He loved the New York Yankees, rock 'n roll, his Harley and herb. In accordance with his wishes, he was cremated, and he had requested his ashes be scattered over the Pacific Ocean.

In rather quick succession after my brother's death came the deaths of my mother's sister Justine and my father's brother Jack. They were the last two of that generation to go. The Grim Reaper is now busy with the next generation: my brother Joe, three of my Uncle Jack's kids, two of my Aunt Virginia's kids, and one of my Aunt Justine's kids. It seems these days that the only events that stir me from my mountain aerie are funerals. The Catholic religion remains strong in my extended family, and as I attend the funeral masses of my relatives and listen to the somewhat clichéd homilies of the priests, I sincerely envy those who have not lost their faith as I have, whose belief system guarantees reunion of the good in heaven for eternity.

Every once in a while, I wake up in the morning staring death in the face. Not that I'm having a heart attack or anything, just with the stark realization that I'm going to die, just like everybody else, and as I stretch out the miles from my seventieth birthday, that event will most likely come sooner rather than later. On the one hand, death is the most natural of events, one of the very few experiences we all share. On the other hand, contemplating "non-existence" is utterly terrifying, although, on occasion, putting a bullet in my head or some other means of self-destruction has seemed a more tolerable, if less rational, solution than living through whatever the next week might hold for me.

I suppose I believe—believe but don't really know—that there is some sort of existence beyond death, although I probably don't believe the classic Christian heaven/hell scenario (shame on me, I guess, if I meet old St. Peter at the pearly gates, and he says to me, "See, it all does exist, and how's your tolerance for heat these days?"). The question for me is whether there is any consciousness of that continued existence: if somehow the consciousness that is me remains intact or whether it dissipates into something larger to be reformed and repackaged in a way that "me" as a consciousness ceases to exist.

I mean, there it is. Despite all the angst and worry and pain and complications of existence, I don't want to not exist. I suppose there is some evidence—from those who have "died" and come back—that there is some sort of consciousness after death. Most of the major religions have that as a basic tenet for the faithful to hang on to: heaven, nirvana, some blissful state or place where all the trappings of mortal existence fall away, a place or state you can dream about and aspire to that somehow gives meaning to all the pain and suffering that life has foisted on us. But there is always a catch. This blissful state is not guaranteed; you can achieve it only if you are "good," if you follow the rules that define "goodness." If you don't, of course, then, according to Christian dogma, your continued existence is an eternal replication of suffering, or according to the Buddhists, you have to keep doing it all over again until you finally get it right. So, I'm torn about what I want to believe. I am terrified of non-existence, but since I haven't exactly followed the "goodness rules," I'm not all that enthused about eternal damnation. Maybe non-existence is not that bad after all. Maybe non-existence is the blissful state we are all waiting for.

A year after my brother Joe's death, his daughter Dawn organized a memorial ceremony for the scattering of his ashes in the Pacific. Family and friends gathered on a beach south of San Diego, a few hundred yards from the Mexican border. There was no one else on the beach; a recent sewage spill from Tijuana and remnants from a pipeline rupture the previous year had rendered this once pristine stretch of sand an ecological disaster area. We tried our best to ignore the smell and the patches of sticky, black sludge under our feet as we paid tribute to Joe. We shared our stories of him, some funny, some sad, all spotlighting his big heart and free spirit and the unbearable fact that he was gone too soon. A friend of Joe's daughter, a surfer, had volunteered to take the ashes out the requisite hundred yards offshore—the legal requirement—to spread them in the ocean. The surf was angry that day, and the young man on his surfboard had a difficult time knifing his way through the waves. As he was struggling through the water, we on the shore were listening to some of Joe's favorite songs over a loudspeaker. Finally, after about five or so minutes, he reached a spot beyond where the waves were breaking and prepared to release the ashes. Then, a strange and wonderful thing happened. The loudspeaker was playing one of Joe's favorite songs, "Free Bird," and a large seabird swooped in over the surfer and circled over his head as he was pouring the ashes into the ocean. When he was finished and headed for the shore, the bird turned and flew languidly out to sea. I don't believe in much anymore, but as I watched that bird until it disappeared over the horizon, it was hard for me NOT to believe that Joe's spirit had at last found the freedom he craved.

Chapter 18

To Russia for Love

The receptionist buzzed me on the intercom.

"There's someone here to see you, and I *know* you're going to want to meet her!"

Since my initial trip to the Soviet Union in 1987, I had made several more under various circumstances, and I used to joke that my telephone number was probably printed on every restroom wall in Moscow: *Going to New York? Call Peter.* In the late eighties and early nineties, the phone calls from Russians had become a steady flow. They were generally of two varieties.

The first was from Russians who were coming to the United States for the first time and were flying through Kennedy Airport. They had heard all the horror stories about how huge and scary JFK was, and they were asking me to meet them after their international flight and help them make the connection to the domestic flight taking them to wherever they were going. On some occasions, the domestic connection was not until the next day, so I would bring them home, let them stay overnight in my apartment, and I'd bring them back out to the airport the next day.

The second type of phone call was more problematic and becoming more frequent. It was from Russians who were in the United States on a visitor's visa and were looking for some type of off-the-books work. At first, I had tried to be sympathetic and as helpful as I could, although I had no real possibilities to offer anyone. As the frequency of such calls began increasing, I became curter in my replies. As soon as I sensed the direction the conversation was taking, I bluntly asked, "Do you have a green card?" Of course, none of them did, and I quickly concluded the conversation by saying I couldn't help them.

The woman waiting for me at the front desk of the Institute where I had been working since the demise of my Wall Street career had called me under those auspices. She had accompanied a Russian businessman to the U.S. as an interpreter. The business had taken no more than a week or so, and the woman had noticed that the visitor's visa she had entered the country on was good for a year. When the businessman had returned to Russia, she had decided to stay in the U.S. to see what might develop. For several months, she had been traveling around the country, visiting various Americans she had previously met in Moscow, but she was now back in New York, with still about six months left on her visa, short on money, and looking to earn some so she could continue to stay. So there it was: another off-the-books job request. For some gloriously fateful reason, rather than asking if she had a green card, I said, "Let's have lunch."

I suppose it wasn't quite so serendipitous as that. I was at a place, both professionally and personally, where I was looking for a big change in my life. Professionally, I had been working as Director of Administration for the foreign policy think tank for almost five years, the longest stint in one job I had managed in my "career" up to that point. It had initially been exciting and challenging, but the organization was growing rapidly, and my one-man-band style of management was not keeping up. The Board of the Institute decided to hire a Chief Operating Officer over me, and it was soon clear that she and I didn't see eye to eye, and she was setting me up for a termination so she could bring in her own person. I preempted her by submitting a three-month resignation notice to John Mroz, the Institute's president, and was now playing out my remaining time there.

On the personal side, I was in the middle of a divorce from my second wife, Beverly, the dancer with the loft in lower Manhattan. As with my previous marriage, family and social pressure had finally pushed us to "legalize" our long-term relationship, but despite the common protestations that marriage doesn't change anything, it did change things. We had been together for seven years prior to marriage, and the marriage barely lasted two. Among the many issues between us, the fact that my wife—who had recently received a significant inheritance from her grandmother—was determined to keep our finances separate (she said she was afraid I would give her money to my ne'er-do-well brother) was a particular bone of contention for me. In retrospect, the separate finances ultimately made the divorce somewhat less complicated, but there was one thing we owned together—a weekend cabin upstate in Carmel, NY—that was gumming up the works. I loved the place and was trying to find some way to buy out her share, but she was determined to keep it from me. When we first split up, I moved out of the loft where we had lived to an apartment back in Brooklyn, but it was becoming impossible for me to pay the rent on the apartment and the mortgage on the place upstate. I told my estranged wife that I was going to use the cabin for a weekend and then just moved in. She was, of course, apoplectic, but there wasn't anything she could do about it. It had the dual benefit for me of reducing my housing costs (although the transportation costs to get to the city every day from Carmel for work made it pretty much a wash) and putting additional pressure on her to work out some sort of settlement so we could finalize the divorce.

This was my second, utterly failed attempt at marriage, and I pretty much expected it would be my last. The old hippie anarchism was still alive and well in me. Although I had been mostly successful at concealing it in my work life,

I was bouncing off the walls in my personal life. The routine of married life both attracted and repelled me, a comfort and utterly boring. I had been living my life in two-to-three-year bursts, periodically needing to cut ties with the past and strike out in some unknown new direction. This had been my longest relationship and longest job up to that time—oh, my God, stability!—and the pressure within me to break free and run was building.

In the early years of our relationship, we'd had a wild and crazy sex life. We tried just about everything at least once: no bounds, no inhibitions, no strings. Considering this was the dawn of the age of AIDS, we were extraordinarily lucky that our uninhibited behavior didn't have any consequences. Yet perhaps it did. Once we were married, the music turned off, and the lights turned on, and I was looking for the door. I needed to run again; it was only a question of when and where.

This was all happening in the fall of 1991. In August, there had been a coup attempt against Gorbachev by hardliners in the Communist Party leadership who opposed Gorbachev's policies of *glasnost* and *perestroika*. The coup collapsed after two days, and Gorbachev returned to power, but it was Boris Yeltsin who stood on a tank and became the public face of the resistance to the coup. Yeltsin had cut his teeth as a regional leader of the Communist Party and was an early supporter of Gorbachev's reforms. He later became a vocal critic of the reforms as being too moderate. He was elected in early 1991 as president of the reconstituted Russian Republic, and when the Soviet Union dissolved in late 1991 as the various republics declared themselves to be independent countries, Gorbachev lost his power and Yeltsin, as head of the largest now-independent republic, emerged as unquestioned leader.

It seemed to me that history was in the making there, that something new and exciting was possibly going to rise from the ashes, and I wanted to be there when it happened. It was an added bonus that the threat I would leave for Russia put additional pressure on my wife to reach a divorce settlement. My plan was to head off to Russia for a year or so, see what kind of adventure I could fall into, then return to the U.S. and find a new road to travel.

All that played into my lunch invitation. Natasha, the young woman on the phone, had mentioned that she had worked as a high school English teacher in the Soviet Union before she turned to the more lucrative interpreting profession, so I figured that perhaps I could convince her to give me some Russian language lessons in preparation for my looming Russian adventure. Natasha sounded interesting on the phone, but I wasn't quite prepared for the fact that she was drop-dead gorgeous to boot.

Natasha

At lunch, I proposed the language lessons to her. She seemed a little disappointed that was all I had, but I guess she figured a bird in the hand, so she agreed. We made an appointment for the first lesson, but two days later, she called me and said she had gotten a live-in babysitting job for a dentist and his wife who lived down in the Village. She said she would be glad to do the language lessons if we could schedule them during her off time from babysitting, and I agreed.

The first two or three meetings took place in the evenings at the Institute where I worked. We would go through some formal lessons, then sit and chat for a while. It was probably clear very quickly that I was attracted to her, so she let me know that she wasn't interested in any relationship but was willing to become friends if that developed. I agreed to be "only friends," all the while plotting how I might maneuver things to become something more.

I asked her out to the movies and made a huge mistake that almost ended things before they even started. Since we were "only friends," I didn't pay for her ticket, figuring that my paying for the ticket would then constitute a "date." Certainly, I wanted it to be a "date," but since we were "only friends" going out to the movies together, I just thought we would each pay for our own ticket, as any two friends going to the movies would. I later learned that she thought this to be despicable, that I was some kind of miserly cheapskate who wouldn't even pay for a movie ticket for a poor Russian girl, and that except for the fact that she needed the money I was giving her for the language lessons, she probably wouldn't have had anything to do with me after that.

Soon, it became more and more difficult to arrange the lessons in the evenings during the week as her responsibilities as a babysitter increased. Her employers gave her Saturday and Sunday off, but she had to be back by seven on Sunday night. I suggested we could do the lessons at my place up in Carmel on the weekends. She could take the train up on Saturday morning, which I would pay for, and I could drive her back to the city on Sunday evening. She was wary of this arrangement at first—I was, of course, excited about the possibilities it presented—but she ultimately agreed because her life as a babysitter was getting more and more oppressive, and she needed some time and space away from it.

We spent the weekends that fall in radiant friendship. The time spent together became less and less about Russian language lessons and more and more about enjoying one another's company. We talked endlessly about everything, sitting in the morning drinking coffee on the rocks in the middle of the stream that ran through the property or swinging languidly for hours in the hammock in my backyard. She had an infectious laugh and a sharp, sarcastic sense of humor. She wanted to learn all about English curse words, and given my extensive knowledge and practice, I was only too glad to comply with her wishes.

Despite her professed desire to be "only friends," I very much wanted it to become more. It seemed that our weekends together had already been moving in that direction, and I finally decided that this next weekend was going to be the one. I was going to kiss her and see what happened.

This was a big step for me. I have always been painfully shy about making the first move with a woman. After the first move, I am fine, but getting past it has always been a problem for me. Many of the relationships I've had have been with women who got tired of waiting for me and just made the first move themselves. This was okay with me; it eliminated the necessity for me to initiate anything. I just went along for the ride, although those rides tended to be short-lived. Both my marriages had started on such a basis, and neither had been particularly successful. Natasha was a woman that I wanted, and I knew she wasn't going to start anything. It was up to me.

The weekend I had designated in my mind arrived and went as usual. There were the perfunctory language lessons, endless conversations, laughing, joking, and enjoying the pleasure of each other's company. But no kiss. I hadn't planned a particular time to try, just assuming that when the time arrived, I would know it, but as we fell into the usual patterns of our weekends together, I couldn't bring myself to break the pattern with a kiss. Too quickly, Sunday afternoon arrived, and it was time for me to drive her back to the city. I was kicking myself because I had blown my chance. I was just too timid to pull it off.

As we were getting into my car, I just summoned up every ounce of courage I could muster. I jumped out of the car and asked Natasha to follow me. She looked puzzled but came along. I led her out to the little bridge that spanned the stream at the back of the property. I didn't wait for anything, fearing that any delay would dissipate my resolve. When we reached the middle of the little bridge, I turned to her, took her in my arms, and kissed her—the first kiss on a bridge, which would become our lifelong tradition. It was a long, languorous kiss. Natasha again looked puzzled, but to my surprise and delight, she didn't resist.

We said almost nothing to each other on the drive back to the city, each of us, I think, trying to figure out what had just happened and how we were going to respond to it. There was no second kiss when I dropped her off, just perfunctory business arrangements for the following weekend. Sometime during the week, she called me and said she had something to do in the city during the day on Saturday, and she wouldn't be able to make it up to Carmel. I said I could drive into the city Saturday evening and pick her up, and she reluctantly agreed. I would meet her in front of the New York City Library on the corner of Fifth Ave. and 42nd Street at 5 p.m. I got there a little before five and waited.

And waited.

And waited.

Finally, a little after 7 p.m., she showed up with another guy whom she introduced as "just a friend." I think they were both surprised I was still there, and I think the guy was more than a little disappointed. He was probably playing the same just-a-friend-but-hoping-for-more game that I was. At first, I was afraid that it would turn into three friends in New York on a Saturday night, but Natasha quickly and gently shooed the other guy off. She had a speech for me she had been rehearsing all week, and she wanted an audience of one—me—when she delivered it. I suggested a dinner in the city before heading upstate, and we went to the Prince Street Bar down in SoHo.

There, over dinner, she delivered her speech. Apparently, she told me she liked me a lot, but she wasn't ready for any kind of romantic relationship and didn't want me to think that anything along those lines was going to happen, and while she enjoyed the kiss, she didn't want me to do that anymore, and if I agreed to be just friends, she would agree to continue coming to the cabin on the weekends. I say "apparently" because this is what she told me years later that she said, and I apparently agreed. I didn't hear a word of it, though. All I knew was that I had spent two hours worrying that I might not see her again, and that had only redoubled my desire for her. I just wanted to be with her, under any circumstances, because I was convinced that the sparks between us were too hot not to ignite at some point.

They did.

A weekend soon after that, our playful physicality just naturally evolved, and we became lovers. It was such a different experience for me. All my previous relationships had started with sex, which then became the central element of the relationship. This was different, and we both quickly realized that our carefully nurtured friendship was turning into deep, passionate love. It was a beautiful time, but soon the cruel dilemma of our situation started to manifest itself.

Our paths had crossed, but those paths were headed in different directions. I was soon off to Russia to chase my latest adventure. I just assumed at first that Natasha would be coming with me, but she was making more money as a live-in babysitter than she had ever made in the Soviet Union, and her employer was promising to sponsor her for a green card, so the lure of the American dream was tugging insistently at her consciousness. In the end, I got on the plane to Moscow alone, and my Russian girlfriend stayed in the United States.

There were the usual pronouncements of love and fidelity and promises to wait when I left, but in my heart, I was skeptical. I had been through several long-distance relationships, and they ultimately never worked. At some point, one would meet someone close by, and the local relationship would supersede the long-distance one. I felt I had found something special with Natasha, and I didn't want to lose it, but I had little confidence that we could make the long-distance situation work for any length of time.

Over the course of the next several months, I wrote her numerous passionate love letters, some pleading, some demanding, some blatantly erotic. Occasionally, we were able to get a phone connection, but the calls always seemed to degenerate into hurt feelings and unfulfilled expectations. My life in Moscow was not great, but the sheer newness and strangeness of it kept the adrenaline flowing. I had an apartment that one of my Afghantsi friends had found for me, and I managed to pick up a few odds and ends of work for some paltry sums of rubles. I had a small grant that I had gotten from one of the board members of the Institute I used to work for, but mostly, I was living off my credit cards, and I was fast approaching the point where the cards would be maxed out. Yet, somehow, I was sure that if I could convince Natasha to come back to Russia, everything would turn out all right.

I had one last trick up my sleeve. The twenty-fifth anniversary of Vietnam Veterans Against the War was scheduled for the spring of 1992 in New York City, and I had always planned to attend. I already had my return ticket to the U.S., but I had never told Natasha of my plans. The night before my plane was scheduled to leave, I managed to get a phone call from Moscow to Natasha. I didn't tell her I would be in NYC the next day. The next night, I bought a single red rose and called Natasha from the phone booth down the block from where she was living. She commented on how good the connection was, and I told her if she came outside, the connection might be even better.

I started walking up the street toward the apartment building where she was staying, and I saw her come flying out the front door and running down the block into my arms. I gave her the rose and told her I loved her. I never really knew what Natasha's plans were before I showed up that night, but she quit her job the next day and told me she was coming back to Russia with me.

The happy couple shortly after returning to Russia.

Now that she had ostensibly changed her plans for me, I was going to have to change my plans for her. If I wanted to be together with her—and I surely did—then my plan to stay in Russia for a year would need to be significantly revised. I had convinced her to return home, but now I would have to commit to a much longer time there to be with her.

It turned out to be nine years.

Shortly after we had returned to Russia, I proposed to her, and she said yes, although marriage wasn't something she wanted to jump into quickly. It was like, yeah, we'll get married sometime in the indistinct future. That worked for me. After two failed marriages, I wasn't looking to plunge headfirst into another one. We did move in together, however. Babushka Tonia, Natasha's grandmother, had been given a tiny one-room apartment by the government as the widow of a soldier killed in the Great Patriotic War (WWII to those in the West). Babushka Tonia, however, preferred to stay at the family dacha in Bakovka, so Natasha and I were allowed to move into the apartment.

Babushka Tonia was a wisp of a woman in her eighties who looked like a strong wind would blow her away. She was actually the sister of Natasha's grandmother, who had died of cancer at the age of forty-three and had begged her sister to take care of her children when she was gone. Tonia had married just before the war and had a child of her own when her husband was sent off as a soldier to defend Moscow from the onslaught of the Germans and was killed in the effort. Tonia was living with her husband's family at the time, and because of the shortages brought on by the war, her husband's family refused to provide food or milk for Tonia's baby, and the baby died of starvation.

The apartment she gave us was on the fourteenth floor of a building located in Sovhoz Moskovskii, a suburb about ten kilometers southwest of the Moscow Outer Ring Road along Kievskaya Shosse. Moskovskii, at the time, was the largest greenhouse complex in the country. Natasha's father had been the chief engineer of the complex before Natasha's parents divorced and he moved away. Natasha's mother still lived in Moskovskii in the same apartment where Natasha had grown up.

The first order of business for me was to improve my income. It seemed that my prospects were limited. Despite Natasha's best efforts, I was not fluent in Russian, and I was limited to short, functional everyday phrases that could get me from here to there, but not much more. My comprehension was a bit better, but there are many other factors involved in comprehension other than spoken language, like context, facial expression, intonation, and body language. In addition, Natasha and I were inseparable once we were both in Russia. One key motivator to learning a language is that the environment forces you to learn it. I had a built-in translator wherever I went, so that environmental compulsion was never there for me. It seemed somewhat unlikely that any fledgling Russian company—nor any of the sprinkling of American entrepreneur/gold-diggers trying to make their fortunes in the burgeoning gangster/capitalist economy of Russia—would have a need for a non-Russian-speaking employee.

There was, however, another promising sector for employment that was starting to develop. The U.S. government was ramping up its foreign aid program in Russia. The United States Agency for International Development (USAID) started throwing money around in Russia, and soon, a number of U.S. non-profit organizations—most of whom had no prior experience in the former Soviet Union—started setting up shop in Moscow in anticipation of grabbing their share of those development dollars floating around.

I had no prior experience in the international development field, and I remembered USAID from Vietnam as primarily a cover for the CIA. After several interviews with various organizations, I was offered a job with an organization called World Learning. I was not their first choice, but when the preferred candidate declined, they turned to me. The project director who interviewed me was an old hippie whom I made sure to regale with some of my VVAW yarns. Also, the fact that I was already located in Moscow saved them some money in terms of the relocation costs associated with bringing someone from the States. So, after scuffling around for nine months, picking up a few rubles here and there in income, and mostly maxing out my credit cards to pay expenses, I now had a real job with a real hard currency salary to go with it.

Hard currency meant dollars instead of rubles. In the early nineties, there were two economies in Moscow: the hard currency economy and the ruble economy. The hard currency economy was much more expensive, but the goods were imported and of higher quality. There were hard currency grocery stores and clothing stores. Many so-called luxury items like computers, cellphones, appliances, and such were only available for hard currency. In the ruble economy, goods were much less costly, but they were generally lower-quality Russian-made goods and available in limited supply. The key element of the hard currency stores was that most of them accepted credit cards, while in those days, ordinary Russian stores dealing in rubles did not. For me, in the first months I was there, this was critical. Despite the enormous disparity in food prices between the hard currency stores and the ruble stores, I shopped at the hard currency stores with my credit cards since I had very little cash available in dollars or rubles. Many expats living in Moscow at the time lived exclusively on the hard currency economy, making Moscow one of the most expensive cities in the world. Once Natasha returned and I got my job, we were able to take advantage of both economies, buying everyday items like food on the cheaper ruble economy but having the wherewithal to shop on the hard currency economy for those things unavailable otherwise.

My landing a hard currency job also altered the timing of our marriage plans. The job came with "benefits" like healthcare and, much to Natasha's delight, a paid R&R out of the country. These things were only available to her, however, if we were married. I was scheduled to go to the U.S. for three weeks of orientation and training for my new job, so we decided that Natasha would come with me and that we would "legalize" our marriage with a city hall ceremony while there and then do a full-blown Russian wedding with family after we returned.

It turned out to be not as easy as we expected. Natasha had to apply for a visitor's visa at the U.S. Embassy in Moscow, and despite the fact that she had previously received such a visa and had returned to Russia within the legally mandated time limit, her visa request was denied the first time she applied. The consular officials had a built-in assumption that any young, single Russian woman looking to get a visitor's visa was probably planning to find and marry an American man in order to stay in the U.S. Certainly, marriage was in our plans, but staying in the U.S. at that point was not.

In those days, there was no waiting period if you were

rejected; you could reapply the next day if you wanted. So, we did. This time, I accompanied Natasha to the embassy. Natasha filled out the paperwork and handed it in, and then we sat in a room with all the other applicants. When her name was called, she went to one of the windows at the front of the room for her interview. I was not allowed to accompany Natasha to the window, but I stood about three feet behind her and stared hard at the consular officer while he interviewed her.

He approved the visa.

Later that day, after Natasha had picked up her passport with the visa in it, by chance, we met the young consular official who had interviewed her outside the embassy. He told us that approving the visa was a risk for him, that according to the procedure he was supposed to follow, she should have been rejected. He also mentioned the supposition of marriage and staying in the U.S. attached to young Russian females, and we assured him that he had made the right decision and nothing like that was in our plans.

I had one more hurdle to overcome to take Natasha's hand in marriage—the approval of her father. Ivan Streltsov had been born in a small town near Voronezh, the descendant of Cossacks who served in the *streltsy* (shooters), an elite unit of the Imperial Army that, among other things, served as the bodyguards for the Czars. After completing his compulsory military service as a young man, Ivan was standing on a train platform waiting for the train to take him home when he saw a train getting ready to leave, heading in the opposite direction. On a whim, he jumped on this train instead and ended up in Vladivostok on the far eastern coast of the Soviet Union. There, he met up with a kindly sea captain who hired him onto his crew, and Ivan began a ten-year stint in the Russian Merchant Marine before he met Natasha's mother, who convinced him to give up the sea for her.

Ivan was salt of the earth, unassuming, and with a ready smile and a crushing handshake despite missing the tips of several fingers. I suspect he had some serious doubts about this strange American who wanted to marry his daughter, but he was always cordial and hospitable to me when Natasha and I visited him and his second wife. One night, the women disappeared, and I was left alone with Ivan, with me sitting on the couch and Ivan in a chair across from me. Between us was a low table with four bottles of vodka and an array of *zakuski*—appetizers such as cold cuts and pickled vegetables that Russians eat immediately after downing a shot of vodka—that had been provided by Ivan's wife, Katya. I was concerned that it was just the two of us; Ivan spoke no English, and my Russian left much to be desired. I quickly realized that this was not about talking; it was about drinking. Ivan kept laughing and pouring shots, and I kept looking him in the eye and downing the shots he poured. I pretty much knew I would never be able to keep up with Ivan, but I did my best before I finally rolled over on the couch and fell asleep. Apparently, I did enough.

I passed the test.

I left for the States a few weeks before Natasha to undertake my orientation and training in D.C., then met her in New York over the Christmas holidays. We went to City Hall, applied for a marriage license, and made our appointment for the ceremony two days later. There was a small jewelry shop across Broadway from City Hall, and we went there to see about rings. We bought two simple gold wedding bands, but there was one—very expensive—engagement ring that Natasha clearly had fallen in love with. I had bought her a relatively inexpensive engagement ring in Russia when I proposed to her—I am always a stickler for proper ceremonies, so I had made the full-blown down-on-my-knees-with-the-ring-in-hand proposal—but this ring was a real flasher. She wanted it, so I slapped down my American Express credit card to pay for it. Except Amex decided they wouldn't approve the purchase unless I could prove I had sufficient funds in a bank account somewhere to cover it. My profligate use of my credit cards in Russia had come back to haunt me. I hadn't yet received my first paycheck from my new job, so my bank account was leaner than a junkyard dog. I didn't have the funds, Amex wouldn't approve the purchase, and we left the store utterly embarrassed.

Two days later, we tied the legal knot, then Natasha flew back to Moscow, and I went back to D.C. to finish my orientation and training. I didn't forget about that ring. I finally got my first paycheck, which just barely covered the price of the ring. I cashed my check rather than putting it into the bank and went back to New York to the little jewelry shop across from City Hall with a wad of cash in my pocket. I wasn't going to entrust this transaction to Amex again. The ring had not been sold, so I bought it. When I presented the ring to Natasha on my return to Moscow, it pretty much wiped out whatever remaining doubts that might have lingered from the movie ticket incident. I was not the miserly cheapskate I had seemed to be then.

As part of the bureaucratic process associated with two people of differing citizenships marrying, it was necessary to register our marriage certificate at the American Embassy upon our return to Russia. This was the first step in setting us up for moving back to the States if and when we decided to do so. The process was relatively routine and was handled by the consular section of the Embassy. When I approached the consular window, who was sitting there but the officer who had approved Natasha's visa and whom we had assured when we met him outside the embassy that we were not going to get married when we were in the States. If he recognized me, he didn't show it. Hey, at least we came back like we said we would.

Although we were "legal," the quickie City Hall ceremony didn't really suffice. We both craved a massive celebration with family and friends, so we decided on a church wedding in Russia the following July. I invited my parents to attend, and, somewhat to my surprise, they agreed to come. In addition, to my greater surprise, my mother's father also agreed to come, along with my mother's sister, my cousin, and my niece. My grandfather was ninety-five years old and confined to a wheelchair, so it was no small effort for him to travel anywhere, much less to Russia. Given my untraditional paths in life, I didn't think I was necessarily his favorite grandson, but I was the oldest grandson, and perhaps more importantly, it had been one of his dreams in life to see Red Square before he died.

Several months before the wedding was to take place, Natasha went to one of the biggest Orthodox cathedrals in Moscow to arrange the ceremony. They told her no problem, just come back a week or two before the event to make the final arrangements. The day after we picked up my family contingent from the States, we went back to the cathedral to make the final arrangements.

Disaster struck.

It seems we had chosen a date that was within the Fast of Peter and Paul, an observance in the Orthodox Church that is similar to Lent. The representative at the cathedral said sorry that we didn't notice this before, but no marriage ceremonies are performed during the period of the Fast. We had all these plans for a marriage celebration, and suddenly, no place for the ceremony.

Luckily, my family had arrived a week or so before the marriage was scheduled, so we asked a friend of Natasha's to take them on some sightseeing tours while Natasha and I were racing all around Moscow, trying to find a church where we could get married. At one church, after Natasha had again been refused, she was walking back to the car, crying. An old woman asked her what was the matter, and Natasha tearfully told her the sad tale. The old woman said there was one remote possibility; she had heard that the Patriarch of the Russian Orthodox Church had once granted a special dispensation for a wedding during the Fast of Peter and Paul.

Skeptical but desperate, we drove to the headquarters of the Russian Orthodox Church at the Danilov Monastery and just walked in, not knowing where to go or who to talk to. We ended up meeting with the bishop on duty, who listened to Natasha's story, asked her, then me, a few questions, and then told Natasha to write the story down on a piece of paper. Natasha wrote four pages; she didn't want to leave out any of the details. The bishop read what she had written, smiled, and then dictated a one-paragraph summary of her story, which Natasha wrote down. He told us to wait, then returned in about forty-five minutes with the dispensation signed by Patriarch Alexey. The only stipulation was that the marriage needed to be performed in a small, out-of-the-way church, not at the big cathedral downtown.

That was an easy choice: the Transfiguration Church at Peredelkino, a small village located about forty minutes from the center of Moscow. Peredelkino had been something of a writer's colony since the 1930s, famous as the place where Boris Pasternak wrote *Dr. Zhivago*. The house where Pasternak had lived—and ultimately died—in Peredelkino had been turned into a museum, and Pasternak was even buried in the Peredelkino cemetery. Peredelkino is the next village over from Bakovka, the village where Natasha had been born and where her mother's family still kept the former family house as a dacha. The Transfiguration Church was the family's church, and many of Natasha's ancestors were buried in the Peredelkino cemetery. We drove directly to Peredelkino from the Patriarchy with dispensation in hand and arranged the wedding for the original day planned. I had the sense that perhaps the wedding could have been arranged without the dispensation if enough dollars were to change hands, but Natasha claimed this was just a manifestation of my cynical nature.

We had a traditional Russian Orthodox ceremony, with candles and crowns and the like, and a beautiful choir singing in the background. After the ceremony—which Natasha later told me had been shortened somewhat in deference to my visiting relatives—there was a quick round of vodka shots and champagne in the parking lot in front of the church. My dad and Natasha's dad were already starting to bond, despite no common spoken language between them, two old seamen with a taste for the grape. During these festivities, my grandfather was sitting in his wheelchair near the entrance to the church, and several old women entering the church dropped some rubles in his lap, apparently mistaking him for a beggar. I don't think my cranky old grandfather appreciated the humor in the situation.

After the wedding, I plunged into my new job, working as the Country Director for the first "NGO Development Project" in Russia. This was supposedly a project where American NGOs would partner with nascent Russian NGOs, and the American organizations would help the Russian ones develop their capacity. The program funded forty-three "partnerships." Many of these consisted of little more than an exchange of mutual collaboration faxes between the two organizations, and, of course, the American organizations were the ones who applied for, received, and controlled the funds. As the program was getting up and running, we had a visit from some muck-ity-muck USAID bureaucrat from Washington. I was called upon to brief him on the program, and, in my neophyte zeal, I was waxing philosophical about how we were going to prepare and strengthen the Russian organizations so that, soon, they could start receiving USAID funds directly. He sat there for a few moments, listening to me and polishing his glasses, then told me abruptly, "This program is not about giving money to Russian organizations. This program is about giving money to American organizations."

Lesson learned.

I lasted in the job for two years, becoming more cynical about the work as I went on. I immensely enjoyed working with the Russian organizations and the idealists in them, testing out their newfound freedom wings as they tried to build a better society from the ruins of the old. Many hoped, as did I, that the way forward was to examine the past and retain those elements of life worth preserving—a world-class education system free and available to all; a health care system that, while lacking a bit in quality, was free and available to all; a social safety net that provided the basics of life for all; and a strong sense of common purpose and cooperation—even while taking advantage of the opportunities the new freedoms and burgeoning post-Soviet economy might provide.

However, the U.S. government—and its principal agent, USAID—had a far different agenda. Their aim was to destroy every last vestige of the previous communist society—both the good and the bad—and replace it with a cutthroat capitalist economy that would make the states of the former Soviet Union dependent on—and ultimately subservient to—the will of the U.S. government.

Under any circumstances, the first stage of capitalism is gangsterism. Without significant regulation, unfettered capitalism is violent and merciless. People tend to forget that men like Astor, Vanderbilt, Rockefeller, Carnegie, and Morgan amassed their fortunes using tactics that are today the hallmarks of organized crime: intimidation, violence, corruption, conspiracies, and fraud. They were the robber barons before slick public relations techniques later dubbed them "captains of industry" and philanthropists.

The initial insertion of capitalist economics into the former Soviet Union followed the same pattern as early American capitalism. A few unscrupulous men quickly amassed fortunes, achieving their ends by any means necessary with few legal or societal restraints to hinder them. The risk of success could be high. Wealthy businessmen could turn overnight into bullet-riddled corpses, as Paul Tatum—an American entrepreneur and owner of a Moscow hotel—found out in 1996 when his dispute with his Russian partners was resolved by the business end of a Kalashnikov machine gun in a Moscow Metro station. Every legitimate business had to have a *krisha*, or "roof" in Russian. It was protection money the company paid to the local Russian mafia to continue to operate. Of course, if your business was highly profitable, your *krisha* could suddenly become your partner or could simply expropriate the business and make it their own.

For ordinary Russians, the onslaught of the capitalist economy was devastating. The communist economy—while bureaucratic, repressive, and offering limited possibilities—had been predictable. If you followed the rules, you could be fairly certain of a frugal but comfortable life. You didn't have to worry about a job or where to live, or whether your kids would get a decent education. In the early nineties, nothing was certain anymore for ordinary Russians. As the assets of the State were sold off or simply expropriated by private interests, there was no longer a guarantee of work. Factories were closed, and enterprises stopped paying their workers, some of whom continued showing up to work for months, even though they were not being paid, because they didn't know what else to do. Whole towns were plunged into economic desperation as the factories the towns had been built around ceased to function. The average life span of a Russian male dropped precipitously from sixty-five in 1987 to fifty-seven in 1994. Needless to say, large portions of the Russian population were following the example of their erstwhile leader, Boris Yeltsin, and popping the top off the vodka bottle at every opportunity.

I could see all this happening around me, but I seldom ventured outside of the safe cocoon of family and work that I had constructed. As the in-country head of a program responsible for handing out U.S. government money, I was the guest of honor wherever I went. I made the rounds of conferences and workshops, giving speeches promoting the "Third Sector" and generally relishing the special attention afforded me. When the confrontation between Yeltsin and the parliament over his highly unpopular "shock therapy" economic reforms—proposed and promoted, of course, by the U.S. government—turned violent in October of 1993, I stayed in our apartment and watched it all on CNN like the rest of the world. Unlike some other expats who later bragged about how close they were able to get to the tanks that were shelling the parliament building, I wanted no part of any armed confrontation. Been there, done that.

My lack of desire to feed my adrenaline addiction was due to another momentous event on the horizon in my family life: Natasha and I had decided to try to have a baby. I had long since given up any hope or even desire to have children of my own. I had settled into the role of perpetual uncle: visit, play, and go. Leave the responsibility of child-rearing to others. I didn't know if I could be a good father. I didn't know if I could shoulder the commitment that fatherhood required, particularly at the age of forty-seven, as I was then. My experience in life was of needing to periodically pick up and go, leaving everything behind, and starting over somewhere new. In my mind, children were a lifetime responsibility, and I wasn't sure if it was a responsibility I was capable of taking on. Of course, I was already a father, at least biologically so, and had already reneged—however inadvertently—on my fatherly responsibilities, but I wasn't aware of any of that at the time. What I knew was that fatherhood was going to fundamentally alter the trajectory of the rest of my life. It was a risk, but the love I felt for Natasha made the risk seem worthwhile.

Once we confirmed Natasha's pregnancy in late 1994, a key decision for us to make was where she would give birth. Many prospective parents—particularly expats—didn't trust the Russian medical establishment, and those who could afford it left Russia to give birth in the U.S. or Europe. We seriously considered this option, but in early 1995, the city of Moscow opened a modern, state-of-the-art birthing clinic, available for free to all but with special arrangements for those who could pay. We visited the clinic, met with the doctors, and made our choice: Natasha would give birth in Russia.

The cost for "special arrangements"—about $400—was nothing compared to the cost of leaving the country. For our money, Natasha got a private room, a better menu, and the services of the best doctor at the clinic. A key element of the "special arrangements" for me was to be present at the birth of my child. In Russia, fathers were not even allowed into the hospital when their wives gave birth, much less be present at the birth itself. A common sight was a man standing outside the hospital, looking up at the window where his wife was holding the newborn child for the father to see. The husband didn't get to see his wife and child in person until four days after the birth when they were released from the hospital.

The doctors were extremely wary of me being present at the birth. The head doctor told me there would be lots of blood and maybe I would faint at the sight. I told her I had been in Vietnam and that the sight of lots of blood was something I had experienced before. In the end, they reluctantly agreed, primarily because I was paying for it.

On May 25, 1995, my son, Danila, was born. About a year and a half later, on January 1, 1997, my daughter, Anastasia, was born. Our son was named after a famous character in Russian fairy tales, Danila Master, the hero of "The Stone Flower" and "The Mountain Master." Natasha and I both loved the name Anastasia, but the Russian nickname for Anastasia was Nastia. We were worried that sticking a girl with that name in an English-speaking environment would not be doing her any favors, but when we came up with Stacia as an alternative nickname, our fears were allayed. For me, the die of fatherhood was irrevocably cast. I was in it up to my eyeballs, with all the joy, pain, confusion, and responsibility that went along with it. After Anastasia was born, Natasha intimated that she was ready for more, but I said we had one of each and that everybody's happy, so let's stop here. I wasn't interested in another sprawling Mahoney clan like the one I had grown up in. I had seen the economic impact of a large family on my parents and how each new mouth to feed kept us in perpetual debt.

I lost my Country Director job shortly before Danya was born. I had excellent relations with USAID and with the Russian organizations we were trying to help, but I was not too good at the politics of dealing with American development organizations, particularly my own home office. This ultimately cost me my job. My stint as Country Director, however, had made me known to most of the players in the USAID NGO sector, so I was able to scrape together enough work as a consultant to keep food on the table, but the work was sporadic and not nearly as lucrative as my previous job.

One of the first gigs I got was working for the Russian American Press and Information Center or RAPIC. 1996 was a presidential election year in Russia, and Boris Yeltsin was in serious trouble. His shock therapy economic reforms were wildly unpopular, and the Communist candidate for president—Gennady Zyuganov—seemed poised in the early going to soundly defeat Yeltsin. A Russian journalist associated with RAPIC had developed a network of regional journalists from around the country and was assembling their reports into a newsletter named *"Vybor Regioni,"* or "Choice of the Regions." I edited the English language version of this newsletter.

The first reports only confirmed the conventional wisdom. Yeltsin was despised, both by the regional leaders who wanted more autonomy from Moscow and the general populace that had borne the brunt of his disastrous economic policies. People wanted to go back to the relative safety and comfort of the old regime. Zyuganov, the communist, was clearly the choice of the regions. As the weeks went by, however, things began to change. More and more reports were claiming that massive amounts of money were being poured into the regions, and soon, regional leaders who had previously heaped scorn on Yeltsin began to sing his praises. Pensions and back wages, which had not been paid, in some cases for years, were suddenly up to date. The Yeltsin campaign was throwing around money like a drunken sailor, and, given the reputation of the man himself, it was an apt description. It had the desired effect. Despite suffering a serious heart attack weeks before the run-off election, Yeltsin handily beat Zyuganov to remain the Russian president. But there was much discussion about where all this money had come from. A Russian friend of mine—whose company did large amounts of public relations for the Yeltsin campaign and received generous compensation for its efforts—had no doubt about its origin: he was convinced the money came from the U.S. government.

Shortly after the election, my friend Gleb—who had traded in his beat-up old Zhiguli for a chauffeur-driven Mercedes—came to me with a job offer. I had met Gleb on a flight from New York to Moscow, and it turned out he was an avid basketball player. When I told him I also enjoyed playing hoops, he invited me to participate in a weekly two-hour run he was involved in at a university gym near Yugo Zapadnaya metro station, which was only about twenty minutes from where I lived in Moskovskii. Although I hadn't played for a number of years, I eagerly accepted his offer. When I first got there, I quickly realized this was no casual schoolyard pick-up game. This was more like the Russian version of "The Cage" at West 4th Street in New York City: highly skilled and motivated hoopsters who played for keeps and took no prisoners. I was totally out of my league. The fact that I was the only American who had crashed this all-Russian game made it all the sweeter for many of them to wipe the floor with my face.

It was a struggle, but I kept coming back for more. The athleticism I had relied on when I was younger was long gone. The first time I jumped up for a rebound, I was back on the floor before the ball even got to me. I used to stay in the air a lot longer than that! But one thing I had going for me was defense. As a benchwarmer in high school, my job in practice had been to play defense against the starters. I got pretty good at it and enjoyed shutting down the hotshot BMOC. I wasn't about to shut down anyone in this game, but I made them work hard for what they got. I set screens, boxed out, made the extra pass, and occasionally scored a put-back. Over time, I earned the respect of the other players, not for my skills, which didn't match theirs, but for my love of the game, which did.

Gleb's job offer to me was to work in the new joint venture he was creating with some Russian and European partners, apparently funding it in part with some of his proceeds from the election. The pay would be minimal, in rubles, but I would get a piece of equity in the firm. If the venture succeeded, there would be a hefty pay-off for me down the line. I decided, literally, to go for the gold. If I couldn't be part of a new and exciting transformation of society, then maybe I could make some bucks instead.

The idea was a good one: to create a Western-style book club in Russia. Russians love books, and one of the achievements of communist society was a close-to-one-hundred-percent literacy rate among the population. Outside of the major metropolitan areas, however, books were hard to come by. *Knijni Klub Dvatsit Pervoi Vek*—Twenty-First Century Book Club—signed contracts with all the major Russian publishing firms for their product. We produced our first catalog and started to solicit memberships. Within six months, we had more than a million registered members, and sales from the first catalog were strong. But distribution was an ongoing issue—the Russian Post Office was not one of communism's success stories. Still, enough books arrived and were paid for that we turned a small profit. We put together a second catalog that was even more ambitious than the first and sent it out to our million-plus members. We were poised to reap the fruits of our labors.

Instead, we reaped the whirlwind.

On 17 August 1998, the Russian government devalued the ruble, defaulted on domestic debt, and declared a moratorium on repayment of foreign debt. A few short weeks after that, the ruble had lost two-thirds of its value against the dollar. Most of the major Russian publishing companies had started printing their books in Europe. European printers were more reliable than Russian printers at that point and delivered a much higher quality product. The publishers got caught in an untenable bind: they had major hard currency expenses but a ruble income. Eighty percent of the books in our second catalog were ones we couldn't deliver because the publishers were unable to pay their printing bills.

The ruble crisis sounded the death knell for the book club. As with any start-up, we were operating on a thin margin. There was no backup financing available during the crisis, and with no funds, things quickly fell apart. I was back on the Moscow streets with no job, diminishing funds, and a family to take care of.

The ruble crisis also sounded the death knell for the Yeltsin regime. We woke up one morning and found out that Yeltsin had resigned, and an unknown bureaucrat named Vladimir Putin had been appointed acting president. Putin was a former KGB agent who had started his political career in the Saint Petersburg city government of Mayor Anatoly Sobchak. When Sobchak lost the mayoral election in 1996, Putin moved on to Moscow and—like Stalin had—made himself useful in a variety of anonymous bureaucratic positions where he could wield behind-the-scenes power. Most Russians had never even heard of him before he succeeded Yeltsin.

By this time, I had had my fill of Russia. The feelings of adventure had long since worn off, and the difficulty of daily life was becoming a burden. After the failure of the book club, I had no real prospects there other than a continued scuffling for a meager existence. I wanted more than that for my family, and it seemed that would only be possible back in the States. Natasha and I had often talked about returning to the U.S., but it had always been a somewhat theoretical conversation. I think Natasha was hoping that I would agree to stay in Russia, and, at times, I considered the possibility. But now, I was set on leaving, and when Natasha sensed my determination, she agreed. The biggest issue for her was telling her parents, particularly her mother. For nine years, I had been golden to them, the man who brought their daughter back to Russia. Now, inevitably, I would be the man who took their daughter away from them again.

I started looking for stateside jobs, hoping to parlay my USAID work in Russia into some type of a position in a home office somewhere. I assumed we would end up in the Washington, D.C., area since that was where most of the USAID contractors had their offices. It didn't work out that way. I did a telephone interview with a small environmental organization in Vermont that had a USAID-funded program running in Russia. They called me back and actually flew me to the States for an in-person interview. I remember walking around the streets of Montpelier, breathing the clean fresh air, basking in the quiet serenity of this rural state capitol, and thinking how wonderful it would be to bring my family back to live in Vermont rather than some congested metropolitan area like D.C. or New York. My wish was granted. I got the job.

I had left for Russia as an unrepentant adventurer, running

away from the failures of my past as I had so many times before. I returned to the States nine years later with a wife, two kids, and the awesome, terrifying responsibility of being the head of a family.

Running away was no longer an option.

Chapter 19

A Letter to My Children

Dear Danya and Anastasia:

This book is for you, my children. If no one else ever reads what I have written here but you, then my efforts will not have been in vain. I wanted you to know who I was and what I did before I became your dad.

Neither of you probably remembers much about our arrival in America. You were both so young. It was a traumatic time for me. I had a job, but we had little else. The remnants of my previous stateside life consisted of a few boxes of memorabilia in my brother Henry's garage. We were literally starting from scratch. But we did it. Your mother and I worked hard, saved our money, and within a year, we had a car and a house, and our little family had settled into a quiet, laid-back life in rural Vermont. The house was small, but it was ours.

I was concerned about how you two would adjust. Neither of you spoke English when we first arrived in the States. I thought you would need to get special language education before you could start attending school. But I was surprised when the school just put you into classes without any preconditions. I had read about how kids your age were just sponges for language, but I didn't really believe it until I saw you guys just flip the switch and start speaking English within a few weeks. What particularly amazed me was when you, Danya, who learned to read in English but already knew the Russian alphabet, just picked up a Russian book and started reading it.

That first year back from Russia was one of the happiest times I can remember, but our little world got turned upside down by my job. The organization I worked for had decided to bid on a USAID project in Ukraine and wanted to put me in the bid as the in-country Director of Finance and Administration. After finally getting us back to America and settled, I had no desire to pack up everyone and leave again, but I agreed because I didn't think we had a chance to win the bid. Unfortunately, we won. I negotiated that I would go for a year only, but after uprooting the family to Kyiv, when the year was up, I was told there was no job for me back in the home office.

On the street again.

I wanted desperately to keep our family in our little house in the woods in Vermont, but there just wasn't any work there unless you were a lumberjack or a ski bum. After three months of fruitless searching, I finally landed a job in Boston at double the rate of pay I had previously been making. Thus began our life as middle-class suburbanites.

In writing this book, I've thought a lot about the choices in life I made and why I made them. I've always been an idealist, even as many of the ideals I have committed to—religion, patriotism, the anti-war movement, international development—have become tarnished in the light of day. It is ironic that the one ideal I never aspired to, the American Dream, is the one that I seem to have been most successful at. I never set out to chase the Dream; I was just trying to provide for my family.

It is that decision, however, that troubles me the most. Oh, I had long since given up my activist life before you guys came into my life. My pursuit of "universal justice" had degenerated into political arguments with friends and relatives and occasional op-eds in the local newspaper. I wanted to protect you, and I made the choice that the best way to do that was to create a little cocoon of safety around you, to fill it with all the material things my middle-class income could afford, and provide you with the best education to give you a chance to pursue your dreams.

I tried to retain my principles, unlike so many others I knew whose moral and political outlook morphed with age and affluence, but I felt powerless to change the big things that were wrong in the world, so I stopped trying and merely cheered from the sidelines for those who never stopped. Yet in that decision, I think I failed you. And I must take my rightful place in the Boomer generation, which had such promise and delivered so little.

Boomers had the potential to be a revolutionary generation, a demographic bulge with the numbers and the power to alter the trajectory of post-war militarism, but we utterly failed in the task that was given us. We in this country have been dancing on the edge of the precipice for years now. The dustbin of history is littered with the carcasses of great nations that failed to respect the ideals they were founded on, nations whose lust for power outstripped their ability to wield it. We could very well be poised to join them.

Sure, when Boomers were young, some of us were loud, irreverent, and irritatingly visible, and many of the causes we championed were forced into the mainstream agenda through our advocacy and actions. But the anthem of the sixties counterculture—sex, drugs, and rock 'n roll—was more about self-indulgence than progressive politics and paved the way for the greed-soaked materialism that followed. Oh, sure, we were able to effect marginal changes in the perception of acceptable norms for things like civil rights, women's rights, and LGBTQ rights, but, as the age of Trumpism has clearly demonstrated, the racism, sexism, and homophobia that has always permeated American society had only retreated into the shadows. For a time, it was expressed only in groups of like-minded bigots, but it was ready to slither out into the light of day once the orange-haired buffoon made bigotry acceptable again. Sure, we want to take credit for forcing an end to the Vietnam War, but we never changed the rampant militarism of post-WWII America, and American soldiers have continued to fight and die in foreign countries for no reason that has anything to do with the national security of this country. Sure, we want to take credit for bringing down a president—Nixon—who abused the power of his office, but our government is now even more unaccountable to the people it is supposed to represent. Sure, there are still hard-core, determined, unreconstructed progressives among the Boomers, but we are a minority, as we always have been. The simple fact is that Boomers have formed the core of support for every conservative president to be elected since Nixon in 1972, culminating in the abomination who disgraced the Oval Office as the forty-fifth president, demonstrating again the quintessential American penchant for believing the spiel of the snake oil salesman.

I naïvely thought that Bernie Sanders could be the savior of the Boomers, that his bids for the presidency could finally bring the ideals we had fought for into the halls of power. Despite the enormous enthusiasm he generated and despite the fact that the policies he advocated—branded as extreme and radical by those who had the most to lose if they were implemented—came to be supported by a majority of the people, it was all a quixotic exercise in futility. Bernie's greatest attribute was that he's a truly decent man. It was also, ultimately, his greatest weakness. His innate decency required him to play by the rules, even as those who opposed him broke the rules, changed the rules, or simply ignored the rules whenever it suited them. Bernie challenged the establishment, and the establishment rose up in all its might and smashed him into submission. So our American system of government of the people, by the rich, for the rich continues unabated.

The American political cycle continues. Republicans take power and, somehow, are able to implement anything and everything they and their bankrollers can come up with. Ordinary people get fed up with being pissed on by the rich and decide to vote for the Democrats. Democrats take power and, somehow, can't get shit done. Oh, we tried, they say, but this, that, or some other thing prevented us from accomplishing what we said we would. People get pissed off at the Democrats because they do almost nothing, then vote again for Republicans, and the cycle starts all over again. And it is the Boomers—that scared, selfish generation I am a part of, clutching at the material things that define our existence—that have been the backbone of this depressing and destructive American political cycle.

Boomers are dying off; we are no longer the statistical majority. The world is now yours, my children. I don't know if the world created by the failures of my generation can be saved or if this book will be nothing more than pages fluttering in the nuclear wind or rotting away in the coming environmental disaster. Perhaps it is too late. Perhaps Mother Earth has had enough of this cancer called humanity and is about to apply radiation or chemotherapy to rid herself of us.

I don't know.

I do know that if we are to survive, we must find a more just, more humane approach to organizing our economic activity than capitalism. I know that humans must learn again that we are a part of nature, not the masters of it, and learn again how to live in harmony with our environment. I know we must find a way to govern ourselves for the benefit of all and not be ruled over by governments that protect themselves and the interests of the few at the expense of the aspirations of the many. And I know that we will need to do more than simply vote to achieve such a goal. I know that humans have used war and violence against one another, it seems, since our advent as a species, but we have reached the point where this trait, if continued, will lead to our extinction.

I tried and failed to change the world, but I tried. I don't need to be silent when asked the question, "Where were you when ...?" I hope that each of you, in turn, will be able to answer that question with pride. I'm not going to give you clichés about only needing love or unattainable utopias that can be imagined but never achieved. All I can give you is this book. I hope that reading about my life can help you understand what you must do in the world I have left you. I don't have the answers; you must find them yourselves. But know one thing: of all the things I have ever done in my life, you two are my greatest accomplishments.

All my love,
Dad

About Atmosphere Press

Founded in 2015, Atmosphere Press was built on the principles of Honesty, Transparency, Professionalism, Kindness, and Making Your Book Awesome. As an ethical and author-friendly hybrid press, we stay true to that founding mission today.

If you're a reader, enter our giveaway for a free book here:

SCAN TO ENTER
BOOK GIVEAWAY

If you're a writer, submit your manuscript for consideration here:

SCAN TO SUBMIT
MANUSCRIPT

And always feel free to visit Atmosphere Press and our authors online at atmospherepress.com. See you there soon!

About the Author

PETER P MAHONEY served in Vietnam as an infantry lieutenant. After returning home, he joined Vietnam Veterans Against the War. In 1972, he was indicted for conspiracy to incite a riot at the Republican convention, the Gainesville Eight case.

In 1983, he worked for the New York Vietnam Veterans Memorial Commission. He helped to collect letters written to and from Vietnam. Excerpts of these letters were engraved on the memorial, and were published in a book called *Dear America: Letters Home From Vietnam*. The dedication of the memorial and a ticker tape parade took place in 1985.

After a long career in international development, he retired in 2017.

He is married with two children and lives in Warren, Vermont.

www.ingramcontent.com/pod-product-compliance
Lightning Source LLC
Chambersburg PA
CBHW072211150726

48002CB00005B/1762